A LIFE WITH

C000133122

MARY SHELLEY

M E R I D I A N

Crossing Aesthetics

Werner Hamacher

Editor

Stanford

University

Press

———————

Stanford

California

A LIFE WITH

MARY SHELLEY

BARBARA JOHNSON

With a Foreword by Cathy Caruth

Introduction by Mary Wilson Carpenter

And Essays by Judith Butler and Shoshana Felman

Stanford University Press
Stanford, California

©2014 by the Board of Trustees of the Leland Stanford Junior University.
All rights reserved.

Introduction ©2014 Mary Wilson Carpenter. All rights reserved.

Barbara Johnson, "The Last Man," in *The Other Mary Shelley: Beyond Frankenstein*, edited by Audrey Fisch, Anne Mellor, and Esther Schor, pp. 258–266 (© Oxford University Press, 1993). Reprinted by permission of Oxford University Press.

Barbara Johnson, "My Monster/My Self," in Barbara Johnson, *A World of Difference*, pp. 144–154 (© The Johns Hopkins University Press, 1987). Reprinted by permission of The Johns Hopkins University Press.

Barbara Johnson, "Gender Theory and the Yale School," in *A World of Difference*, pp. 32–41 (© The Johns Hopkins University Press, 1987). Reprinted by permission of The Johns Hopkins University Press.

No part of this book may be reproduced or transmitted in any form or by any means, electronic or mechanical, including photocopying and recording, or in any information storage or retrieval system without the prior written permission of Stanford University Press.

Printed in the United States of America on acid-free, archival-quality paper

Library of Congress Cataloging-in-Publication Data

Johnson, Barbara, 1947-2009, author.
  [Essays. Selections]
  A life with Mary Shelley / Barbara Johnson ; with a foreword by Cathy Caruth ; introduction by Mary Wilson Carpenter ; and essays by Judith Butler and Shoshana Felman.
      pages cm. — (Meridian, crossing aesthetics)
  Includes index.
  ISBN 978-0-8047-9052-9 (cloth : alk. paper) —
  ISBN 978-0-8047-9125-0 (pbk. : alk. paper)
  1. Shelley, Mary Wollstonecraft, 1797-1851—Criticism and interpretation.
  2. Johnson, Barbara, 1947-2009—Criticism and interpretation. I. Title.
  II. Series: Meridian (Stanford, Calif.)
  PR5398.J66 2014
  823.7—dc23

ISBN 978-0-8047-9126-7 (electronic)

Typeset by Bruce Lundquist in 10.9/13 Adobe Garamond

Contents

Acknowledgments

The editors wish to thank a number of colleagues, students, and assistants who helped us to review the manuscript and to facilitate our work on it. Margie Ferguson generously shared with us her memories and facts, and read—and enriched—the Introduction. Christina Leon, Perry Guevara, and above all, Patrick Blanchfield were the first to read the manuscript of "Mary Shelley and Her Circle," yielding precious, thoughtful help at the initial stages. Dr. Amy Jamgochian offered editorial insight and tirelessly facilitated the preparation of the manuscript for publication. Dane Prim-erano helped as a scrupulous library researcher, as a discriminating critical reader, and finally as a companion-interlocutor, first in checking and veri-fying correctness of quotations, later in contributing insightful feedback on the writing and the editing and in offering thereby—throughout the various stages of the process—unwavering support and reliable, loyal as-sistance (both technical and intellectual) without which this last volume could not have been brought to fruition. Eyal Peretz was, as always, a val-ued intellectual interlocutor, an uncompromising critic, and a generous friend and supporter. Finally, thanks are due to Werner Hamacher for his encouragement, his unconventional support, and his exquisite editorial sensitivity.

Barbara Johnson's essay "The Last Man" was first delivered as a lec-ture in French followed by a public discussion, at a conference held in Cerisy, France, and published in its French original as Barbara Johnson, "Le dernier homme," in *Actes du colloque de Cerisy: Les fins de l'homme—à partir du travail de Jacques Derrida, 23 juillet–2 août 1980,* ed. Philippe Lacoue-Labarthes and Jean-Luc Nancy (Paris: Galilée, 1980). This text was later translated into English by Bruce Robbins, and published in its

English version in the collective volume, *The Other Mary Shelley: Beyond Frankenstein*, ed. Audrey Fisch, Anne K. Mellor, and Esther H. Schor (New York and London: Oxford University Press, 1993), pp. 258–266. Reprinted by permission of Oxford University Press.

"My Monster/My Self" was first published as Barbara Johnson, "My Monster/My Self" in *diacritics*, Summer 1982, and later republished in Barbara Johnson's book, *A World of Difference* (Baltimore and London: Johns Hopkins University Press, 1987), pp. 144–154. Reprinted by permission of The Johns Hopkins University Press.

"Gender Theory and the Yale School" was first delivered as a lecture at the conference "Genre Theory and the Yale School," and published in its first version in the review *Genre*, Summer 1984. It was later republished in a revised version in Johnson's book *A World of Difference*, pp. 32–41. Reprinted by permission of The Johns Hopkins University Press.

Cathy Caruth

Foreword

As the title of this book suggests, *Barbara Johnson: A Life with Mary Shelley* offers, in a single collection, Barbara Johnson's influential and pathbreaking essays on the Romantic writer Mary Shelley written over the course of Johnson's lifetime. These essays provide essential insights into the work, and the life, of Mary Shelley, and more specifically, into the entanglement of Mary Shelley's life and writing. The original and daring works collected in this volume also sketch out a trajectory from the beginning to the end of Barbara Johnson's own brilliant career, and offer a glimpse of the inextricability of this career—of its far-reaching literary critical, theoretical, and feminist innovations—from the writing, and (theorized) life, of Mary Shelley.

Prefaced by a lucid description of Johnson's critical and theoretical development written by Mary Wilson Carpenter, a scholar of nineteenth-century British women's writing, the book consists of two parts, each involving essays by Barbara Johnson about Mary Shelley as well as critical interpretations of Barbara Johnson's writing by a major philosophical or literary theorist. In Part One, Johnson's early essays on Mary Shelley (or inspired by the image of Mary Shelley's monster) are followed by a critical commentary offered by the leading feminist philosopher Judith Butler. In Part Two, Johnson's last book, *Mary Shelley and Her Circle*—written during her final illness and finished just weeks before she died—is followed by a critical commentary written by the eminent literary critic and theorist Shoshana Felman. We thus come to understand Johnson's vision of the intricate relation between Mary Shelley's life and writing by discovering the ways in which Johnson's work is, in its turn, bound up with her reading of—her life "with"—Mary Shelley. And we likewise discover the profound significance of these interwoven lives and works by recognizing the way in which Johnson's conceptual and existential imperatives are commented on—and continue to resonate in—the inspiring essays of the women-critics who contribute to this volume, and who live, write, and think *with* Barbara Johnson.

In thus providing an inventive critical overlay of the work of Mary Shelley and of Barbara Johnson, this book affords new genealogical perspectives on late twentieth-century and early twenty-first-century critical thought. In her innovative readings of Mary Shelley's work, and in particular of her most famous novel, *Frankenstein*, Johnson began to shift the definition of Romanticism from its focus on great male poets to its interplay of these famous writers with the novelistic writing of Mary Shelley, who, always on the margin, implicitly (as Johnson suggested) narrated the complexity of the woman writer's position in her own literary texts. During a period when the literary theoretical scene was drawing its own lines back to its Romantic forebears—particularly in the cutting-edge deconstructive writing of the 1980s—Barbara Johnson thus opened up a new line between contemporary thought and a different romanticism, one which gave birth to a genre of literary, theoretical, and (indirectly) autobiographical writing exemplified, in stunning originality, by Johnson's own work. At the same time, by drawing together Johnson's work on Mary Shelley with the work of influential feminist critics and theorists, *Barbara Johnson: A Life with Mary Shelley* allows us to recognize another alternative genealogy, one that binds the feminist critical writing of the 1980's—whose legacy is practiced also by the feminist commentators in this book—to the newly thought Romanticism that Johnson had herself reconfigured. Proceeding from Barbara Johnson's own interest, beginning with her work on Mary Shelley's *Frankenstein*, in the origination of new kinds of lineages—in previously unrecognized ways in which literature, and criticism, are engendered and reproduced—this volume thus provides fresh genealogical narratives of Barbara Johnson's original vision and of an era of contemporary theory that profoundly altered our relation to our texts and to our lives.

This collection thus proceeds by "circling back"—in the evocative phrase of Shoshana Felman from her "Afterword"—to the beginning of Johnson's work on Mary Shelley and to the manner in which that work moves forward through the entirety of Johnson's career and through her enduring influence on the world of criticism and theory. In so doing, these essays, as a collection, do for Barbara Johnson what Felman says Johnson does for Mary Shelley: they write "her impossible autobiography," and thus provide a narrative group and a "circle of listening"[1] that, like the listening of Mary Shelley near the fire on that rainy night of the famous ghost story contest—the writing competition that would lead to the creation of *Frankenstein*—becomes a generative moment and perpetuates the origination of a new genre of critical writing in which autobiography, theory, and literature are closely intertwined. The circle of women readers and writers in this book does not exactly reproduce or mimic that original circle at the fire (which, after reading Johnson's *Mary Shelley and her Circle*, we cannot understand anymore as a single circle), nor do the women commentators in this book simply circle around Barbara Johnson, since in the process of reading her work they have been, unwittingly, pulled into a circle around Mary Shelley. Barbara Johnson, Mary Wilson Carpenter, Judith Butler, and Shoshana Felman indeed form, together, part of a circle of women listeners and writers that did not quite yet exist for Mary Shelley and even now may be less a completed circle than a call for others to join a future narrative and critical group.

Johnson herself, with her satirical wit and—even in the face of her own imminent death—her refusal of excessive pathos, would perhaps characterize this collection in a less tendentious manner. In "Gender Theory and the Yale School"—included in this volume and discussed here by both Carpenter and Felman—Johnson draws attention to the male-centeredness of the early volume *Deconstruction and Criticism*, which consisted of five male critics of the so-called "Yale School." Johnson relates how, "at the time of the publication of . . . *Deconstruction and Criticism*, several of us—Shoshana Felman, Gayatri Spivak, Margaret Ferguson, and I—discussed the possibility of writing a companion volume inscribing female deconstructive protest and affirmation centering not on Percy Bysshe Shelley's 'The Triumph of Life' (as the existing volume was originally slated to do) but on Mary Shelley's *Frankenstein*."[2] That female counter-manifesto, Johnson says, "might truly have illustrated the Girardian progression 'from mimetic desire to the monstrous double.' Unfortunately, this *Bride of Deconstruction and Criticism* never quite got off the ground."[3] Inspired here by the spark of Johnson's still recent life, the women who write in this volume may finally have animated that long-forgotten monstrous Bride[4]—a vision of the book that, I am sure, they would consider a compliment and that, as Johnson reminded us in her discussion of Dr. Frankenstein's creation, also calls upon us to recognize its own inherent beauty.

In reading this book we must, then, attend to the different interwoven strands of life, of death, of autobiography, of criticism, and of theory that make up the complex relationship between Barbara Johnson and Mary Shelley, and that constitute the subtle resonances between the insights of Johnson's readers and her own foundational work. These writers, in a posthumous conversation with Barbara Johnson, also dramatize for us the emergence and evolution of a mode—or modes—of reading and thinking that have, collectively, produced a lasting impact on contemporary critical thought.

Mary Shelley, as Barbara Johnson tells us in her last work—published here for the first time—tended first to the living Percy Bysshe Shelley and later to the dead one, a task that was truly, for her, a matter of the heart. The three women in this volume, who write so beautifully of Barbara Johnson's life and work, also tended to Barbara Johnson in her life: both as interlocutors while she lived, and as friends and supporters at the end of her life. They now form a posthumous circle that precisely crosses between death and life—the lives and deaths of Mary Shelley and of Barbara Johnson—in order to transmit the revitalizing force of Barbara Johnson's creativity, and singular originality, which cannot be exhausted by any genealogy, and cannot be reduced to any school or lineage.

Barbara Johnson tells us that the ghost stories that had inspired the writing contest behind *Frankenstein* had to do with "the uncanniness of death," but Mary Shelley's novel was concerned with "what gave life." This volume, too, occasioned by Johnson's early death, is also, ultimately, about *what gives life*: in the work, and in the lives (and deaths), of the great women writers who are at its center. They are all, indeed, as Felman writes of Johnson, "theorists who became storytellers," women who both write and narrate—who narrate a life as they write their critical and theoretical appraisals of another woman's work—in order to pass on to us the spark of life communicated, across time and writing, from one woman in the circle to the next.

May 2013

Mary Wilson Carpenter

Introduction

> Where to start speaking of the end? But on the other hand, isn't it
> always from the end that one starts?
>
> Barbara Johnson

The quotation above is taken from "The Last Man," an essay originally written in French for a 1980 colloquium held in Cerisy, France, and organized as a response to Jacques Derrida's work, especially his essay "Les fins de l'homme."[1] In 1980 Johnson was an Assistant Professor of French and the Literature Major (an undergraduate program taught by faculty from Comparative Literature and other departments) at Yale, and already internationally known for her work in deconstructionist theory. Her dissertation, *Défigurations du langage poétique: La seconde révolution baudelairienne* (Paris: Flammarion), had been published in 1979, and her first English collection of essays, *The Critical Difference: Essays in the Contemporary Rhetoric of Reading* (Johns Hopkins University Press) was published in the same year as "Le dernier homme," 1980. Her translation of Derrida's 1972 work, *La dissémination*, would be published as *Dissemination* in 1981. But her essay on Mary Shelley's novel *The Last Man* (1826), reprinted in this volume, was the beginning of her published writings on Mary Shelley. It marked her first publication in the field of "women's studies," one of whose areas was the rediscovery and critical analysis of works by women writers previously excluded from the academic canon. The last book manuscript she completed before her death in August 2009 was "Mary Shelley and Her Circle," published here for the first time. Mary Shelley was thus the subject for Johnson's beginning in feminist theory and criticism and also for her end.

In "The Last Man," she questions, "Why couldn't such a story be entitled *The Last Woman?* . . . Would the idea that humanity could not end with a woman have something to do with the ends of *man?*"[2] The idea that a woman's story, unless it was written for the "ends" of man, was somehow monstrous, unthinkable, had already emerged in her teaching at Yale. There, in a 1978 course titled "Man and His Fictions: Narrative Forms," and team-taught with Peter Brooks, Barbara Guetti, and Joseph Halpern, Johnson had lectured in a course section titled "Life Stories" on Rousseau's *Confessions*. The course included no texts by women writers in this year or the next, in which Johnson did not teach. In the fall of 1980, the course had been retitled as the gender-neutral "Narrative Forms." Now team-taught by Johnson, David Marshall, and J. Hillis Miller, the section "Life Stories" included Mary Shelley's *Frankenstein*, and Johnson was the lecturer for this text. Seminar discussion compared *Frankenstein* and Rousseau's *Confessions* as "life stories." In her essay "The Last Man," Johnson begins with *Frankenstein*, proposing that "to speak of Mary Shelley's *Frankenstein* is immediately to approach the question of *man* indirectly through what has always been at once excluded and comprehended by its definition, namely, the *woman* and the *monster*" (p. 259). Citing Rousseau's statement that "the most useful and least advanced of all human knowledge seems to me to be that of man," Johnson suggests that Mary Shelley's novel demonstrates on the contrary that "if one translates in this way the command to know oneself as a command to know *man*, one risks losing contact monstrously with what one doesn't know" (p. 261). Johnson thus begins her first essay on Mary Shelley's work with a comparison between *Frankenstein* and Rousseau's writing as writing about "man and his fictions," a project that seems to both critique and anticipate the teaching of the Yale course.

She characterizes *The Last Man* as Mary Shelley's "story of the one who remains" (p. 262). The narrator—the last survivor of a universal plague— is witness, survivor, scribe, or the same role Mary Shelley plays at the moment she writes her novel. Commenting that Mary Shelley's life was also a series of survivals at the time of her writing of *The Last Man* (her mother had died in giving her birth, three of her own four children had died, Percy had drowned, and Byron had just died in Greece), Johnson suggests that "at the age of twenty-six, she considered herself the last relic of an extinct race" (p. 263). Mary Shelley paints her own mourning on "a universal scale" (p. 263). But since that universal scale was the one which characterized the writings of the Romantic poets, she "does more than give a universal vision of her mourning; she mourns for a certain type of universal vision" (p. 263). Beyond mourning, however, "the image of a certain conception of *man* . . . will be progressively demystified through-out the novel that follows . . . The story of *The Last Man* is in the last analysis the story of modern Western man torn between mourning and deconstruction" (p. 265).

With this insightful reading of Mary Shelley's apocalyptic novel, John-son leads the way in the then emerging field of Mary Shelley studies by proposing that her work mounts a deconstructive critique of Romanti-cism. Anne K. Mellor, in her introduction to the 1993 edition of *The Last Man*, which includes Johnson's essay in its bibliography, comments that Mary Shelley articulates "a critique so total that the novel becomes the first literary example of what we now call deconstruction."[3] Esther Schor, in her introduction to *The Cambridge Companion to Mary Shelley* (2003), describes *Frankenstein* as "the century's most blistering critique of Romantic egotism."[4]

At the time of Johnson's essay on *The Last Man*, this and *Frankenstein* were the only two of Mary Shelley's novels in print. *The Last Man* had been published by the University of Nebraska Press, edited by Hugh J. Luke, Jr., in 1965. In the same year the Signet Classic paperback edition of *Frankenstein*, an edition widely used for teaching purposes, was first pub-lished. This edition reprints the 1831 third edition of the novel, published some thirteen years after the first edition and nine years after Percy Bysshe Shelley's death. It was for the 1831 edition that Shelley wrote her now famous "Author's Introduction" characterizing the novel as "my hideous progeny." The 1965 Signet Classic edition—the only edition ever cited by Johnson—also contains an "Afterword" by Harold Bloom. Bloom's explanation of what makes *Frankenstein* an important book, "though it is only a strong, flawed novel with frequent clumsiness in its narrative and characterization" is that "it contains one of the most vivid versions we have of the Romantic mythology of the self, one that resembles Blake's *Book of Urizen*, Shelley's *Prometheus Unbound*, and Byron's *Manfred*," and that it was precisely because Mary Shelley's novel "lacks the sophistication and imaginative complexity of such works, [that] *Frankenstein* affords a unique introduction to the archetypal world of the Romantics" (p. 215).

Bloom's 1965 statement was only a pithy summary of the general view of most *Frankenstein* critics at the time. In her 1988 critical biography, *Mary Shelley: Her Life, Her Fiction, Her Monsters*, Mellor notes that "before Ellen Moers's ground-breaking discussion of *Frankenstein* in *The New York Review of Books* in 1973, literary scholars and critics had for the most part discussed

Mary Shelley's career merely as an appendage to her husband's, dismissing *Frankenstein* as a badly written children's book even though far more people were familiar with her novel than with Percy Shelley's poetry."[5] By the time of Johnson's writing of "Le dernier homme," however, some revolutionary feminist readings of *Frankenstein* had appeared. In addition to Moers's *Literary Women* (1976), which included her reading of the novel as an instance of "Female Gothic," a "phantasmagoria of the nursery," Marc A. Rubenstein's "'My Accursed Origin': The Search for the Mother in *Frankenstein*" had appeared in *Studies in Romanticism* (Spring 1976).[6] Sandra Gilbert and Susan Gubar had published *The Madwoman in the Attic* (1979), whose chapter "Horror's Twin: Mary Shelley's Monstrous Eve" identifies the monster, though created male, as "a female in disguise," a figure for the author's sense of namelessness and deformity.[7] George Levine and U. C. Knoepflmacher's critical anthology *The Endurance of Frankenstein* (1979) included Knoepflmacher's much-cited essay "Thoughts on the Aggression of Daughters," as well as other feminist critical essays on the novel.[8] In 1980, the same year in which Johnson published "Le dernier homme," her colleague at Yale Mary Poovey published "My Hideous Progeny: Mary Shelley and the Feminization of Romanticism" in *PMLA*.[9]

Johnson's position at Yale when she wrote "Le dernier homme" was probably central to her decision to both teach and write on Mary Shelley. As described in the Foreword to this volume, she and some of her Yale feminist colleagues tossed around the notion of writing a female counter-manifesto to the Yale School's entirely male-centered *Deconstruction and Criticism*, centered on *Frankenstein* rather than Percy Bysshe Shelley's "The Triumph of Life." Though that idea never quite got off the ground, Johnson refers to it in "Le dernier homme," commenting that "perhaps it was not *Frankenstein* but rather *The Last Man*, Mary Shelley's grim depiction of the gradual extinction of humanity altogether, that would have made a fit counterpart to 'The Triumph of Life.' Percy Bysshe Shelley is entombed in both, along with a certain male fantasy of Romantic universality. The only universality that remains in Mary Shelley's last novel is the plague" (p. 33).[10]

Johnson was also active at Yale in the Women's Studies Program. After the admission of women as undergraduates in 1969, momentum gathered to include women's studies in the curriculum. By 1976 the Women's Studies Task Force was formed, and in May 1979 the Yale faculty approved the institution of the Women's Studies Program. Johnson was included as one of the "Core Faculty" along with Silvia Arrom, Nancy Cott (who became program chair in 1980), Faye Crosby, Margaret Homans, Lydia Kung, Catherine MacKinnon, Susan Olzak, and Mary Poovey.[11] Janet Todd was later to describe Yale as one of two institutions (the other was Princeton) that could boast more than one major feminist critic, naming Barbara Johnson, Shoshana Felman, and Margaret Homans, though Todd did not feel that either Yale or Princeton could be described as a "feminist establishment."[12] Felman's foundational feminist essay, "Women and Madness: The Critical Phallacy," was first published in 1975.[13] Homans published her groundbreaking *Women Writers and Poetic Identity: Dorothy Wordsworth, Emily Brontë, and Emily Dickinson* in 1980.[14]

Johnson's now classic essay on *Frankenstein*, "My Monster/My Self," was published in a feminist issue of *diacritics*, "Cherchez La Femme: Feminist Critique/Feminine Text," edited by Cynthia Chase, Nelly Furman, and Mary Jacobus, in 1982.[15] But this was not the first time Johnson had appeared as a feminist critic in an American academic journal. *Critical Inquiry* had published a feminist issue the preceding year, Winter 1981, and the "Editor's Introduction" begins with a quotation from Johnson's *The Critical Difference*:

> If human beings were not divided into two biological sexes, there would probably be no need for literature. And if literature could truly say what the relations between the sexes are, we would doubtless not need much of it then, either . . . It is not the life of sexuality that literature cannot capture; it is literature that inhabits the very heart of what makes sexuality problematic for us speaking animals. Literature is not only a thwarted investigator but also an incorrigible perpetrator of the problem of sexuality.[16]

For Elizabeth Abel, Johnson's thesis here represents the turn in deconstructive criticism from "notions of textual difference" to "the complexities of sexual difference," which, though "more pervasively engrained in our culture, have largely been confined to the edges of critical debate" (*Writing and Sexual Difference*, p. 1). Johnson herself, however, having dissected the Yale School's gender politics in "Gender Theory and the Yale School," gleefully applies her critical scalpel to her own work:

> In order to end with a meditation on a possible female version of the Yale School, I would like now to turn to the work of a Yale daughter. For this purpose I have chosen to focus on *The Critical Difference* by Barbara Johnson. What happens when one raises Mary Jacobus's question: 'Is there a woman in

this text?' The answer is rather surprising. For no book produced by the Yale School seems to have excluded women as effectively as *The Critical Difference*. No women authors are studied. Almost no women critics are cited. And, what is even more surprising, there are almost no female characters in any of the stories analyzed. *Billy Budd*, however triangulated, is a tale of three *men* in a boat. . . . In a book that announces itself as a study of difference, the place of the woman is constantly being erased. (*World of Difference*, p. 39)

Nevertheless, she acknowledges that "this does not mean, however, that the question of sexual difference does not haunt the book from the beginning" (p. 39). Quoting the same passage quoted in Abel's introduction, Johnson sees *The Critical Difference* as able only to describe "the escape of the difference it attempts to analyze" (p. 40).

Johnson, according to Diane Long Hoeveler, was "one of the first American critics to link feminism and deconstruction." What Hoeveler finds most interesting in Johnson's reading of *Frankenstein* is "her recognition of the novel as dominated by its 'description of a primal scene of creation . . . where do babies come from? And where do stories come from? In both cases, the scene of creation is described, but the answer to these questions is still withheld.'"[17] She quotes Johnson's generative perception that "*Frankenstein*, in other words, can be read as the story of the experience of writing *Frankenstein*" (*World of Difference*, p. 49).

Perhaps even more interesting, however, is the fact that Johnson both begins and ends her essay with the question of autobiography, specifically the monstrosity of female autobiography. She begins with the statement that "to judge from recent trends in scholarly as well as popular literature, three crucial questions can be seen to stand at the forefront of today's preoccupations: the question of mothering, the question of the woman writer, and the question of autobiography" (*World of Difference*, p. 144). Tellingly, her reflection begins with a comment on *popular* as well as scholarly literature: the essay—which is actually composed as a review essay of Nancy Friday's *My Mother/My Self* (1977) and Dorothy Dinnerstein's *The Mermaid and the Minotaur* (1976), against which Mary Shelley's *Frankenstein* is juxtaposed—demonstrates her grounding in the "real world," or that figurative term which, as she comments in her introduction to *A World of Difference*, denotes nothing other than "perceptions of the boundaries of institutions" (p. 3). Reading all three books together from her position in view of those boundaries, she works out her stunning analysis of *Frankenstein* as Mary Shelley's monstrous autobiography, the woman writer's story of giving birth to her "hideous progeny." The monstrousness of female autobiography, she concludes, is due to "the fact of self-contradiction that is so vigorously repressed in women" (p. 153). In all three of the books discussed, "the monstrousness of selfhood is intimately embedded within the question of female autobiography" (p. 154). And how could it be otherwise, she ponders, since the very shape of human life stories has always been modeled on the man? "Rousseau's—or any man's—autobiography consists in the story of the difficulty of conforming to the standard of what a *man* should be. The problem for the female autobiographer is, on the one hand, to resist the pressure of masculine autobiography as the only literary genre available for her enterprise, and, on the other, to describe a difficulty in conforming to a female ideal which is largely a fantasy of the masculine, not the feminine, imagination" (p. 154). It seems clear, in other words, that "My Monster/My Self" was gestated in the Yale course that was originally conceived as "Man and His Fictions: Narrative Forms."

In 1982–83, Johnson was a Fellow at the Mary I. Bunting Institute at Radcliffe College in Harvard University. Feminist theory was electrifying the academic world at this point, and the Cambridge-Boston area was particularly explosive. So many feminist talks, lectures, meetings, films, conferences, and other events were being held in the numerous academic institutions in the metro Boston area that Ruth Perry, founding director of the Women's Studies Program at MIT, began compiling and publishing a monthly newsletter titled "Women's Studies Around Boston" in 1984. The Boston Area Colloquium on Feminist Theory was first held at Northeastern University in the spring of 1982. By 1983–84, when Johnson began her career as a Professor of Romance Languages and Literatures and Comparative Literature at Harvard, the third colloquium series was being held, now cosponsored by Harvard and Wellesley.

The battle to establish women's studies programs and to include women writers in such already established departments as Afro-American studies, as well as English and other modern language departments, was being fought on multiple academic fronts, including that of Harvard. Dean Henry Rosovsky established the Committee on Women's Studies in 1978, initially chaired by Edward Keenan, Dean of the Graduate School of Arts and Sciences. In late 1983, Dean Keenan appointed Professor Susan Suleiman of the Department of Romance Languages and Literatures as Chair of the Committee, to take office in 1985. In September

1984, Johnson was Acting Chair of the Committee, and she and Suleiman worked together to plan a degree-granting program, coordinating courses throughout the Faculty of Arts and Sciences that included a "gender component," and also finding funding for lectures and symposia.[18] In 1985, the Committee on Women's Studies at Harvard and the Women's Studies Program at MIT jointly sponsored a conference on pornography that occasioned intense debate from feminists "of different viewpoints," most notably Women Against Pornography and the Feminists Against Censorship Task Force.[19] From 1991 to 1993, Johnson was Chair of the Committee on Women's Studies at Harvard, in which she was succeeded by Suleiman in 1993 and in 1995 by Alice Jardine of the Department of Romance Languages and Literatures.

This era also saw the beginning of Johnson's work on African American women writers. In the fall of 1983 she taught her first course, "Black Women Writers." There were no women faculty in the Afro-American Studies Department at that point, and Johnson's course pioneered the teaching of black women writers at Harvard. She offered a course with this title again in 1985 and one titled "African American Women Writers" in 1990, as well as a course titled "The Slave Narrative" in 1995. From 1990 to 1991, she was Chair of the Department of Afro-American Studies, where she vigorously promoted the hiring of new faculty members. In 1984 she published "Metaphor, Metonymy and Voice in Zora Neale Hurston's *Their Eyes Were Watching God*" in *Black Literature and Literary Theory*, edited by Henry Louis Gates, Jr., and in 1985 a second essay on Hurston, "Thresholds of Difference: Structures of Address in Zora Neale Hurston," was published in *Critical Inquiry* and reprinted in *Race, Writing, and Difference*, also edited by Gates.[20]

In the fall of 1995, Johnson taught an undergraduate seminar at Harvard titled "Mary Shelley and Her Circle." By this time, critical interest in Mary Shelley had mushroomed. More than half of all students of Romanticism now read *Frankenstein*; the novel was a staple in such courses as "The Gothic," "Women's Literature," and "The Post-Human"; and it was included in both *The Norton Anthology of English Literature* and *The Longman Anthology of British Literature*, the leading undergraduate anthologies.[21] *MLA Approaches to Teaching Shelley's "Frankenstein"* had been published in 1990.[22] Both scholarly and paperback editions of Mary Shelley's other novels and short fictions had become available (Schor, pp. 1–2). Complete editions of Mary Shelley's letters and journals had also been

English 90ij
Mary Shelley and Her Circle
Fall 1995
B. Johnson, 4th Floor, Emerson
Office Hours Tu 10-12, 2-4
call 495-4186 for appt.

Syllabus

Sept 18   Introduction

Sept 25   Mary Wollstonecraft, _Mary_

Oct 2   Mary Wollstonecraft, _A Vindication of the Rights of Woman_

Oct 9   (holiday--no class; start reading Godwin)

Oct 16   William Godwin, _Political Justice_

Oct 23   Mary Wollstonecraft, _Maria_

Oct 30   Percy Bysshe Shelley, letter to Godwin*, "Queen Mab,"
         "Mont Blanc"

Nov 6   Mary Shelley, _Frankenstein_
        Lord Byron, "Prometheus"

        SHORT PAPER DUE

Nov 13   John Polidori, _The Vampyre_

Nov 20   Lord Byron, "Manfred"
        Mary Shelley, _Matilda_
        Percy Shelley, "The Cenci"

Nov 27   Percy Shelley, Introduction to _Revolt of Islam_*,
         "Prometheus Unbound"

Dec 4   Percy Shelley, "Ode to Liberty," "Hellas," "The Triumph
         of Life"
        letter by Mary Shelley on death of Shelley*
        material on death of Shelley and Byron in _Byron's Poetry_

Dec 11-18 Mary Shelley, _The Last Man_

Jan 9   FINAL PAPER DUE

published. Johnson's essay "Le dernier homme," now published in English translation as "The Last Man" in *The Other Mary Shelley: Beyond Franken-stein* (1993), had begun to surface in the fertile field of Mary Shelley studies. Johnson's second essay on Mary Shelley, "My Monster/My Self," had been reprinted in *Mary Shelley's Frankenstein* (1987), edited by Harold Bloom, and was widely quoted.[23] It was to be reprinted the following year in the Norton Critical Edition of *Frankenstein*.[24] The syllabus for Johnson's course (reproduced below) included readings in the work of Mary Wollstonecraft Godwin and William Godwin, Percy Bysshe Shelley and Lord Byron, and "poor Polidori," Byron's physician who later committed suicide.

The course was designed to present Mary Shelley not as an appendage to the "great Romantics," but as a major writer whose work deserved to be studied in itself, as well as in its intersections with that of her illustri-ous parents, husband, and other members of the famous literary "circle" among whom she lived and wrote—and all of whom she long survived.

In 2009, Johnson, now disabled by a progressive neurological condi-tion which had forced her retirement from teaching, worked on "Mary Shelley and Her Circle" (she had already completed several other books post-retirement, including a translation of Mallarmé's *Divagations* (2007), *Persons and Things* (2008), and *Moses and Multiculturalism* (published posthumously in 2010). *Mary Shelley and Her Circle* is in essence a long reflective essay on this other "last woman," this other woman surviving beyond or outside her literary circle. Johnson explores Mary Shelley's rela-tions to the mother who died giving her birth and to her radical feminist works, to her philosopher-novelist father and his ambivalent treatment of his feminist wife's daughter, and most especially to Mary Shelley's com-plex and difficult relation to her narcissistic husband, who continually sought and received all kinds of adoration and celebration that inevita-bly relegated Mary to the margins. Byron and his short-lived physician Polidori also figure in this strange circle that surrounded Mary Shelley at the point at which she produced her "hideous progeny." The book, like so much of Johnson's work, seems to emerge directly from her teach-ing. At times it displays an almost conspiratorial tone, as if initiating stu-dents into the hitherto unknown realm of the haunted woman writer and her haunting productions. At other moments, Johnson presents with deadpan humor the unvarnished truths of both sexual and textual inter-sections in Mary Shelley's circle. Ultimately, Johnson proposes, Mary Shelley desired to become what Percy Bysshe Shelley had been, a god-like sole creator, "someone capable of having progeny alone" (Epilogue, p. 8). Although Johnson did not intend this book to be her last work, the book ties together a continuing thread in her work that began in 1980, while she was still an assistant professor at Yale, and that continued to engage her thought throughout her life. It is a fitting subject for the final work of Barbara Johnson, famed scholar and beloved teacher who eagerly joined in the crucial work of lifting other women writers out of obscurity and into those literary circles where still other students of women's lives and literature could learn to know them.

A LIFE WITH MARY SHELLEY

PART ONE

Early Essays

Barbara Johnson

The Last Man[1]

When considering a subject as broad as "the ends of man," one can only ask oneself: *Where to start?* Where to start speaking of the end? But on the other hand, isn't it always from the end that one starts? Isn't every narrative in fact constructed beginning with the denouement, as every project is constructed beginning with its goal? Isn't the end precisely that which never ceases to be repeated, which one is never done with? If man is truly, as Derrida says, "that which relates to its end," he is also that which is never finished with ending. Thus the question would not be to know how to *begin* speaking of the end, but how to *finish* speaking of it, how to narrate something other than the interminable death of the penultimate, how to be finished with the end?

This is perhaps the question that Nietzsche poses in *Human, All-Too-Human* when he writes, under the heading of "First and Last Things," "We look at everything through the human head and cannot cut this head off; while the question remains, What would be left of the world if it had been cut off?"[2] The end of man would seem then to be that which cannot be *lived* by any man. But what exactly is "human" in Nietzsche's statement, "*we* look at everything through the *human* head"? The human, here, is apparently something that says "we." And what if men were reduced only to "I"? Would the word "man" still have the same meaning if there were only one left? Would the end of man take place *before* or *after* the death of the last man? Would the final cut take place only after the death of the last man, or would it consist of his testimony, his unprecedented experience of survival? In other words, what would be the relation between the last representative of the human race and the end of man?

It is the limit-narrative of decapitation, of the cutting off of the human head with which we look at all things, that Mary Shelley attempted in a novel entitled *The Last Man*. This very long narrative, written by a woman whose birth coincides with the bloodiest moments of the French Revolution, is one of the first versions of the idea—which has become so commonplace in our atomic age—of the total extinction of the human species. Postrevolutionary but preatomic, this prophetic novel could perhaps tell us something about the strange temporality of the end of man.

In fact, in the current context Mary Shelley merits our interest in more than one respect. If she risks appearing somewhat marginal today, it's precisely her marginality that has always earned her a certain celebrity. That marginality was of two kinds: one, she lived surrounded by writers whose works strongly marked the thought and literature of the epoch: her father, William Godwin, liberal philosopher and author of *Political Justice*; her mother, Mary Wollstonecraft, author of *A Vindication of the Rights of Woman*; her husband, Percy Bysshe Shelley, Romantic poet and disciple of Godwin; and the many friends of Shelley, in particular the poet Byron. Aside from this marginality in the very center of the Romantic circle, Mary Shelley knew a second sort of famous nonexistence as the anonymous author of *Frankenstein*, a novel that she wrote at the age of nineteen and whose mythic power has only increased since, independently of the name and even the notion of the author. In the shadow of her parents, her husband, and her own work, Mary Shelley thus lived the Romantic period through its folds and margins. If I put the accent in this way on her marginality, it's not in order to discover for her a new centrality, but in order to analyze the new manner in which the question of marginality is inscribed in and agitates her work.

To speak of Mary Shelley's *Frankenstein* is immediately to approach the question of *man* indirectly through what has always been at once excluded and comprehended by its definition, namely, the *woman* and the *monster*. It's undoubtedly not an accident if the conjunction of these two categories of beings has traversed history under the reassuring form of fables of the "beauty and the beast" genre—which always end by confirming the superior glory of man, since the beast is transformed into a man with whom the woman falls in love. In *Frankenstein*, the end of the story is far from reassuring, but it is precisely because the monster is not monstrous enough.

Frankenstein, as everyone knows, is the story of a scientist who, trying to create a man in his laboratory, succeeds in manufacturing a monstrous being who ends up turning against his creator. It's the creator who is called "Frankenstein" and not the monster, who has no name, but the universal tendency to call the monster by the name of its creator is far from insignificant. Contrary to what the cinematic versions of *Frankenstein* have led us to believe, Mary Shelley's monster is not manufactured with a criminal's brain, and its creator is not crazy. Aside from a certain physical ugliness, Shelley's monster is the exact realization of the dream of its creator, to whom the project of discovering the secrets of life and of making use of them to manufacture a man had seemed the consummation of science and an inestimable benefit for humanity. But there is one detail which the creator had not foreseen: his own reaction to his creature. When he sees the yellowish eye of the one he had constructed and animated with so much effort open, Frankenstein is seized with horror and flees from the laboratory, abandoning the giant newborn to his fate. This creature whose features are roughly sutured but whose heart is good tries to find a place among men, but men always reject him with horror. Choosing to reside in the shadow of a country cottage, unknown to its inhabitants, the monster acquires a full humanist education by listening to the French lessons given by the country folk to an Arab woman. The monster, who has developed a tender sympathy for these country people, finally tries to win recognition from them, but like all human beings, they are incapable of enduring his monstrous appearance. Made furious by loneliness, the monster leaves in search of his creator, whose youngest brother he strangles when he unluckily turns up along the way. When the monster finds Frankenstein, in the shadow of Mont Blanc, he tells him his story and begs his creator to make him a wife of the same species as himself. Touched in spite of himself, Frankenstein the creator agrees to the monster's request and sets about gathering the necessary materials for this new piece of work. But suddenly the image of a new, monstrous Eve forces itself upon him and, frightened by his vision, Frankenstein ends up destroying the rough draft of the female monster. The monster, who has watched this entire process, will never forgive him for the destruction of his mate. Instead of attacking his creator directly, he murders, one after another, all those who are dear to Frankenstein, until the creator is reduced to the same isolation as his creature.

If Mary Shelley thus elaborates a work of science fiction which seems to caution us against the fictions of science, it is not, however, only in order to suggest that there are limits which man has no right to overstep. For far from marking the *limits* of the human, Shelley's monster is nothing but the perfect realization of the humanist project par excellence: mastery of the knowledge of man. The chemical details of Frankenstein's experiment are only the *literalization* of the desire to give oneself a total representation of man, to master the origins of man to the point of being able to create one. The monster is thus not what remains *exterior* to the humanist conception of man; it is the figure of that conception itself to the extent that "man" is precisely a creation of man. This perfectly reasonable monster, whose wickedness is entirely explained by the injustices that are inflicted on him, is a perfect example of man such as he was created by the Enlightenment philosophes, for whom the human being par excellence was Western, rational, and masculine. It's no accident if the humanist-creator can't or doesn't want to create a woman equal to her man, or if the monster's education is presented as a *Westernization*. (The lessons he overhears are those given by Europeans to an Arab woman. It is also interesting to note that, in order to recover from the shock of the catastrophic creation, Frankenstein begins to study, precisely, Oriental languages.) Thus if Mary Shelley's novel constitutes a critique of humanism, that critique is directed not against the hubris of the humanist who takes himself for God, but against the blindness of the humanist who can't see himself. In gathering and sewing materials with the design of creating a human, Frankenstein never doubts for an instant that he knows what a human is. But the creature only has to open his eyes, the object only has to become subject for Frankenstein not to recognize him anymore and for him literally to lose consciousness (or knowledge— "connaissance"—Tr.). The *unknown* is not located in the object of humanism, but in the desiring humanist subject. That which the humanist remains blind to in his efforts to know man is the nature of his own desire to know man. That blindness is moreover represented within the novel by the total lack of explanation concerning the motives which led the creator to reject his creature so violently. This explanatory ellipsis has always been considered a grave defect in the novel by readers who were looking to follow the psychological logic. But it is precisely by this sort of logical flaw, this blind spot in the explanation of human desire, that something like psychology can be elaborated.

The humanist's blindness in relation to his own desire to know is illustrated in an exemplary way by Rousseau in the preface to his *Discourse on the Origin and Causes of Inequality Among Men,* by the way in which he understands the meaning of the inscription of Delphi, "The most useful and the least advanced of all human knowledge seems to me to be that of man; and I dare say that the inscription of the temple of Delphi alone contained a precept more important and more difficult than all the thick volumes of the moralists."[3] As opposed to Rousseau's project, the story of Frankenstein seems to affirm that if one translates in this way the command to know oneself as a command to know *man*, one risks losing contact monstrously with what one doesn't know.

Curiously, in the article by Jacques Derrida on "The Ends of Man," one finds in an unexpected way this idea of monstrosity linked to the critique of a tradition deformed by a humanist view:

> After the war, under the name of . . . existentialism . . . , the thought that dominated France presented itself essentially as humanist. . . . [T]he major concept, the theme of the last analysis, the irreducible horizon and origin is what was then called "human reality." As is well-known, this is a translation of Heideggerian *Dasein*. A *monstrous translation* in many respects, but so much the more significant.[4]

Would this Derridean monster be the modern reincarnation of Shelley's monster? Would monstrosity always exist as a function of humanist translation? Are there nonhumanist monsters? nonmonstrous translations?

In our day the myth of Frankenstein is ceaselessly invoked by the newspapers apropos of babies conceived in a test tube and, more recently, apropos of the creation of new forms of bacteria by the recombination of their genetic codes. In the context of debates over the commercial and juridical status of these new forms of life, the question of man finds itself curiously reopened. Having to decide whether the law governing the distribution of patents applied or not to the invention of living beings, the Supreme Court of the United States decreed that life was indeed susceptible to be patented since, in the words of former Chief Justice Burger (quoted in *Time*), "the issue is 'not between living and inanimate things, but between products of nature—whether living or not—and human-made inventions.'"[5] In other words, it's the opposition between man and nature which here takes over from the worn-out opposition between life and death. All the more so in that, in our day, the legal status of death is itself submitted to the opposition between natural means and technological means of maintaining life. Thus if man is indeed that which is determined beginning with his end, his end is, more and more, that which can be determined only beginning with man.

This question of man suspended between life and death returns us finally to that second untimely meditation of Mary Shelley—untimely for her time but ardently timely for our own—namely, her other novel entitled precisely *The Last Man*. While *Frankenstein* was the story of the one who was superfluous in the world of men, *The Last Man* is the story of the one who is superfluous in a world without men. It's the story of the one who remains. Now, what does this remainder of humanity signify in relation to the question of the ends of man?

But first of all, a question is indispensable: Why couldn't such a story be entitled *The Last Woman*? Or rather, why is it that a novel entitled *The Last Woman* would be automatically interpreted—as one sees in the film of that title by Marco Ferreri—as the story of the last love of a man or else as a narrative of castration? Would the idea that humanity could not end with a woman have something to do with the ends of *man*?

In reality, although the narrator of this book speaks in the first person masculine singular, he belongs, like the monster, to a sort of third sex. He resembles neither the men nor the women of the novel. He serves the function of witness, of survivor, and of scribe. As we will see, it is the same role that Mary Shelley plays at the moment when she writes her novel.

The story of *The Last Man* takes place in Europe near the end of the twenty-first century. The main characters are few: aside from the narrator Lionel Verney and his sister Perdita, we count Adrian and Idris, children of the last king of England; Lord Raymond, hero of the Greek wars; and Evadne Zaimi, a Greek princess who lives in England. In the year 2073, the king of England, father of Adrian and Idris, abdicates to permit the creation of an English republic. The royal family withdraws to Windsor. After many sentimental and political vicissitudes, the narrator Verney marries Idris, the former king's daughter; the hero Raymond marries Perdita, sister of the narrator; Adrian, who had been in love with the princess Evadne, remains alone; and Evadne, in love with Raymond, disappears. Raymond, for whom the tranquil life at Windsor begins to be a burden, gets elected Lord Protector of England and throws himself immediately into innumerable projects for the good of humanity. By a series of accidents, Raymond rediscovers the Greek princess Evadne, reduced to a life of misery and still in love with him. Raymond, who tries to remedy her misery, doesn't speak of the princess to his wife Perdita, but she nevertheless begins to suspect something. As the misunderstanding between the spouses becomes irreparable, Raymond resigns his post and leaves England to join the Greek army once again. The Greeks are about to achieve victory over the Turks; the Greek army needs only to take Constantinople. The Greeks besiege the city. But the besieged city becomes more and more silent. Constantinople has fallen under the sway of the Plague. The armies separate without combat, making way for a plague-ridden peace.

England once again becomes the scene of the action. For several years, the English believe themselves sheltered from the Plague that devastates the entire Orient. But little by little this scourge takes over Europe and England until the last English survivors decide to leave their island to wait for death in a gentler climate. At every step, the circle of the survivors is circumscribed, but nothing stops the progress of the Plague, which is always fatal. Verney, the narrator, is the only one among all human beings to recover from it. He is thus more than a survivor; he is a ghost. When humanity is reduced to three beings—Raymond, Adrian, and the daughter of Raymond and Perdita—these three survivors decide to embark on a sailing ship for Greece. The boat is shipwrecked; Verney remains alone. Searching for a fellow creature, he goes to Rome, where he spends a year writing and waiting. Finally convinced that no one will come meet him in Rome, he climbs to the top of St. Peter's to carve in stone the following inscription: "the aera 2100, last year of the world." Then, accompanied only by his dog, he embarks for unknown shores.

The life of Mary Shelley was also a series of survivals. Beginning with her birth, which cost her mother her life. At the moment when Mary Shelley wrote *The Last Man*, three of her four children had died, her husband Percy Shelley had drowned in a shipwreck, and Byron had just died in Greece. At the age of twenty-six, she considered herself the last relic of an extinct race.

One could thus affirm that in writing *The Last Man* Mary Shelley only painted her mourning on a universal scale. But that universal scale, that universal perspective on human affairs was just the one which ordinarily characterized the writings of the Romantic poets, especially those of Shelley and Byron. Thus Mary Shelley takes over a typically Romantic style in order to say what she sees as the end of Romanticism. In other words, in this novel, Mary Shelley does more than give a universal vision of her mourning; she mourns for a certain type of universal vision.

For that vision is precisely that of Verney and his companions. In going to seek other survivors in Rome, birthplace of *homo humanus*, Mary

Shelley's last man performs the humanist gesture par excellence: he seeks
to live the death of all of humanity. On his way, he leaves two kinds
of messages, two sorts of "please forward": first, in three languages, he
writes, "Verney, last of the race of Englishmen, had taken up his abode
in Rome"; second, in Italian, "Friend, come! I wait for thee." To speak of
oneself in the third person of the past tense is to take oneself for a historical character, that is, a dead man. To make an invitation in the second
person, in the other's language, is still to expect to live. But after a year
of vain waiting in Rome, Verney realizes that he doesn't know how to
speak the other's language anymore, for he doesn't know any longer who
the other might be. It becomes clear that all roads lead to Rome only for
a certain Western culture which can no longer take itself for the voice of
humanity in its entirety. In leaving Rome to seek an unknown otherness,
Verney also stops writing. In designating the year of his departure the last
year of the world, the last man thus marks the survival of humanist discourse, that is, of the possibility of making history. And yet, in setting off
to wander in search of an unknown destiny, smitten with a culture that
he knows to be obsolete, but incapable of forging for himself a postplague
discourse, Verney could not symbolize better the very condition of modern Western man. How indeed can one survive humanism? How can one
create a language that is postplague, that is, postuniversal?

But what does the Plague signify in this book? In *The Plague*, Albert
Camus writes, "In this respect our townsfolk were like everybody else,
wrapped up in themselves; in other words they were humanists: they dis-
believed in pestilences. A pestilence isn't a thing made to man's measure."[6]
It is evident that, for Mary Shelley as well, the Plague is that which man's
measures can neither foresee nor master. All systems for the amelioration
of man's lot pass in review in this novel, only to end in a blind alley in
front of the Plague. The Plague is at once that which stops all systems
of meaning from functioning and that against which those systems are
necessarily erected.

But just before having them swallowed up by the scourge, Mary Shelley outlines a critique of each of the projects of reform dear to her father
William Godwin and her husband Percy Shelley. In other words, each
time we are about to draw a lesson from the narrative of political events,
the Plague arrives to erase the question. The book does indeed contain a
series of critiques, but *there is no relation* between these critiques and the
train of events. The Plague itself seems neither entirely unavoidable nor

entirely avoidable. Where the poet Percy Shelley, apropos of the French Revolution, spoke of an inadequacy, a "defect of correspondence between the knowledge existing in society and the improvement or gradual abolition of political institutions,"[7] Mary Shelley sees not a defect of correspondence but a *lack of relation* between acquired knowledge and the scene of action.

But the Plague is not only that which stops us from drawing lessons from human events. For it enters the plot at a very precise and significant moment of the novel. The Western world is about to fend off definitively the threat of the East. The Greeks need only to take Constantinople for victory to be complete. But the capture of Constantinople will never happen. Where Western man expects to encounter and to master his other, he finds himself faced with the absolute Other. The novel never tells us the political consequences of this suspension of the final confrontation between East and West. The question of the relation or of the nonrelation between East and West remains open, precisely by the way in which it is badly posed. The Plague, which extends out over the entire world from the point of encounter between East and West, is thus in a sense that which replaces the victory of the West over the East. Its lethal universality is a nightmarish version of the desire to establish a universal discourse, to spread equality and fraternity throughout the world. Thus the universal empire of the Plague would not be only, as Camus suggests, what is *excluded* from Western humanism; it would also be its *inverted image*.

It is not an accident if *The Last Man* begins with praise of England, that England which was mistress of the world's most powerful empire:

> I am the native of a sea-surrounded nook, a cloud-enshadowed land, which, when the surface of the globe, with its shoreless ocean and trackless continents, presents itself to my mind, appears only as an inconsiderable speck in the immense whole; and yet, when balanced in the scale of mental power, far outweighed countries of larger extent and more numerous population. So true it is, that man's mind alone was the creator of all that was good or great to man, and that Nature herself was only his first minister. England, seated far north in the turbid sea, now visits my dreams in the semblance of a vast and well-manned ship, which mastered the winds and rode proudly over the waves. In my boyish days she was the universe to me. When I stood on my native hills . . . the earth's very centre was fixed for me in that spot, and the rest of her orb was as a fable, to have forgotten which would have cost neither my imagination nor understanding an effort.[8]

This image of England as mental mastery, inviolable insularity, self-sufficient centrality, is in fact the image of a certain conception of *man* which will be progressively demystified throughout the novel that follows. But this pitiless demystification is narrated as a series of privations and unendurable sorrows. At each step, one loses again a fatherland which never existed. The story of *The Last Man* is in the last analysis the story of modern Western man torn between mourning and deconstruction.

In a certain sense, one can say that modern literature begins with this end of man, at the moment when the last man leaves Rome without knowing what language to speak to it. It is interesting to note that in the novel by Maurice Blanchot also entitled *The Last Man*, one no longer finds any traditional narrative landmarks. Even the certainty that this is indeed a *narrative* is acquired only in the form of a strange joy, on the last page of the book, "Later, he asked himself how he had entered the calm. He couldn't talk about it with himself. Only joy at feeling he was in harmony with the words: 'Later, he. . . . '"[9] In this end of the book, it's thus a certain relation to language which ends by at once confirming and denying the end, solitude, the possibility of speaking.

Before this last page, Blanchot's book presents itself as a monologue cut into two unequal parts. In the first part, there is an "I," a "he," and a "she" who find themselves in a sort of asylum. After the break between the two parts, the word "event" appears, but the reader no longer knows who is speaking, nor to whom, nor of whom, nor of what event. In other words, in Blanchot's *Last Man* all that remains of traditional "lastmanism" is the questions which the theme obliges us automatically to ask. For a book entitled *The Last Man* is manifestly an impossible book. If the last man is a "he," who is writing the book? If the last man is an "I," who is reading it? Unless the reader is dead . . .

But the reader is inscribed in Mary Shelley's book precisely as dead. At the moment when Verney decides to write the story of the end of man, he begins with the following dedication:

> TO THE ILLUSTRIOUS DEAD.
> SHADOWS, ARISE, AND READ YOUR FALL!
> BEHOLD THE HISTORY OF THE
> LAST MAN.

If man is the one to whom the end is important, it is evident that Verney possesses the most important story that has ever been told. But those to whom that story is important are all necessarily dead. In a certain sense, the story of the end interests only the dead. For to the living, what matters isn't the end, but the future perfect.

Indeed, from the title on, *The Last Man* presents itself as a particularly striking example of the functioning of the future perfect. While normally the future perfect is the tense itself where the meaning of a story is tied up, *The Last Man* promises the reader only a future in which he will not be able to have read the novel. By his reading, the reader only approaches retrospectively his own elimination, while the last man continues beyond his end. But the temporality of this narrative is further complicated by a supplementary fold, an author's introduction which tells us that this story of the last man that we have under our eyes is in reality only the imperfect and doubtless deformed translation of certain inscriptions found in 1818 on scattered leaves in the cavern of the Sybil of Cumae. What is at issue is thus a translation made in the nineteenth century of a prophecy uttered in Antiquity which takes the form of a narrative written by a man of the twenty-first century on the subject of the end of man. The end of man, in other words, will have always already coincided with the moment of predicting, the moment of translating, and the moment of writing. Unless, however, this is an error of translation.

Barbara Johnson

My Monster / My Self

To judge from recent trends in scholarly as well as popular literature, three crucial questions can be seen to stand at the forefront of today's preoccupations: the question of mothering, the question of the woman writer, and the question of autobiography. Although these questions and current discussions of them often appear unrelated to each other, it is my intention here to explore some ways in which the three questions *are* profoundly interrelated. To attempt to shed some new light on each by approaching it via the others, I shall base my remarks upon two twentieth-century theoretical studies—Nancy Friday's *My Mother/My Self* and Dorothy Dinnerstein's *The Mermaid and the Minotaur*—and one nineteenth-century gothic novel, *Frankenstein; or, The Modern Prometheus*, written by Mary Shelley, whose importance for literary history has until quite recently been considered to arise not from her own writings but from the fact that she was the second wife of poet Percy Bysshe Shelley and the daughter of the political philosopher William Godwin and the pioneering feminist Mary Wollstonecraft.[1]

All three of these books, in strikingly diverse ways, offer a critique of the institution of parenthood. *The Mermaid and the Minotaur* is an analysis of the damaging effects of the fact that human infants are cared for almost exclusively by women. "What the book's title as a whole is meant to connote," writes Dinnerstein, "is both (*a*) our longstanding general awareness of our uneasy, ambiguous position in the animal kingdom, and (*b*) a more specific awareness: that until we grow strong enough to renounce the pernicious forms of collaboration between the sexes, both man and woman will remain semi-human, monstrous" (p. 5). Even as

Dinnerstein describes convincingly the types of imbalance and injustice the prevailing asymmetry in gender relations produces, she also analyzes the reasons for our refusal to abandon the very modes of monstrousness from which we suffer most. Nancy Friday's book, which is subtitled "The Daughter's Search for Identity," argues that the mother's repression of herself necessitated by the myth of maternal love creates a heritage of self-rejection, anger, and duplicity that makes it difficult for the daughter to seek any emotional satisfaction other than the state of idealized symbiosis that both mother and daughter continue to punish themselves for never having been able to achieve. Mary Shelley's *Frankenstein* is an even more elaborate and unsettling formulation of the relation between parenthood and monstrousness. It is the story of two antithetical modes of parenting that give rise to two increasingly parallel lives—the life of Victor Frankenstein, who is the beloved child of two doting parents, and the life of the monster he single-handedly creates but immediately spurns and abandons. The fact that in the end both characters reach an equal degree of alienation and self-torture and indeed become indistinguishable as they pursue each other across the frozen polar wastes indicates that the novel is, among other things, a study of the impossibility of finding an adequate model for what a parent should be.

All three books agree, then, that in the existing state of things there is something inherently monstrous about the prevailing parental arrangements. While Friday and Dinnerstein, whose analyses directly address the problem of sexual difference, suggest that this monstrousness is curable, Mary Shelley, who does not explicitly locate the self's monstrousness in its gender arrangements, appears to dramatize divisions within the human being that are so much a part of being human that no escape from monstrousness seems possible.

What I will try to do here is to read these three books not as mere studies of the monstrousness of selfhood, not as mere accounts of human monsterdom in general, but as autobiographies in their own right, as textual dramatizations of the very problems with which they deal. None of the three books, of course, presents itself explicitly as autobiography. Yet each includes clear instances of the autobiographical—not the purely authorial—first-person pronoun. In each case the autobiographical reflex is triggered by the resistance and ambivalence involved in the act of writing the book. What I shall argue here is that what is specifically feminist in each book is directly related to this struggle for female authorship.

The notion that *Frankenstein* can somehow be read as the autobiography of a woman would certainly appear at first sight to be ludicrous. The novel, indeed, presents not one but three autobiographies of men. Robert Walton, an arctic explorer on his way to the North Pole, writes home to his sister of his encounter with Victor Frankenstein, who tells Walton the story of his painstaking creation and unexplained abandonment of a nameless monster who suffers excruciating and fiendish loneliness, and who tells Frankenstein *his* life story in the middle pages of the book. The three male autobiographies motivate themselves as follows:

> [Walton, to his sister:] "You will rejoice to hear that no disaster has accompanied the commencement of an enterprise which you have regarded with such evil forebodings. I arrived here yesterday, and my first task is to assure my dear sister of my welfare." (p. 15)

> [Frankenstein, with his hands covering his face, to Walton, who has been speaking of his scientific ambition:] "Unhappy man! Do you share my madness? Have you drunk also of the intoxicating draught? Hear me; let me reveal my tale, and you will dash the cup from your lips!" (p. 26)

> [Monster, to Frankenstein:] "I entreat you to hear me before you give vent to your hatred on my devoted head." [Frankenstein:] "Begone! I will not hear you. There can be no community between you and me." [Monster places his hands before Frankenstein's eyes:] "Thus I take from thee a sight which you abhor. Still thou canst listen to me and grant me thy compassion. . . . God, in pity, made man beautiful and alluring, after his own image; but my form is a filthy type of yours, more horrid even from the very resemblance." (pp. 95, 96, 97, 125)

All three autobiographies here are clearly attempts at persuasion rather than simple accounts of facts. They all depend on a presupposition of resemblance between teller and addressee: Walton assures his sister that he has not really left the path she would wish for him, that he still resembles *her.* Frankenstein recognizes in Walton an image of himself and rejects in the monster a resemblance he does not wish to acknowledge. The teller is in each case speaking into a mirror of his own transgression. The tale is designed to reinforce the resemblance between teller and listener so that somehow transgression can be eliminated. Yet the desire for resemblance, the desire to create a being like oneself—which is the autobiographical desire par excellence—is also the central transgression in Mary Shelley's novel. What is at stake in Frankenstein's workshop of filthy creation is precisely the possibility of shaping a life in one's own image: Frankenstein's monster can thus be seen as a figure for autobiography as such. Victor Frankenstein, then, has twice obeyed the impulse to construct an image of himself: on the first occasion he creates a monster, and on the second he tries to explain to Walton the causes and consequences of the first. *Frankenstein* can be read as the story of autobiography as the attempt to neutralize the monstrosity of autobiography. Simultaneously a revelation and a cover-up, autobiography would appear to constitute itself as in some way a repression of autobiography.

These three fictive male autobiographies are embedded within a thin introductory frame, added in 1831, in which Mary Shelley herself makes the repression of her own autobiographical impulse explicit:

> The publishers of the standard novels, in selecting *Frankenstein* for one of their series, expressed a wish that I should furnish them with some account of the origin of the story. . . . It is true that I am very averse to bringing myself forward in print, but as my account will only appear as an appendage to a former production, and as it will be confined to such topics as have connection with my authorship alone, I can scarcely accuse myself of a personal intrusion. (p. vii)

Mary Shelley, here, rather than speaking into a mirror, is speaking as an appendage to a text. It might perhaps be instructive to ask whether this change of status has anything to do with the problem of specifically feminine autobiography. In a humanistic tradition in which *man* is the measure of all things, how does an appendage go about telling the story of her life?

Before pursuing this question further, I would like to turn to a more explicit version of surreptitious feminine autobiography. Of the three books under discussion, Nancy Friday's account of the mother/daughter relationship relies the most heavily on the facts of the author's life in order to demonstrate its thesis. Since the author grew up without a father, she shares with Frankenstein's monster some of the problems of coming from a single-parent household. The book begins with a chapter entitled "Mother Love," of which the first two sentences are "I have always lied to my mother. And she to me" (p. 19). Interestingly, the book carries the following dedication: "When I stopped seeing my mother with the eyes of a child, I saw the woman who helped me give birth to myself. This book is for Jane Colbert Friday Scott." How then, can we be sure that this huge book is not itself another lie to the mother it is dedicated to? Is autobiography somehow always in the process of symbolically killing the mother off by telling her the lie that we have given birth to ourselves? On page 460, Nancy Friday is still not sure what kind of lie she has told. She writes: "I am suddenly afraid that the mother I have depicted throughout this book is false." Whose life is this, anyway? This question cannot be resolved by a book that sees the "daughter's search for identity" as the necessity of choosing *between* symbiosis and separation, *between* the mother and the autonomous self. As long as this polarity remains unquestioned, the autobiography of Nancy Friday becomes the drawing and redrawing of the portrait of Jane Colbert Friday Scott. The most truly autobiographical moments occur not in expressions of triumphant separation but in descriptions of the way the book itself attempts to resist its own writing. At the end of the chapter on loss of virginity, Nancy Friday writes:

> It took me twenty-one years to give up my virginity. In some similar manner I am unable to let go of this chapter. . . .
>
> It is no accident that wrestling with ideas of loss of virginity immediately bring me to a dream of losing my mother. This chapter has revealed a split in me. Intellectually, I think of myself as a sexual person, just as I had intellectually been able to put my ideas for this chapter down on paper. Subjectively, I don't want to face what I have written: that the declaration of full sexual independence is the declaration of separation from my mother. As long as I don't finish this chapter, as long as I don't let myself understand the implication of what I've written, I can maintain the illusion, at least, that I can be sexual and have my mother's love and approval too. (pp. 331–333)

As long as sexual identity and mother's judgment are linked as antithetical and exclusive poles of the daughter's problem, the "split" she describes will prevent her from ever completing her declaration of sexual independence. "Full sexual independence" is shown by the book's own resistance to be as illusory and as mystifying an ideal as the notion of "mother love" that Friday so lucidly rejects.

Dinnerstein's autobiographical remarks are more muted, although her way of letting the reader know that the book was written partly in mourning for her husband subtly underlies its persuasive seriousness. In her gesture of rejecting more traditional forms of scholarship, she pleads not for the validity but for the urgency of her message:

> Right now, what I think is that the kind of work of which this is an example is centrally necessary work. Whether our understanding makes a difference or

not, we must try to understand what is threatening to kill us off as fully and clearly as we can. . . . What [this book] is, then, is not a scholarly book: it makes no effort to survey the relevant literature. Not only would that task be (for me) unmanageably huge. It would also be against my principles. I *believe* in reading unsystematically and taking notes erratically. Any effort to form a rational policy about what to take in, out of the inhuman flood of printed human utterance that pours over us daily, feels to me like a self-deluded exercise in pseudomastery. (pp. viii–ix)

The typographical form of this book bears out this belief in renouncing the appearance of mastery: there are two kinds of notes, some at the foot of the page and some at the back of the book; there are sections between chapters with unaligned right-hand margins which are called "Notes toward the next chapter." And there are boldface inserts which carry on a dialogue with the controversial points in the main exposition. Clearly, great pains have been taken to let as many seams as possible show in the fabric of the argument. The preface goes on:

> I mention these limitations in a spirit not of apology but of warning. To the extent that it succeeds in communicating its point at all, this book will necessarily enrage the reader. What it says is emotionally threatening. *(Part of why it has taken me so long to finish it is that I am threatened by it myself.)* (p. ix; emphasis mine)

My book is roughly sutured, says Dinnerstein, and it is threatening. This description sounds uncannily like a description of Victor Frankenstein's monster. Indeed, Dinnerstein goes on to warn the reader not to be tempted to avoid the threatening message by pointing to superficial flaws in its physical makeup. The reader of *Frankenstein*, too, would be well advised to look beyond the monster's physical deformity, both for his fearsome power and for his beauty. There are indeed numerous ways in which *The Mermaid and the Minotaur* can be seen as a modern rewriting of *Frankenstein*.

Dinnerstein's book situates its plea for two-sex parenting firmly in an apparently twentieth-century double bind: the realization that the very technological advances that make it possible to change the structure of parenthood also threaten to extinguish earthly life altogether. But it is startling to note that this seemingly contemporary pairing of the question of parenthood with a love-hate relation to technology is already at work in Mary Shelley's novel, where the spectacular scientific discovery of the secrets of animation produces a terrifyingly vengeful creature who attributes his evil impulses to his inability to find or to become a parent. Subtitled "The Modern Prometheus," *Frankenstein* itself indeed refers back to a myth that already links scientific ambivalence with the origin of mankind. Prometheus, the fire bringer, the giver of both creation and destruction, is also said by some accounts to be the father of the human race. Ambivalence toward technology can thus be seen as a displaced version of the love-hate relation we have toward our own children.

It is only recently that critics have begun to see Victor Frankenstein's disgust at the sight of his creation as a study of postpartum depression, as a representation of maternal rejection of a newborn infant, and to relate the entire novel to Mary Shelley's mixed feelings about motherhood.[2] Having lived through an unwanted pregnancy from a man married to someone else only to see that baby die, followed by a second baby named William—which is the name of the monster's first murder victim—Mary Shelley, at the age of only eighteen, must have had excruciatingly divided emotions. Her own mother, indeed, had died upon giving birth to her. The idea that a mother can loathe, fear, and reject her baby has until recently been one of the most repressed of psychoanalytical insights, although it is of course already implicit in the story of Oedipus, whose parents cast him out as an infant to die. What is threatening about each of these books is the way in which its critique of the *role* of the mother touches on primitive terrors of the mother's rejection of the child. Each of these women writers does in her way reject the child as part of her coming to grips with the untenable nature of mother love: Nancy Friday decides not to have children, Dorothy Dinnerstein argues that men as well as women should do the mothering, and Mary Shelley describes a parent who flees in disgust from the repulsive being to whom he has just given birth.

Yet it is not merely in its depiction of the ambivalence of motherhood that Mary Shelley's novel can be read as autobiographical. In the introductory note added in 1831, she writes:

> The publishers of the standard novels, in selecting *Frankenstein* for one of their series, expressed a wish that I should furnish them with some account of the origin of the story. I am the more willing to comply because I shall thus give a general answer to the question so very frequently asked me—how I, then a young girl, came to think of and to *dilate* upon so very hideous an idea. (p. vii; emphasis mine)

As this passage makes clear, readers of Mary Shelley's novel had frequently expressed the feeling that a young girl's fascination with the idea of monstrousness was somehow monstrous in itself. When Mary ends her introduction to the reedition of her novel with the words, "And now, once again, I bid my hideous progeny go forth and prosper," the reader begins to suspect that there may perhaps be meaningful parallels between Victor's creation of his monster and Mary's creation of her book.

Such parallels are indeed unexpectedly pervasive. The impulse to write the book and the desire to search for the secret of animation both arise under the same seemingly trivial circumstances: the necessity of finding something to read on a rainy day. During inclement weather on a family vacation, Victor Frankenstein happens upon the writings of Cornelius Agrippa and is immediately fired with the longing to penetrate the secrets of life and death. Similarly, it was during a wet, ungenial summer in Switzerland that Mary, Shelley, Byron, and several others picked up a volume of ghost stories and decided to write a collection of spine-tingling tales of their own. Moreover, Mary's discovery of the subject she would write about is described in almost exactly the same words as Frankenstein's discovery of the principle of life: "Swift as light and as cheering was the idea that broke in upon me" (p. xi), writes Mary in her introduction, while Frankenstein says: "From the midst of this darkness a sudden light broke in upon me" (p. 51). In both cases the sudden flash of inspiration must be supported by the meticulous gathering of heterogeneous, ready-made materials: Frankenstein collects bones and organs; Mary records overheard discussions of scientific questions that lead her to the sudden vision of monstrous creation. "Invention," she writes of the process of writing, but her words apply equally well to Frankenstein's labors, "Invention . . . does not consist in creating out of the void, but out of chaos; the materials must, in the first place, be afforded: it can give form to dark, shapeless substances but cannot bring into being the substance itself" (p. x). Perhaps the most revealing indication of Mary's identification of Frankenstein's activity with her own is to be found in her use of the word "artist" on two different occasions to qualify the "pale student of unhallowed arts": "His success would terrify the artist" (p. xi), she writes of the catastrophic moment of creation, while Frankenstein confesses to Walton: "I appeared rather like one doomed by slavery to toil in the mines, or any other unwholesome trade than an artist occupied by his favorite employment" (p. 55).

Frankenstein, in other words, can be read as the story of the experience of writing *Frankenstein*. What is at stake in Mary's introduction as well as in the novel is the description of a primal scene of creation. *Frankenstein* combines a monstrous answer to two of the most fundamental questions one can ask: Where do babies come from? and Where do stories come from? In both cases, the scene of creation is described, but the answer to these questions is still withheld.

But what can Victor Frankenstein's workshop of filthy creation teach us about the specificity of *female* authorship? At first sight, it would seem that *Frankenstein* is much more striking for its avoidance of the question of femininity than for its insight into it. All the interesting, complex characters in the book are male, and their deepest attachments are to other males. The females, on the other hand, are beautiful, gentle, selfless, boring nurturers and victims who never experience inner conflict or true desire. Monstrousness is so incompatible with femininity that Frankenstein cannot even complete the female companion that his creature so eagerly awaits.

On the other hand, the story of Frankenstein is, after all, the story of a man who usurps the female role by physically giving birth to a child. It would be tempting, therefore, to conclude that Mary Shelley, surrounded as she then was by the male poets Byron and Shelley, and mortified for days by her inability to think of a story to contribute to their ghost-story contest, should have fictively transposed her own frustrated female pen envy into a tale of catastrophic male womb envy. In this perspective, Mary's book would suggest that a woman's desire to write and a man's desire to give birth would both be capable only of producing monsters.

Yet clearly things cannot be so simple. As the daughter of a famous feminist whose *A Vindication of the Rights of Woman* she was in the process of rereading during the time she was writing *Frankenstein*, Mary Shelley would have no conscious reason to believe that writing was not proper for a woman. Indeed, as she says in her introduction, Mary was practically born with ink flowing through her veins. "It is not singular that, as the daughter of two persons of distinguished literary celebrity, I should very early in life have thought of writing. . . . My husband . . . was from the first very anxious that I should prove myself worthy of my parentage and enroll myself on the page of fame" (pp. vii–viii). In order to prove herself worthy of her parentage, Mary, paradoxically enough, must thus usurp the parental role and succeed in giving birth to *herself* on paper. Her declaration of existence as a writer must therefore figuratively repeat the matricide that her physical birth all too literally entailed. The connection between literary creation and the death of a parent is in fact suggested in the novel by the fact that, immediately after the monster's animation, Victor Frankenstein dreams that he holds the corpse of his dead mother in his arms. It is also suggested by the juxtaposition of two seemingly unrelated uses of italics in the novel: Mary's statement that she had *"thought of a story"* (which she inexplicably italicizes twice) and the monster's promise to Frankenstein, *"I will be with you on your wedding night,"* which is repeatedly italicized. Both are eliminations of the mother, since the story Mary writes is a tale of motherless birth, and the wedding night marks the death of Frankenstein's bride, Elizabeth. Indeed, Mary herself was in fact the unwitting murderous intruder present on her own parents' wedding night: their decision to marry was due to the fact that Mary Wollstonecraft was already carrying the child that was to kill her. When Mary, describing her waking vision of catastrophic creation, affirms that "his success would terrify the artist," she is not giving vent to any ordinary fear-of-success syndrome. Rather, what her book suggests is that what is at stake behind what is currently being banalized under the name of female fear of success is nothing less than the fear of somehow effecting the death of one's own parents.

It is not, however, the necessary murderousness of any declaration of female subjectivity that Mary Shelley's novel is proposing as its most troubling message of monsterdom. For, in a strikingly contemporary sort of predicament, Mary had not one but *two* mothers, each of whom consisted in the knowledge of the unviability of the other. After the death of Mary Wollstonecraft, Mary's father, William Godwin, married a woman as opposite in character and outlook as possible, a staunch, housewifely mother of two who clearly preferred her own children to Godwin's. Between the courageous, passionate, intelligent, and suicidal mother Mary knew only through her writings and the vulgar, repressive "pustule of vanity" whose dislike she resented and returned, Mary must have known at first hand a whole gamut of feminine contradictions, impasses, and options. For the complexities of the demands, desires, and sufferings of Mary's life as a woman were staggering. Her father, who had once been a vehement opponent of the institution of marriage, nearly disowned his daughter for running away with Shelley, an already married disciple of Godwin's own former views. Shelley himself, who believed in multiple love objects, amicably fostered an erotic correspondence between Mary and his friend Thomas Jefferson Hogg, among others. For years, Mary and Shelley were accompanied everywhere by Mary's stepsister Claire, whom Mary did not particularly like, who had a child by Byron, and who maintained an ambiguous relation with Shelley. During the writing of *Frankenstein*, Mary learned of the suicide of her half-sister Fanny Imlay, her mother's illegitimate child by an American lover, and the suicide of Shelley's wife Harriet, who was pregnant by a man other than Shelley. By the time she and Shelley married, Mary had had two children; she would have two more by the time of Shelley's death and watch as all but one of the children died in infancy. Widowed at age twenty-four, she never remarried. It is thus indeed perhaps the very hiddenness of the question of femininity in *Frankenstein* that somehow proclaims the painful message not of female monstrousness but of female contradictions. For it is the fact of self-contradiction that is so vigorously repressed in women. While the story of a man who is haunted by his own contradictions is representable as an allegory of monstrous doubles, how indeed would it have been possible for Mary to represent feminine contradiction *from the point of view of its repression* otherwise than precisely in the *gap* between angels of domesticity and an uncompleted monsteress, between the murdered Elizabeth and the dismembered Eve?

It is perhaps because the novel does succeed in conveying the unresolvable contradictions inherent in being female that Percy Shelley himself felt compelled to write a prefatory disclaimer in Mary's name before he could let loose his wife's hideous progeny upon the world. In a series of denials jarringly at odds with the daring negativity of the novel, Shelley places the following words in Mary's mouth:

> I am by no means indifferent to the manner in which whatever moral tendencies exist in the sentiments or characters it contains shall affect the reader; yet my chief concern in this respect has been limited to . . . the exhibition of the amiableness of domestic affection, and the excellence of universal virtue. The opinions which naturally spring from the character and situation of the hero are by no means to be conceived as existing always in my own conviction; nor is any inference justly to be drawn from the following pages as prejudicing any philosophical doctrine of whatever kind. (pp. xiii–xiv)

How is this to be read except as a gesture of repression of the very specificity of the power of feminine contradiction, a gesture reminiscent of Frankenstein's destruction of his nearly completed female monster? What is being repressed here is the possibility that a woman can write anything that would *not* exhibit "the amiableness of domestic affection," the possibility that for women as well as for men the home can be the very site of the *unheimlich*.

It can thus be seen in all three of the books we have discussed that the monstrousness of selfhood is intimately embedded within the question of female autobiography. Yet how could it be otherwise, since the very notion of a self, the very shape of human life stories, has always, from Saint Augustine to Freud, been modeled on the man? Rousseau's—or any man's—autobiography consists in the story of the difficulty of conforming to the standard of what a *man* should be. The problem for the female autobiographer is, on the one hand, to resist the pressure of masculine autobiography as the only literary genre available for her enterprise, and, on the other, to describe a difficulty in conforming to a female ideal which is largely a fantasy of the masculine, not the feminine, imagination. The fact that these three books deploy a *theory* of autobiography as monstrosity within the framework of a less overtly avowed struggle with the raw materials of the authors' own lives and writing is perhaps, in the final analysis, what is most autobiographically fertile and *telling* about them.

Barbara Johnson

Gender Theory and the Yale School[1]

I hope that by the end of this paper I will not have bitten off more of the hand that feeds me than I can chew.

> —From the original introduction to
> "Gender Theory and the Yale School"

In January 1984, shortly after the death of Paul de Man, I received a call from Robert Con Davis and Ronald Schleifer inviting me to attempt the painful and obviously impossible task of replacing de Man in a conference entitled "Genre Theory and the Yale School" in which Geoffrey Hartman, Hillis Miller, and Paul de Man had been asked to speak about genre theory in relation to their own work. I was invited to speak, however, not about *my* own work but about de Man's. The reasons for this are certainly understandable. I could easily sympathize with the conference organizers' impulse: there is nothing I could wish more than that de Man had not died. But the invitation to appear as de Man's *supplé-ment*—supplemented in turn by a panel on de Man with participants of my own choosing—gave me pause. For it falls all too neatly into patterns of female effacement already well established by the phenomenon of the Yale School—and indeed, with rare exceptions, by the phenomenon of the critical "school" as such. Like others of its type, the Yale School has always been a Male School.

Would it have been possible for there to have been a female presence in the Yale School? Interestingly, in Jonathan Culler's bibliography to *On Deconstruction*, Shoshana Felman's book *La Folie et la chose littéraire* is described as "a wide-ranging collection of essays by a member of the 'école de Yale.'"[2] Felman, in other words, *was* a member of the Yale School, but only in French. This question of the foreignness of the female language will return, but for now, suffice it to say that there was no reason other than gender why Felman's work—certainly closer to de Man's and Derrida's than the work of Harold Bloom—should not have been seen as an integral part of the Yale School. At the time of the publication of the Yale School's nonmanifesto, *Deconstruction and Criticism*, several of us— Shoshana Felman, Gayatri Spivak, Margaret Ferguson, and I—discussed the possibility of writing a companion volume inscribing female decon- structive protest and affirmation centering not on Percy Bysshe Shelley's "The Triumph of Life" (as the existing volume was originally slated to do) but on Mary Shelley's *Frankenstein*. That book might truly have illus- trated the Girardian progression "from mimetic desire to the monstrous double." Unfortunately, this *Bride of Deconstruction and Criticism* never quite got off the ground, but it is surely no accident that the project was centered around monstrosity. As Derrida puts it in "The Law of Genre" (which is also, of course, a law of gender), "As soon as genre announces itself, one must respect a norm, one must not cross a line of demarcation, one must not risk impurity, anomaly, or monstrosity."[3] After all, Aristotle, the founder of the law of gender as well as of the law of genre, considered the female the first distortion of the genus "man" en route to becoming a monster. But perhaps it was not *Frankenstein* but rather *The Last Man*, Mary Shelley's grim depiction of the gradual extinction of humanity alto- gether, that would have made a fit counterpart to "The Triumph of Life." Percy Bysshe Shelley is entombed in both, along with a certain male fan- tasy of Romantic universality. The only universality that remains in Mary Shelley's last novel is the plague.

It would be easy to accuse the male Yale School theorists of having avoided the issue of gender entirely. What I intend to do, however, is to demonstrate that they have had quite a lot to say about the issue, often without knowing it. Before moving on to a female version of the Yale School, therefore, I will begin by attempting to extract from the es- says in *Deconstruction and Criticism* and related texts an implicit theory of the relations between gender and criticism. For the purposes of this paper, I will focus on the four members of the Yale School who have actually taught full time at Yale. Since Derrida, the fifth participant in *Deconstruction and Criticism*, has in contrast consistently and explic- itly foregrounded the question of gender, his work would demand far more extensive treatment than is possible here. I will confine myself to the more implicit treatments of the subject detectable in the writings of Bloom, Hartman, Miller, and de Man.

Geoffrey Hartman, ever the master of the throwaway line, has not failed to make some memorable remarks about the genderedness of the reading process. "Much reading," he writes in *The Fate of Reading*, "is indeed, like girl-watching, a simple expense of spirit." And in *Beyond Formalism*, he claims: "Interpretation is like a football game. You spot a hole and you go through it. But first you may have to induce that opening."[4]

In his essay in *Deconstruction and Criticism*, Hartman examines a poem in which Wordsworth, suddenly waylaid by a quotation, addresses his daughter Dora with a line from Milton's *Samson* that harks back to the figure of blind Oedipus being led by his daughter Antigone:

> A little onward lend thy guiding hand
> To these dark steps, a little further on![5]

This is certainly a promising start for an investigation of gender relations. Yet Wordsworth and Hartman combine to curb the step of this budding Delilah and to subsume the daughter under the Wordsworthian category of "child," who, as everyone knows, is *Father* of the man. While the poem works out the power reversal between blind father and guiding daughter, restoring the father to his role of natural leader, the commentary works out *its* patterns of reversibility between Wordsworth and Milton. "Let me, thy happy guide, now point thy way / And now precede thee." When Wordsworth leads his daughter to the edge of the abyss, it is the abyss of intertextuality.

While brooding on the abyss in *The Fate of Reading*, Hartman looks back at his own precursor self and says: "In *The Unmediated Vision* the tyranny of sight in the domain of sensory organization is acknowledged, and symbol making is understood as a kind of 'therapeutic alliance' between the eye and other senses through the medium of art. I remember how easy it was to put a woman in the landscape, into every eyescape rather; and it struck me that in works of art there were similar centers, depicted or inferred" (p. 6). Yet the woman in Wordsworth's poemscape is precisely what Hartman does not see. And this may be just what Wordsworth intended. In the short paragraph in which Hartman acknowledges that there may be something oedipal about this Oedipus figure, he describes the daughter as *barred* by the incest prohibition. The poem would then transmit a disguised desire for the daughter, repressed and deflected into literary structures. Yet might it not also be that Wordsworth so often used incest figures in his poetry as a way, precisely, of barring the reality of the woman as other, a way of keeping the woman in and *only* in the

eyescape, making a nun out of a nymph? For the danger here is that the
daughter will neither follow nor lead, but simply leave:

> the birds salute
> The cheerful dawn, brightening for me the east;
> For me, thy natural leader, once again
> Impatient to conduct thee, not as erst
> A tottering infant, with compliant stoop
> From flower to flower supported; but to curb
> Thy nymph-like step swift-bounding o'er the lawn,
> Along the loose rocks, or the slippery verge
> Of foaming torrents.

The family romance takes a slightly different form in Hillis Miller's essay,
"The Critic as Host." In that essay, Miller discusses Booth's and Abrams's
image of deconstructive criticism as "parasitical" on the "obvious or uni-
vocal reading" of a text. Miller writes:

> "Parasitical"—the word suggests the image of "the obvious or univocal read-
> ing" as the mighty oak, rooted in the solid ground, endangered by the insidi-
> ous twining around it of deconstructive ivy. That ivy is somehow feminine,
> secondary, defective, or dependent. It is a clinging vine, able to live in no
> other way but by drawing the life sap of its host, cutting off its light and air. I
> think of Hardy's *The Ivy-Wife.* . . .
>   Such sad love stories of a domestic affection which introduces the parasitical
> into the closed economy of the home no doubt describe well enough the way
> some people feel about the relation of a "deconstructive" interpretation to "the
> obvious or univocal reading." The parasite is destroying the host. The alien has
> invaded the house, perhaps to kill the father of the family in an act which does
> not look like parricide, but is. Is the "obvious" reading, though, so "obvious"
> or even so "univocal"? May it not itself be the uncanny alien which is so close
> that it cannot be seen as strange? (*Deconstruction and Criticism*, p. 218)

It is interesting to note how effortlessly the vegetal metaphor is sexualized in Miller's elaboration of it. If the parasite is the feminine, then
the feminine must be recognized as that uncanny alien always already
in the house—and in the host. What turns out, in Miller's etymological
analysis, to be uncanny about the relation between host and parasite—
and by extension between male and female—is that each is already inhabited by the other as a difference from itself. Miller then goes on to describe
the parasite as invading virus in the following terms: "The genetic pattern

of the virus is so coded that it can enter a host cell and violently reprogram all the genetic material in that cell, turning the cell into a little factory for manufacturing copies of itself, so destroying it. This is *The Ivy-Wife*, with a vengeance" (*Deconstruction and Criticism*, p. 222). Miller then goes on to ask, "Is this an allegory, and if so, of what?" Perhaps of the gender codes of literature, or of criticism. But this image of cancerous femininity may be less a fear of takeover than an extreme version of the desire to deny difference. There is perhaps something reassuring about total annihilation as opposed to precarious survival. The desire to deny difference is in fact, in a euphoric rather than a nightmarish spirit, the central desire dramatized by the Shelley poems Miller analyzes. The obsessive cry for oneness, for sameness, always, however, meets the same fate: it cannot subsume and erase the trace of its own elaboration. The story Shelley tells again and again is the story of the failure of the attempt to abolish difference. As Miller points out, difference is rediscovered in the linguistic traces of that failure. But a failed erasure of difference is not the same as a recognition of difference—unless, as Miller's analysis suggests, difference can be recognized only in the failure of its erasure.

If the parasite is both feminine and parricidal, then the parasite can only be a daughter. Miller does not follow up on the implications of a parricidal daughter, but Harold Bloom, whose critical system is itself a garden of parricidal delights, gives us a clue to what would be at stake for him in such an idea. In *A Map of Misreading* he writes:

> Nor are there Muses, nymphs who *know*, still available to tell us the secrets of continuity, for the nymphs certainly are now departing. I prophesy though that the first true break with literary continuity will be brought about in generations to come, if the burgeoning religion of Liberated Woman spreads from its clusters of enthusiasts to dominate the West. Homer will cease to be the inevitable precursor, and the rhetoric and forms of our literature then may break at last from tradition.[6]

In Bloom's prophetic vision of the breaking of tradition through the liberation of woman, it is as though the Yale School were in danger of becoming a Jael School.[7]

The dependence of Bloom's revisionary ratios upon a linear patriarchal filiation has been pointed out often enough—particularly in the groundbreaking work of Sandra Gilbert and Susan Gubar—that there is no need to belabor it here. I will therefore, instead, analyze the opening

lines of Bloom's essay "The Breaking of Form" as a strong misreading of
the question of sexual difference. The essay begins: "The word *meaning*
goes back to a root that signifies 'opinion' or 'intention,' and is closely
related to the word *moaning*. A poem's meaning is a poem's complaint, its
version of Keats' Belle Dame, who looked *as if* she loved, and made sweet
moan. Poems instruct us in how they break form to bring about meaning, so as to utter a complaint, a moaning intended to be all their own"
(*Deconstruction and Criticism*, p. 1). If the relation between the reader and
the poem is analogous to the relation between the knight-at-arms and the
Belle Dame, things are considerably more complicated than they appear.
For the encounter between male and female in Keats's poem is a perfectly
ambiguous disaster. Rather than a clear "as if," Keats writes: "She looked
at me *as* she did love, / And made sweet moan." Suspicion of the woman
is not planted quite so clearly, nor quite so early. In changing "as" to "as
if," Bloom has removed from the poem the possibility of reading this first
mention of the woman's feelings as straight description. Perhaps Bloom
is here demonstrating what he says elsewhere about the study of poetry
being "the study of what Stevens called 'the intricate evasions of as.'" By
the end of the poem, it becomes impossible to know whether one has
read a story of a knight enthralled by a witch or of a woman seduced and
abandoned by a male hysteric. And the fine balance of that undecidability
depends on the "as."

If the poem, like the woman, "makes sweet moan," then there is con-
siderable doubt about the reader's capacity to read it. This becomes all
the more explicit in the knight's second interpretive assessment of the
woman's feelings: "And sure in language strange she said— / 'I love thee
true.'" The problem of understanding the woman is here a problem of
translation. Even her name can only be expressed in another tongue. The
sexes stand in relation to each other not as two distinct entities but as two
foreign languages. The drama of male hysteria is a drama of premature
assurance of understanding followed by premature panic at the intima-
tion of otherness. Is she mine, asks the knight, or am I hers? If these are
the only two possibilities, the foreignness of the languages cannot be re-
spected. What Bloom demonstrates, perhaps without knowing it, is that
if reading is the gendered activity he paints it as, the reading process is less
a love story than a story of failed translation.

That the question of gender is a question of language becomes even
more explicit in an essay by Paul de Man entitled "The Epistemology of

Metaphor."[8] Translation is at issue in that essay as well, in the very deriva-
tion of the word *metaphor*. "It is no mere play of words," writes de Man,
"that 'translate' is translated in German as '*übersetzen*' which itself translated the Greek '*meta phorein*' or metaphor" (p. 17). In all three words,
what is described is a motion from one place to another. As we shall see,
the question of the relation between gender and figure will have a great
deal to do with this notion of *place*.

De Man's essay begins as follows:

> Metaphors, tropes, and figural language in general have been a perennial
> problem and, at times, a recognized source of embarrassment for philosophi-
> cal discourse and, by extension, for all discursive uses of language including
> historiography and literary analysis. It appears that philosophy either has to
> give up its own constitutive claim to rigor in order to come to terms with the
> figurality of its language or that it has to free itself from figuration altogether.
> And if the latter is considered impossible, philosophy could at least learn to
> control figuration by keeping it, so to speak, in its place, by delimiting the
> boundaries of its influence and thus restricting the epistemological damage
> that it may cause. (p. 13)

This opening paragraph echoes, in its own rhetoric, a passage which oc-
curs later in the essay in which de Man is commenting on a long quotation from Locke. After detailing the reasons for avoiding rhetoric, Locke
nevertheless concludes his discussion of the perils of figuration as follows:
"Eloquence, like the fair sex, has too prevailing beauties in it to suffer itself ever to be spoken against. And it is in vain to find fault with those arts
of deceiving wherein men find pleasure to be deceived" (p. 15). De Man
glosses the Locke passage as follows:

> Nothing could be more eloquent than this denunciation of eloquence. It is
> clear that rhetoric is something one can decorously indulge in as long as one
> knows where it belongs. Like a woman, which it resembles ("like the fair
> sex"), it is a fine thing as long as it is kept in its proper place. Out of place,
> among the serious affairs of men ("if we would speak of things as they are"), it
> is a disruptive scandal—like the appearance of a real woman in a gentleman's
> club where it would only be tolerated as a picture, preferably naked (like the
> image of Truth), framed and hung on the wall. (pp. 15–16)

Following this succinct tongue-in-cheek description of the philosophical tradition as a men's club, de Man goes on to claim that there is "little

epistemological risk in a flowery, witty passage about wit like this one," that things begin to get serious only when the plumber must be called in, but the epistemological damage may already have been done. For the question of language in Locke quickly comes to be centered on the question, "What essence is the proper of man?" This is no idle question, in fact, because what is at stake in the answer is what sort of monstrous births it is permissible to kill. Even in the discussion of Condillac and Kant, the question of sexual difference lurks, as when de Man describes Condillac's discussion of abstractions as bearing a close resemblance to a novel by Ann Radcliffe or Mary Shelley, or when Kant is said to think that rhetoric can be rehabilitated by some "tidy critical housekeeping." De Man's conclusion can be read as applying to the epistemological damage caused as much by gender as by figure: "In each case, it turns out to be impossible to maintain a clear line of distinction between rhetoric, abstraction, symbol, and all other forms of language. In each case, the resulting undecidability is due to the asymmetry of the binary model that opposes the figural to the proper meaning of the figure" (p. 28). The philosopher's place is always within, not outside, the asymmetrical structures of language and of gender, but that place can never, in the final analysis, be proper. It may be impossible to know whether it is the gender question that is determined by rhetoric or rhetoric by gender difference, but it does seem as though these are the terms in which it might be fruitful to pursue the question.

In order to end with a meditation on a possible female version of the Yale School, I would like now to turn to the work of a Yale daughter. For this purpose I have chosen to focus on *The Critical Difference* by Barbara Johnson.[9] What happens when one raises Mary Jacobus's question: "Is there a woman in this text?" The answer is rather surprising. For no book produced by the Yale School seems to have excluded women as effectively as *The Critical Difference*. No women authors are studied. Almost no women critics are cited. And, what is even more surprising, there are almost no female characters in any of the stories analyzed. *Billy Budd*, however triangulated, is a tale of three *men* in a boat. Balzac's *Sarrasine* is the story of a woman who turns out to be a castrated man. And in Johnson's analysis of "The Purloined Letter," the story of oedipal triangularity is transformed into an endlessly repeated chain of fraternal rivalries. In a book that announces itself as a study of difference, the place of the woman is constantly being erased.

This does not mean, however, that the question of sexual difference does not haunt the book from the beginning. In place of a dedication, *The Critical Difference* opens with a quotation from Paul de Man in which difference is dramatized as a scene of exasperated instruction between Archie Bunker and his wife:

> Asked by his wife whether he wants to have his bowling shoes laced over or laced under, Archie Bunker answers with a question: "What's the difference?" Being a reader of sublime simplicity, his wife replies by patiently explaining the difference between lacing over and lacing under, whatever this may be, but provokes only ire. "What's the difference?" did not ask for difference but means instead "I don't give a damn what the difference is." The same grammatical pattern engenders two meanings that are mutually exclusive: the literal meaning asks for the concept (difference) whose existence is denied by the figurative meaning. As long as we are talking about bowling shoes, the consequences are relatively trivial; Archie Bunker, who is a great believer in the authority of origins (as long, of course, as they are the right origins) muddles along in a world where literal and figurative meanings get in each other's way, though not without discomforts. But suppose that it is a *de*-bunker rather than a "Bunker," and a debunker of the arche (or origin), an archie Debunker such as Nietzsche or Jacques Derrida, for instance, who asks the question "What is the Difference?"—and we cannot even tell from his grammar whether he "really" wants to know "what" difference is or is just telling us that we shouldn't even try to find out. Confronted with the question of the difference between grammar and rhetoric, grammar allows us to ask the question, but the sentence by means of which we ask it may deny the very possibility of asking. For what is the use of asking, I ask, when we cannot even authoritatively decide whether a question asks or doesn't ask?

Whatever the rhetorical twists of this magnificent passage, the fact that it is framed as an intersexual dialogue is not irrelevant.

Another essay in *The Critical Difference*, a study of Mallarmé's prose poem "The White Waterlily," offers an even more promising depiction of the rhetoric of sexual difference. The essay begins:

> If human beings were not divided into two biological sexes, there would probably be no need for literature. And if literature could truly say what the relations between the sexes are, we would doubtless not need much of it then, either. Somehow, however, it is not simply a question of literature's ability to say or not to say the truth of sexuality. For from the moment literature begins to try to set things straight on that score, literature itself becomes inextricable

from the sexuality it seeks to comprehend. It is not the life of sexuality that literature cannot capture; it is literature that inhabits the very heart of what makes sexuality problematic for us speaking animals. Literature is not only a thwarted investigator but also an incorrigible perpetrator of the problem of sexuality. (p. 13)

But the prose poem in question ends up dramatizing an inability to know whether the woman one is expecting to encounter has ever truly been present or not. It is as though *The Critical Difference* could describe only the escape of the difference it attempts to analyze. This is even more true of the essay subtitled "What the Gypsy Knew." With such a title, one would expect to encounter at last something about female knowledge. But the point of the analysis is precisely that the poem does not tell us what the gypsy knew. Her prophecy is lost in the ambiguities of Apollinaire's syntax.

There may, however, be something accurate about this repeated dramatization of woman as simulacrum, erasure, or silence. For it would not be easy to assert that the existence and knowledge of the female subject could simply be produced, without difficulty or epistemological damage, within the existing patterns of culture and language. *The Critical Difference* may here be unwittingly pointing to "woman" as one of the things "we do not know we do not know." Johnson concludes her preface with some remarks about ignorance that apply ironically well to her book's own demonstration of an ignorance that pervades Western discourse as a whole: "What literature often seems to tell us is the consequences of the way in which what is not known is not *seen* as unknown. It is not, in the final analysis, what you don't know that can or cannot hurt you. It is what you don't *know* you don't know that spins out and entangles 'that perpetual error we call life'" (p. xii). It is not enough to be a woman writing in order to resist the naturalness of female effacement in the subtly male pseudogenderlessness of language. It would be no easy task, however, to undertake the effort of reinflection or translation required to retrieve the lost knowledge of the gypsy, or to learn to listen with retrained ears to Edith Bunker's patient elaboration of an answer to the question, "What *is* the difference?"

Judith Butler

Afterword
Animating Autobiography:
Barbara Johnson and Mary Shelley's Monster

There remain many good reasons to find Barbara Johnson's 1982 essay "My Monster/My Self" stunning. At the height of "high theory" she was engaging popular feminist texts, such as Nancy Friday's *My Mother/Myself* in a comparative reading with Mary Shelley's *Frankenstein*, without conceding any theoretical rigor; over and against those who would seek to safeguard the literary canon against writing deemed non-canonizable, she insisted on moving between high and low without apology. But the argument is also disorienting: the monster may well be a figure for Mary Shelley's own life story. As Johnson herself points out, it would be difficult to consider Mary Shelley's *Frankenstein* as a female autobiography if only because all the accounts retold within its pages belong to men. Nevertheless, at least two features of the text make it hard to reject the claim that the novel might in some sense be Mary Shelley's autobiographical work; the first is that Victor Frankenstein describes his own creation through metaphors of birth, which suggests that something of women's reproductive capacity is at work in his own form of making; the second is that Shelley and Frankenstein share certain locutions, each regarding their created works as monstrous.

These two points prove to be interrelated, since there is some question about whether giving birth is itself monstrous or is intimately tied to a problem of monstrosity. Johnson makes several remarks about this, but the main one that "stuns" an ordinary reader is that Frankenstein's monster may well provide a refracted and condensed cipher for the murderous impulse that a mother feels toward the child she bears. Thinking about this infanticidal impulse—together with its converse, the matricidal wish pulsing through the child—is surely something quite aversive for feminist theorists of the maternal to encounter, especially those who seek to idealize the scene of early mother-daughter bonding as a pre-Oedipal arcadia. Equally difficult, however, is the task of understanding *Frankenstein* as a story "about" Mary Shelley, given that she appears not at all and that female figures in the novel tend to be flat, compliant, supplementary foils, sacrificial icons of goodness, etc. It is not quite sufficient to say either that the monster reflects Mary Shelley in some mimetic way or that it provides an eloquent metaphor for her private feelings about herself. After all, the monster is not precisely a mirror, but rather the articulation of desire considered aversive and largely disavowed. In Johnson's words, "the desire or resemblance, the desire to create a being like oneself—which is the autobiographical desire itself—is also the central transgression in Mary Shelley's novel" (*World of Difference*, p. 146).[1]

One might object right away that whereas childbearing is a natural phenomenon, the making of Frankenstein's monster is unnatural, but the distinction does not quite hold. After all, the monster is conceived in part through Frankenstein's interest in what animates "the structure of the human frame" (*Frankenstein*, p. 31),[2] and the figure of childbirth in Mary Shelley's introduction to her text seems primarily to characterize her writing. So we might ask whether the monstrous crosses the natural and the unnatural or, rather, establishes that something customarily regarded as aversive and "unnatural" belongs properly to the human frame. Indeed, in Shelley's creation of the character Frankenstein, who within the story creates the monster who seems to share his name, the human frame is animated by a desire that belongs ambiguously to the creator and the form created. And that desire is hardly uniform; as much as it might be described as a desire to give or make life, it is crossed, perhaps inevitably, with a desire to negate the life created or a fear that the life created will take away the creator's own. Perhaps what we call "character" is precisely a stylized negotiation of this set of psychic conflicts.

Johnson makes a few broadly theoretical claims that seem to support this view of the relation between character and psychic states. These remarks are clearly derived from psychoanalysis. The first is that Shelley locates monstrousness not primarily as a function of gender relations, but rather as it "appears to dramatize divisions within the human being that are so much a part of being human that no escape from monstrousness seems possible" (*World of Difference*, p. 145). The second claim centers on the way that division is animated in the relation between author and character: "what is at stake in Frankenstein's workshop of filthy creation is precisely the possibility of shaping a life in one's own image. Frankenstein's monster can thus be seen as a figure for autobiography as such" (*World of Difference*, p. 146). If we understand the character of the monster less as an image that reflects the life of Mary Shelley than as a figure for the predicament of autobiography, we see that the monster cannot be reduced to "projective identification" or any other mimetic operation that would establish a clear parallel between the monster and the author of *Frankenstein*. Rather, as a "figure for autobiography as such" the monster calls into question whether it is really possible to shape a life in one's own image. In the background we can think about Pygmalion, so important for Johnson's own thinking throughout her career, a love that requires that its object turn into a stony and mute form of created perfection. But whereas Pygmalion turns a living being into stone, Frankenstein narrates the process of "infus[ing] life into an inanimate body" (*Frankenstein*, p. 35). The problem with making a living being in this way is not that it fails to achieve verisimilitude with other human forms, but that the creation is itself animated by the murderous impulse and destructive potentiality that belong equivocally to both the creator and the created. The monster describes himself as "an abortion," so in some sense killed in the making, but still alive enough to report on that fact. And what satisfaction do we read in the monster's proclamation, "He is dead who called me into being?" (*Frankenstein*, p. 161). Where does the murderous impulse begin and end, and can we say definitively to whom it belongs?

Is Shelley creating or murdering, and is she herself created (elevated into the pantheon of great writers from whom she is descended) or murdered by what she writes? If Shelley has a desirous and fearful relation to the text she has created, then we might assume that once Frankenstein ceases merely to be a title and a surname and becomes animated as a monstrous figure, the text has already exceeded her control, continuing her own impulse in directions she could not have anticipated. The question "what have I created?" is yet another figure for the monster itself, since the creation already appears as a monster when that question is posed. Something ran off, got out of control, at the moment when the title gave birth to a character by that same name who left his home only to create a monster who roams widely through the landscape and seems to share the name of its creator. Indeed, the title is animated by both

the scientist and his monstrous "progeny," naming a certain form of creation that loses control of what is created. As Frankenstein, the narrator-
scientist, wonders whether he *is* that alien monster he created or whether,
conversely, the monster has made a monster out of him, so the monster,
too, becomes absorbed in a dramatically human form of self-doubt and
self-beratement. Even the monster wonders whether he is that creature
he sees reflected in a "transparent pool," registering surprise and alarm
as he regards himself in that form, suggesting that "monster" is a name
that coincides with that distorted reflexive predicament of seeing oneself
in a way that cannot be assimilated. In an impressively elevated English
prose that was doubtless transferred to him by his twin creators, Shelley
and "Frankenstein," the monster describes his minor mirror stage in the
following way:

> At first I stared back, unable to believe that it was indeed I who was reflected
> in the mirror; and when I became fully convinced that I was in reality the
> monster that I am, I was filled with the bitterest sensations of despondence
> and mortification. Alas! I did not yet entirely know the fatal effects of this
> miserable conformity. (*Frankenstein*, pp. 78–79)

Thus, "Frankenstein" names the text, the scientist, and his monstrous
production, but also the transitive set of effects that each undergoes by
virtue of the other. Of course, one might say that Mary Shelley has created something the effects of which she cannot fathom. Psychologically,
she, the author, unleashes a murderous destructiveness that she may or
may not be able to avow as her own, so that writing this novel is a form
of unleashing—one made particularly acute for women, like Shelley, who
seek to write their way out of a certain marital and kinship bind. Is this
what Barbara Johnson meant to say? And is this the kind of explanation
with which we might be satisfied? It seems to be a true rendering, however
partial, of what is happening here, the beginning of a narrative account
of Mary Shelley through the figure of the monster. Such a psychological
explanation assumes that our task is to discover the psychic workings of
the author. The text is presumed to reflect that inner life, and by decod-
ing the text, we expect to arrive at the truth of that psychic interior. The
text in such an explanation is presumed to mirror the psychic life of its
author, and yet this presumption is undone by the notion that the text is
a refracted and distorted condensation and displacement of a conflictual
set of drives. For instance, what if a series of displacements take place as

the author writes and the character comes into existence, a figure becomes animated who is and is not human in an accepted sense? At stake is the status of the drive as a kind of writing, to be sure, one that does not—and cannot—mimetically reflect its origins. Further, such a psychological reduction implied by the mimetic model remains within the reflexive account of the subject, and fails to understand the pointed challenge to that very idea of authorial creation enacted by the novel. After all, the text elucidates a figure in relation to which its creator is unprepared, appalled, averse, frightened, though also, in some sense, sympathetic, since the figure shares a reality with the one who made it.

So perhaps it is neither a story about Mary Shelley nor a diagnosis of her that we find in *Frankenstein*. Johnson tells her reader rather precisely that the monster is "a figure for" autobiography, not an allegory and not even a meta-psychological story about her life-history. As a "figure," the monster is animated by a set of conflicting trends, and even though this figure moves through a narrative (escaping the bed and room where he was created, exploring polar landscapes, hiding in a hovel from which he can observe human forms of domesticity from a proximate distance, etc.), he is not the same as the story and seems to exist in structural tension with the narration within the story—where is the monster when he is gone? how precisely was he made and animated? what is his fate? Indeed, if the monster is a figure for an autobiographical predicament implied by the wish to shape a life in one's own image, then it seems right to assume that a figure is not the same as the image itself. The figure, rather, names the predicament, disrupting that narcissistic project and exposing its impossibility; it signifies precisely that dimension of the self one cannot bear to see at the same time that it absorbs and enacts the insuperable conflict of the autobiographical project itself. This means that the monster neither contains a "true story" about Mary Shelley nor amounts to a projected "image" of her. The monster does not merely "reflect back" the author or the character but refuses to do so, running off in various directions, unmasterable and destructive. These circuits of reflexivity (the text reflects back the author's inner life, and the monster reflects back Frankenstein's) give way to a story that shows the unmasterable and destructive consequences of trying to compel one's own creation to mirror oneself.

In what sense, then, are we to understand "my monster" and "my self" as connected if the one is not a reflection of the other, if the demand to provide that perfected reflection is disputed and denied within the novel itself? Johnson's essay inserts the backslash between the two parts of that title, miming Nancy Friday's syntactical format to intervene upon Shelley's text. The backslash introduces a form of division explicitly where Mary Shelley's text works the homonymic and polyvalent senses of the name "Frankenstein" (as title, as human character, as monstrous issue, as the whole story of those interrelations). The monster proliferates, or perhaps it is the monstrous that is subject to a wayward logic of replication. It cannot be captured and subdued, suggesting that whatever animates the text takes on a life of its own quite apart from the author's intention or conscious wish. Something unconscious or uncapturable about the wish proves stronger than any conscious hold or narcissistic demand. At one point, Frankenstein tries to chase the monster, only to discover that "the devil eluded my grasp. Suddenly the broad disk of the moon arose and shone full upon his ghastly and distorted shape as he fled with more than mortal speed" (*Frankenstein*, p. 146). Shelley may well be explicitly showing how the monstrous is a by-product of human narcissism, as Johnson suggests, the invariable breakdown of any effort to make and secure an image of oneself purified of all deformity. Indeed, the fixed image seems always to be haunted by a deforming double. Paradoxically, that very effort proves to be a kind of monstrosity that follows from an emphatically narcissistic autobiographical passion to pursue and fix oneself in the form of an image. When the final narrator, Walton, finds Frankenstein dead in the cabin, he describes the spectral double hovering over him: "Over him hung a form which I cannot find words to describe; gigantic in stature, yet uncouth and distorted in its proportions. As he hung over the coffin his face was concealed by long locks of ragged hair; but one vast hand was extended, in colour and texture like that of a mummy. . . . Never did I behold a vision so terrible as his face . . . every feature and gesture seemed instigated by the wildest rage of some incontrollable passion" (*Frankenstein*, p. 158). The monster hangs above the dead body as a "form" but also as a ghostly double or suspended portrait. So there is some question of whether this is a spirit rising from the body, hovering above, an inverted reflection of the one who is gone. As much as the monster is animated by "uncontrollable passion," he is also clearly venting superegoic rage upon himself with "wild and incoherent self-reproaches." A figure for a psyche, then, whose murderous passions and acts stoke forms of guilt understood as moral sadism directed against the self. In what way does this figure of the psyche hang above the text, the emanation of human psychic life as it emerges as a nearly murdered being, bearing a murderous impulse from its creator, murdering others and then turning finally on itself?

Johnson's essay builds on this psychic predicament as it queries the consequences for women writers who must negotiate the condition of being nearly or partially murdered and feeling murderous. In what sense can the monster be read as a woman who writes, who must break with her traditional place and "image" to articulate passion of one kind or another? Johnson asks whether the gendered arrangement of parenting and compulsory reproduction does not ride against a monstrous undertow—that is, whether it doesn't presume and produce some monstrosity as a matter of course. After all, the monstrous must be edited out of the image that the child is compelled to present to the parent, and yet the coercive demand itself makes the parent monstrous. And if the child produces something like, say, a text, or if the child herself turns out to be the kind of "product" (think waste) that does not reflect upon, and augment, the embellished image of the parent, then the child becomes "monstrous" by failing to do the duty of replicating the image in the manner required. So, imperfect replication implies either that the parent is monstrous (for asking for such a thing) or that the child is (by failing to replicate what is required), or that both are. Indeed, Shelley's novel implies that replications never turn out quite as we might expect, that there is something monstrous at the core of replication, and that the desire for the perfect copy of a perfected image is not only monstrous, but breeds forms of monstrosity that expose both the impossibility and the cruelty of such a demand.

Shelley's implicit critique of anthropocentrism underscores the monstrous side of human narcissism that compels its progeny to reflect back the image of its creator (or parent), and which then transfers that very monstrosity to the animated life, the child-monster, who fails. Johnson's take on *Frankenstein* insists as well that certain gendered assumptions make the idea of a young girl narrating herself quite monstrous and, further, that the compulsory character of two-sexed parenting gives a specific cultural organization to both matricidal and patricidal longings. Johnson points out that Mary Shelley was herself regarded as somewhat monstrous for having the kinds of thoughts about monstrosity that appear in *Frankenstein*. Mary Shelley's ideation and even her forms of fascination were understood as deformations of the idea of gender to which she was supposed to correspond. Other biographical remarks enter into Johnson's analysis, but they are not meant to reduce the text to the personal history of Mary Shelley. Rather, a set of correspondences emerge between life and text that further complicate the question of whether a life might be adequately expressed in a text or an image or some work of art.[3]

As a critic, Johnson avails herself of Mary Shelley's world to understand how the prevailing norms regarding gender, marriage, and progeny are registered, reworked, narrated, and figured within the literary text, even as the relation between a life and the work it makes remains problematic both within the story and for anyone who seeks to bring biographical details to bear upon it. For instance, Johnson makes reference to work that speculates on the relevance for the story of Mary Shelley's own "post-partum depression" at the age of seventeen, her first unwanted pregnancy followed by the death of that baby shortly after birth, coupled with the fact that her own mother, Mary Wollstonecraft, died upon giving birth to her. A presentiment of murder lingers in both stories. Was Mary Shelley responsible for the death of her child, or was Mary Shelley the unwitting author of her mother's death? Although medical complications led to both deaths, the fantasy nevertheless can, and does, emerge that the child killed the mother or the baby, or both. Sequence is phantasmatically transfigured into cause, and the daughter who is made to bear the loss of her mother becomes responsible for it; the child who suffers this unbearable loss becomes its cause rather than suffer her insignificance in relation to her most terrible loss, thereby shoring up a negative narcissism—and an imaginary relation to the one who is lost—to ward off the more difficult conclusion that the loss was fully accidental and that the child mattered not at all.

To what extent is reproduction thus linked up with murderous wish, the wish to murder either the parent or the child? Johnson points out that one of the most difficult cultural taboos to overcome is the one encoded in the idea that mothers never want the death of their children. So though neither of those actual deaths (the child, the mother) can be said to be the fault of Mary Shelley, is there not a phantasmatic articulation of those events that attributes intentionality and efficacy to the child's wish? Or, rather, that inflames and instrumentalizes those destructive wishes that both Freud and Klein have affirmed are part of human psychic organization from infancy (the "monstrous" dimension that properly and aversively animates the human frame)? This fact should perhaps cease to surprise us, but as often as the insight is established, it is covered over, pushed into oblivion, so that romanticized images of parent-child bond-ing (especially the fundamental non-violence of the mother-daughter tie) can prevail.[4]

So making use of the biographical details to explain the novel only recapitulates the critical problem posed by the novel itself: how do we un-derstand the way that life is figured in the text, especially if that relation recapitulates the psychosocial scenes in which parents make monstrously narcissistic demands on their progeny? Reproductive metaphors saturate the making or "animating" of the monster just as they do Mary Shelley's own reflections on her writing. So in some ways sexual reproduction has departed from its literal form in this work. Its overdetermination as a central metaphor for both scientific invention and literary writing signals that reproduction is signifying in excess of its purpose, that it is perhaps always already a site overburdened with conflicting aims. Who produces whom, and what is reproduced in the one who is produced? In the novel, we can specify this question: does Frankenstein produce the monster, or does the monster end up establishing the trajectory of Frankenstein's life, effectively authoring him retroactively? Similarly, does the novel, *Frank-enstein*, produce the place of Mary Shelley among the pantheon of writers from whom she descends, fortifying that lineage, or does it establish a non-reproductive form of filiation that fails to conform to the norms of heterosexual reproduction and familial legacy? The alchemical and tech-nological creation of Frankenstein makes natural childbirth unnecessary, could be said as well to "steal" the reproductive capacity of women and even dispense with the necessity of the heterosexual couple for the pur-poses of reproduction, challenging the reproductive basis for the compul-sory heterosexuality of marriage. In a sense, the novel opens the salient question before its time of whether technology can become a way of de-parting from, and criticizing, established familial norms, or whether it figures a kind of monstrosity, associated with eugenics and cloning, and the technological mastery of life processes?

Johnson re-poses the dilemma this way for the twentieth century: "the very technological advances that make it possible to change the struc-ture of parenthood also threaten to extinguish earthly life altogether." She notes "this seemingly contemporary pairing of the question of parenthood with a love-hate relation to technology," which she finds prefigured in Mary Shelley's novel (*World of Difference*, p. 148). Has Frankenstein elimi-nated the need for both mother and father? Can science now function as the new creator, displacing God as well? Does the monster represent the living form of the critique of family, heterosexuality, and religion? Significantly, we're never really presented with the "science" that makes the creation of the monster possible. We understand that Frankenstein read books, studied natural processes, but in the end the making of the monster seems more alchemical than technological. This does not keep the novel from signifying something about technology, especially those technologies that most of us fail to understand. Does the "intervention" of donor insemination or in vitro fertilization produce new modes of parenting or destroy established ones? And what if these technologies are used precisely by established and married heterosexual couples who seek to fulfill their dreams for themselves? In the end, there is no one moral lesson to be derived from such technologies, though *Frankenstein* surely articulates the terror that a technological displacement of conventional kinship might produce. Under what conditions does something so anodyne as "alternative parenting" appear as the destruction of life itself? Or, to ask the same question a different way: to what extent does the "monster" articulate a fantasy of destructiveness localized in the cultural innovation of kin relations? Is the problem that new kin relations will destroy life as we know it, or that some manner of destructiveness runs through every possible kin relation? In other words, the destructive potential attributed to technology to destroy kinship, even life, is possible only if we acknowledge the destructive impulse of progeny toward parents, matricidal or patricidal, and the murderous impulses felt by parents toward their own children, especially when they disrupt the narcissistic compact.

Of course, Shelley's novel does not offer any examples of non-reproductive forms of filiation; its characters mainly end up dead or isolated or psychically destroyed. But the specter of that alternative form of sociability is one reason, to be sure, that Johnson returns to Mary Shelley toward the end of her life to understand the alternative forms of sociability and company that populated her world—a network of friends and writers whom Johnson calls "Mary Shelley's Circle." These forms of affiliation post-date marriage and childbirth and the entire logic of reproductive relations. Although it could be argued that *Frankenstein* effectively counsels against technological modes of reproduction in favor of "natural" family forms, such a view fails to understand the degree to which the natural family form is indicted by the novel. Indeed, technological reproduction does not destroy the family, but articulates the disavowed destructiveness of the family in monstrous form. Frankenstein's passion for his science has him taking a path that feverishly leads him away from his fiancée, his family, and his friends, attenuating and breaking the most treasured social bonds in the pursuit of a lonely and obsessive act of creation. What he creates turns out to be murderous, a being who finally murders himself, suggesting that there is a death drive in the midst of creation, one that seeks to undo social bonds, acting as its corrosive force on the structure of kinship itself. One interpretation is that Frankenstein produces a monster that he fails to recognize as himself. Yet, is this refusal to recognize precisely what keeps kinship going? Is it precisely a refusal to recognize the murderous impulse that traverses and threatens all relational ties?

If we are tempted to reduce the story to a tale of masculine narcissism (womb envy that takes the form of the technological appropriation of properly female reproductive powers and the desire for the disappearance of women), we would probably then miss some of the more complex and disturbing ways that gender functions here. For Johnson, this story about very dramatic men is precisely a way of figuring the absence of women from the larger story of artistic creativity, and it matters that that story is told by a woman who is writing. The problem is not just that women have been excluded (after all, Mary Shelley comes from a mother, Mary Wollstonecraft, who is an established and esteemed writer and philosopher), but that a certain compact emerges whereby the woman writer can establish her creativity (by extension, her sexual independence as well) only by refusing the mother, if not murdering her, in order to exist at all. In this sense, the girl becomes a woman writer through a matricidal impulse, since the mother's demand is precisely that the girl be absorbed into the circuit of the mother's narcissistic desire. And if the mother is already dead, what then? The murder has to be retroactively posited, such that the infant who is emphatically without power at birth still somehow "murders" the mother who dies in childbirth in order to come into existence at all. If the child must "murder" its way into existence, she recommits the crime every time she acts and makes something, asserts existence, which means that to overcome the status of the "appendage" she embraces criminality. The novel *Frankenstein* manages to keep women in their place, and yet the monster may well be carrying that excess of gender that fails to fit properly into "man" and "woman" as conventionally defined. If the monster is really what a "man" looks like when we consider his aggressive form, or if this is really what a "woman" looks like when her own gendered place is destabilized as she starts to write and risk matricide or patricide, then the "monster" functions as a liminal zone of gender, not merely the disavowed dimensions of manhood, but the unspeakable limits of femininity as well.

The monster's story that begins in Book II, Chapter IV of *Frankenstein* has been likened to other "state of nature" narratives in which a pre-civilized creature looks on with wonder as he learns how human society is organized. The monster is not unlike Rousseau's Emile or the uncannily knowing savage dwelling in a state of nature who in eighteenth-century philosophical fictions provides the perspective from which to consider the contingency and even the basic oddness of the cultural organization of familial life and labor. After a night of cold and hunger, he lights upon "a small hut," what he calls his "kennel," which becomes, as it were, the first social form of shelter (*Frankenstein*, p. 73). From the perspective of his poor mimetic substitute for a home, he looks on at the human life next door while they do not see him, remarking on the kinship relations in a language that is impossibly civilized and knowing. The monster is no grunting Neanderthal, but someone who derives pleasure from watching, speculating on the motives that guide the family's actions; he is often sleepless, endeared by his strangers' habits, compelled by their gentleness, interested in institutions like property and wealth; and he begins to read through a mimetic process and, indeed, becomes a reader much like us; by the time the monster starts reading, we become readers who read about how a reader comes into being through following a set of civilizing rules and practices, and see a strange replication of ourselves in the text, and so suffer a minor mirror stage that deflates, rather than inflates, our sense of power. The monster has, after all, a moral sensibility coupled with negative narcissism, expressing sympathy for his neighbors and yet convinced that whereas they are gentle and noble, he is a terrifying sight. He suffers shame at being seen and wretched guilt about what he does. His sense of shame and self-beratement becomes more dramatic as the story unfolds and he finally murders the one who created him. As the monster watches that human family from his proximate distance, he seems to be a sympathetic extension of what he sees, yet its "inverse" form, the disavowed underside of the civilizational, that which is forever purged from the familial. And when they finally see him, his appalling state is confirmed by their manifest "horror and consternation" (*Frankenstein*, p. 94). Significantly, his response is to return to his creator and demand that a female counterpart be made for him. Thus, his exclusion from society can be countered only through his entrance into heterosexual coupling, and that can happen only if someone equally monstrous comes along. In other words, he can be lovers with a non-human human, suggesting that sexuality is possible only where this ambiguity between the human and the non-human is at work. Who asks what part of sexuality is human or animal, and who receives an answer?

∽

Johnson's reading of *Frankenstein* weaves a thread between that book and Nancy Friday's, but also *The Mermaid and the Minotaur* by Dorothy Dinnerstein. In that book, the idea of sexual freedom for women is understood to be matricidal since the daughter must remain sexless in order for the tie to the mother to remain intact. It is not simply that the mother delivers a prohibition against sexuality, but that the daughter must remain pre-sexual to maintain her dependency, her attachment, and her place. Does becoming sexual imply matricide within the context in which the daughter takes the mother's place in relation to the father? And if that incestuous conclusion is not at issue, why would the emergent heterosexuality of the daughter threaten to kill the mother? Does the daughter cease to be progeny at the moment in which she engages sexuality outside of reproductive norms? If the mother's desire is to see her own image replicated and reflected in the daughter, then the daughter's independent desire is wayward, a betrayal and narcissistic wound for the mother, to be sure. The daughter wants something that does not reflect or augment the mother—has she murdered her? And yet, it seems as well that the very power of kinship to govern and mediate sexual relations is reduced, if not displaced, by forms of sexuality unconstrained by (diverting from) reproduction and its attendant norms of marriage and family. The monster's desire seems to be figured spatially to the side of kinship, outside of its domestic structure, looking in. And when he tries to arrange an entry into the couple form or the domestic space, the consequences are disastrous. Is the monster a figure for a form of sexuality that cannot adapt to a social form? Or is it the social form of the household from which it seems perpetually excluded? Is the monster a form of gender that fails to comply with norms that govern recognizability, one that remains too difficult to see, unbound by the visual parameters of the norm? If so, does the monster provide a critical position, feminist and queer, on the compulsory organization of sexuality and kinship?

These questions became important ones for Barbara Johnson, providing a point of departure for thinking about those post-marital forms of alliance and relationality that were inflected in both the life and the work of Mary Shelley. But if we imagine that Johnson saw a utopian promise in the devastations of *Frankenstein*, an unwitting opening toward a post-familial form of kinship and company, then we move too quickly to imagine that "new social forms" constitute the final promise of this analysis. If every social form that engages sexuality and intimacy is also haunted by the potential of aggression and destruction, then any new social form will have to come to terms with this inherent ambivalence. Indeed, social form itself will have to be rethought in light of its constitutive ambivalence. The dismal ending of the monster and his maker might seem to mark an end to a regime, clearing another path. But the point is not to fill that opening with a new social form that will be free of the threat of murderous rage and toxic guilt. Every social form is subject to that death drive that corrodes its claim on immutability and permanence, and this at once establishes the promising mutability of forms of kinship and sociability and warns us against the lure of any social form that promises to deliver us from aggression itself.[5] We achieve human form in light of those social arrangements that allocate recognition. But each of those forms finds itself at some point confronted by liminal figures who fail to conform to the idea of the human established by its norms. That spectral and stunning figure of the monster accompanies any contingent social definition of the human and its supporting relations. It reminds us that forms of relationality are historically contingent, to be sure, but also that sexuality and aggression both ride the uncertain distinction between the human and the inhuman. The question of what is animated there, at the site of that uncertain vacillation, is precisely the problem of the figure, one that shakes and animates the human frame every time we try to tell the story of its life.

PART TWO

Writing in the Face of Death: Johnson's Last Work

Mary Shelley

and

Her Circle

By Barbara Johnson

Edited by Shoshana Felman, Judith Butler, and Mary Wilson Carpenter

Note
The guiding principle of our editorial policy of this last text was one of scrupulous faithfulness to Johnson's authentic style, and to her original manuscript, even though she wrote this last text under duress, and consequently in an abbreviated and condensed manner, nearly always struggling with the sheer physical effort to keep writing and advance her vision, despite inhibiting conditions of severe disease. The interventions of the editors have been deliberately minimal. A few words are added here and there, only so as to clarify, and very seldom to articulate more fully what remains elliptical in the original.

Introduction

A prestigious collection of Romantic texts (letters, diaries, etc., by Percy Bysshe Shelley, Leigh Hunt, Thomas Love Peacock, Lord Byron, Edward John Trelawney, John Keats, and others) was amassed in the Pforzheimer Library under the title *Shelley and His Circle*.[1] But the notion of "circle" in the title of the present book is more restricted. Unlike her husband, Mary Shelley did not always like to surround herself with admirers or imitators, but desired rather to be part of a narrative group. The coalescence of this narrative group is first described in the 1817 preface to her novel *Franken-stein* (the only part of her novel, Mary will say later, entirely written by her husband):

> The season was cold and rainy, and in the evenings we crowded around a blazing wood fire and occasionally amused ourselves with some German stories of ghosts which happened to fall into our hands. (*Frankenstein*, p. xiv)[2]

Mary Shelley's circle is the one listening to ghost stories around the fire. About this circle she says more in her "Author's Introduction" to the 1831 edition of *Frankenstein*, written when the novel was republished for the third time, so as to be included in the Standard British Novels series:[3]

> In the summer of 1816 we visited Switzerland and became the neighbours of Lord Byron. . . .
> But it proved a wet, ungenial summer, and incessant rain often confined us for days to the house. Some volumes of ghost stories translated from the German into French fell into our hands. There was the *History of the Inconstant Lover*, who, when he thought to clasp the bride to whom he had pledged his

vows, found himself in the arms of the pale ghost of her whom he had deserted.
There was the tale of the sinful founder of his race whose miserable doom it
was to bestow the kiss of death on all the younger sons of his fated house. . . .

"We will each write a ghost story," said Lord Byron, and his proposition
was acceded to. There were four of us. The noble author began a tale, a fragment of which he printed at the end of his poem of Mazeppa. Shelley, more
apt to embody ideas and sentiments in the radiance of brilliant imagery and
in the music of the most melodious verse that adorns our language than to
invent the machinery of a story, commenced one founded on the experiences
of his early life. Poor Polidori had some terrible idea about a skull-headed
lady who was so punished for peeping through a key-hole . . . The illustri-
ous poets also, annoyed by the platitude of prose, speedily relinquished their
uncongenial task.

I busied myself *to think of a story*—a story to rival those which had excited
us to this task. . . . I thought and pondered—vainly. I felt that blank inca-
pability of invention which is the greatest misery of authorship. . . ." Have
you thought of a story?" I was asked each morning, and each morning I was
forced to reply with a mortifying negative. (*Frankenstein*, pp. viii–x)

Despite the fact that Mary says there were four participants in the ghost-
story contest, there were both more and fewer authors taunting her for
unproductivity. Two other important secret interlocutors and rival authors were her parents, her mother Mary Wollstonecraft (who died giving
birth to her) and her father William Godwin (who soon remarried):

It is not singular that, as the daughter of two persons of distinguished literary celebrity, I should very early in life have thought of writing (*Frankenstein*,
p. vii),

she writes in that same Introduction. But she was the only contestant
to take the ghost-story contest seriously: Byron and Shelley preferred to
work in more respectable genres,[4] and Polidori's imagination took him
too far. Mary Shelley thus defined her place in literature in a minor genre
(the gothic or sensational novel). Even her husband wanted her to write
as a sign of future writing, and not as something that had value in itself:

My husband, however, was from the first, very anxious that I should prove
myself worthy of my parentage. . . . At this time he desired that I should
write, not so much with the idea that I could produce anything worthy of
notice, but that he might himself judge how far I possessed the promise of
better things hereafter. (*Frankenstein*, p. viii)

Having surrendered the prestigious poetic genres to Byron and Shelley, she chose to compete with other authors for the most vulgar genres of prose. While her husband had not stooped so low since finding fame, her parents had each written novelistic fiction as well as philosophical and social treatises; there was a big genre difference, in William Godwin's writing, between *An Enquiry Concerning Political Justice* (1793) and *Caleb Williams* (1794), and in Mary Wollstonecraft's writing, between *A Vindication of the Rights of Woman* (1792) and *Maria* (1798). Mary Shelley did follow her parents' lead in writing her ghost story, and in thus seeking a direct impact on her readers without the intermediary of prestige. "What terrified me will terrify others," she said (*Frankenstein*, p. xi).

The competition with her parents must have haunted her, though, throughout her life, beyond the inspiration that she got from their gothic novels. Percy Shelley wrote to her father as a great political philosopher before he knew of her existence. And the already-married Shelley had only one role available for young women: adorer. He was used to every young woman in his vicinity falling in love with him, and Mary was no exception. This gave her an edge over her parents for a while, but made the realization that she was one in a series very bitter. When Shelley unexpectedly died in 1822, she was very mad at him. But by that time (after his first wife's suicide) legally married to him, she had an undisputed role as his exclusive widow, a role that she played to the hilt. Nevertheless, Shelley would never write to her, as he had to her father:

> The name of Godwin has been used, to excite in me feelings of reverence and admiration. I have been accustomed to consider him a luminary too dazzling for the darkness which surrounds him. From the earliest period of my knowledge of his principles, I have ardently desired to share, on the footing of intimacy, that intellect which I have delighted to contemplate in its emanations.[5]

Nor would *she* have provided inspirational reading matter on her tomb, as did her mother, who died in childbirth from the act of giving her birth, and whose writings Shelley liked to read with her over the grave. The fact was that Percy had relationships with the writings of both of her parents before her—intellectual relationships, based on their writings. Mary was thus at once conversing and competing equally with *them* in entering the ghost-story contest. Her anger at all of them came out in her first novel, which she was later to refer to as her "hideous progeny."

I propose to study both the people and the texts that Mary tried to take in and to measure up to, in entering into the ghost-story writing-contest. Mary engages in this competition with both her writing and her life. Her passion and her art alike proceed from these generative moments of connection and of difference, of rival stories inscribed within a circle of entangled lives and of entangled texts. I will try not simply to narrate this story of entangled stories, but to view this multiplicity of figures and of texts together, by juxtaposing them rhetorically upon each other, and by reading them synchronically through one another. Imbricated in this web of interwoven living stories, Mary struggles to create "a story of her own," in trying to give value and distinction to her own newborn existence as a female writer. In a competition that is both erotic and aesthetic, she writes to gain prestige and love within this circle of prestigious and dramatically compelling, inter-generational and inter-relational *writing contestants.*

The fact that Mary's monster-tale was more successful than anything written by her parents or her husband, or that Godwin's idealistic hopes for the redistribution of wealth in society served as a pretext for him to live off Percy's money, did not change the value system by which the writings in themselves were judged. Mary, however, had to adjust her-self (unconsciously or consciously) to these lived discrepancies and to the contradictions embodied by those surrounding her. Some of these contradictions and discrepancies found their way into her writing. In Mary's novel *Frankenstein*, the monster kills off the family of his creator for lack of good parenting. In this study I want to look at what Mary was competing with.

CHAPTER ONE

William Godwin

Mary Shelley's father had a period of great celebrity as the author of *An Enquiry Concerning Political Justice* in the early 1790s. Known as "the Philosopher," he was part of the circle around Joseph Johnson, Mary Wollstonecraft's publisher and editor of the *Analytical Review*, which aligned itself with radical and innovative thinkers, British reformers, and supporters of the French Revolution.

Mary and William had met before, but this time, perhaps because the glow of fame endowed Godwin with a sort of aura, they fell in love and became a couple. Both were opposed in principle to the loss of liberty marriage entailed, and they at first retained separate residences and married only when, Mary finding herself once more pregnant (with the future Mary Shelley), they decided they had to render their child legitimate. But Mary Wollstonecraft died in childbirth (1797), and Godwin was taken aback by the negative reaction to his admiring biography of her, *Memoirs of the Author of A Vindication of the Rights of Woman* (1798). Whereas he had applauded her independence and enterprise, the increasingly conservative public thought she was a whore and cried scandal over Godwin's *Memoirs*. The initial enthusiasm over the French Revolution was giving way to Victorian respectability. Godwin married again (1801), much to little Mary's chagrin, this time to a vulgar but competent woman, Mrs. Clairmont, who would take care of Mary Wollstonecraft's two children, one by her husband and the other by her former lover, Gilbert Imlay.

But Mary did take away something from her father—not from the political treatise Percy so much admired, but from his novels, particularly
the first, entitled *Things as They Are, or The Adventures of Caleb Williams*
(1794). Reminiscent of the pursuit of the monster by Frankenstein, *Caleb
Williams* is the story of the relentless pursuit by a guilty aristocrat of an
innocent commoner, whose only fault, like Pandora, is his curiosity. Both
Frankenstein and *Caleb Williams* revolve around a pursuit, and a mystery.
While both of Mary's parents had written novels, her father—even when
attacked—remained prestigious, whereas her mother was considered
scandalous. From this Mary learned that the difference between the sexes
was not so much biological as *narrative*. The "proper lady," to use Mary
Poovey's critically ironic term, did not narrate.[1]

Thus the picture we get of a woman in *Frankenstein* is a composite,
made up of a split (an incommensurability) between a non-narrative
image of female beauty, and an eloquently narrative, authoritative, speaking, and violent male narrator. Mary Shelley's women have often been
criticized for being idealized images of the "Angel of the House": no one
could suspect them of feminism. In *Frankenstein*, for instance, Victor's
mother is the orphan of an old friend of his father's—most women have
only fathers, never mothers.

> [H]er father died in her arms, leaving her an orphan and a beggar. This last
> blow overcame her, and she knelt by Beaufort's coffin weeping bitterly, when
> my father entered the chamber. He came like a protecting spirit to the poor
> girl, who committed herself to his care; and after the interment of his friend
> . . . Caroline became his wife. (*Frankenstein*, p. 32)

Victor's future wife, Elizabeth, seems almost genetically destined to be
idealized:

> Among these [children] there was one which attracted my mother far above
> all the rest. She appeared of a different stock. The four others were dark-
> eyed, hardy little vagrants; this child was thin and very fair. Her hair was the
> brightest living gold, and despite the poverty of her clothing, seemed to set
> a crown of distinction on her head. Her brow was clear and ample, her blue
> eyes cloudless, and her lips and the moulding of her face so expressive of sen-
> sibility and sweetness that none could behold her without looking on her as
> of a distinct species, a being heaven-sent, and bearing a celestial stamp in all
> her features. (*Frankenstein*, p. 34)

A third beautiful woman, Justine, reveals her connection with the monster by structurally taking his place in the plot of the trial and the punishment: Justine is mistakenly, unjustly executed for the crime of the murder of William, which the monster had committed: [2]

> And on the morrow Justine died. Elizabeth's heart-rending eloquence failed to move the judges from their settled conviction in the criminality of the saintly sufferer. . . . I might proclaim myself a madman [—Victor tells himself in self-justification of his silence—], but not revoke the sentence passed upon my wretched victim. (*Frankenstein*, pp. 84–85)

The plots of many of these novels turn around a crime and an injustice. The damning evidence against the "saintly sufferer" was a locket, which William had been wearing, and which had been found in her pocket, containing a *picture* of Caroline Beaufort. Women are beautiful and mute images, not tellers of tales.

Tales were usually told with one of two purposes in mind, and the tales in *Frankenstein* are no exceptions; they either convey a lesson, or gain sympathy. Frankenstein says to Walton, who is searching for the North Pole:

> Unhappy man! Do you share my madness? Have you drunk also of the intoxicating draught? Hear me; let me reveal my tale, and you will dash the cup from your lips! (*Frankenstein*, p. 26)

And the monster says to his creator:

> [L]isten to me and grant me thy compassion . . . Hear my tale; . . . The sun is yet high in the heavens; before it descends to . . . illuminate another world, you will have heard my story and can decide. (*Frankenstein*, p. 97)

As if to emphasize the incommensurability between telling and seeing, the monster puts his hands in front of his creator's face:

> [T]hus I take from thee a sight which you abhor. Still thou canst listen to me and grant me thy compassion. (*Frankenstein*, p. 97)

The monster tries to evoke sympathy through narrative eloquence in only one other character, the blind old patriarch, de Lacey.

Mary Shelley learned many of her narrative techniques from her father, not from his treatises (*Political Justice*) but from his novel *Caleb*

Williams. In fact, the narrator of her later novel, *The Last Man* (1826, her second "science fiction" novel), is very similar to the narrator of *Caleb Williams*.

> Thus untaught in refined philosophy . . . I wandered among the hills of civilized England as uncouth a savage as the wolf-bred founder of old Rome. (Mary Shelley, *The Last Man*, p. 9)[3]

> I was born of humble parents. . . . But I had an inquisitive mind . . . (Godwin, *Caleb Williams*, p. 5)[4]

Both novels present characters who seek a mentor or an educated double—a double whose encounter will help cultivate their mind and thus transform their life:

> It was not his rank—after all that I have said, surely it will not be suspected that it was Adrian's rank, that, from the first, subdued my heart of hearts, and laid my entire spirit prostrate before him . . . Even at this early age, he was deep read and imbued with the spirit of high philosophy. (*The Last Man*, pp. 17–18)

> Mr. Falkland questioned me respecting my learning. . . . When Mr. Falkland had satisfied his curiosity, he proceeded to inform me that he was in want of a secretary, that I appeared to him sufficiently qualified for that office, and that, if . . . I approved of the employment, he would take me into his family. (*Caleb Williams*, p. 7)

Here, however, the narrative resemblance ceases between the figures of the doubles in the father's and the daughter's novels. In Mary's novel, the narrator's double is the aristocratic Adrian, son of a king who abdicates, remains benevolent, unmarried, and dies. In Godwin's novel, the aristocratic double, Falkland, illustrates in contrast the tyrannical epitome of the abuse of power and of rank: aware that his domestic Caleb Williams knows his guilty secret, Falkland stalks him and takes revenge on him unmercifully. Mary's storyteller, Lionel Verney, becomes the narrator of all narrators, "The Last Man." As the last man, he becomes a writer: "I turned author myself" (*The Last Man*, p. 113). This enables him to dwell in the scene of autobiographical writing, as Rousseau was the first to do. "Thus long, I have cradled my heart in retrospection of past happiness, when hope was" (*The Last Man*, p. 173).

William Godwin fantasized the narrative position of an impartial spectator in *Political Justice*:

> [T]he soundest criterion of virtue is, to put ourselves in the place of an impartial spectator, of an angelic nature . . . (*Political Justice*, pp. 173–174)[5]

John Bender relates this to the Foucauldian image of acculturation, the Panopticon.[6] This was a prison with a central post affording one a view of every prisoner. The Benthamite Panopticon may never have been built, but there is a radical difference between modern prisons based on surveillance and medieval dungeons based on oblivion. In many of these novels, prisons indeed are central, and, after all, the storming of the Bastille, which started the French Revolution, was an attack on a state prison. I will never forget hearing John Bender say at Harvard[7] that this fantasy of total surveillance better fits the omniscient narrator than any prison.

Political Justice employs many of the terms then in current use in political theory—particularly the concepts of tyranny and slavery—but Godwin goes further than his predecessors. While others were speaking about the rights of man, Godwin was arguing *against anything* that constrains the subject, anything fixed in advance, even voluntarily.

> Now one of the principal means of information is time. . . . But . . . if we bind ourselves today to the conduct we will observe two months hence. . . . [We are] certainly not less improvident than he who lives by anticipating the stores of fortune. (*Political Justice*, p. 220)

Thus Godwin is against marriage as a sexual "monopoly" and against any promise whatsoever, since promises try to bind the future by present perspectives. Laws, government, and punishment all suffer from the same evil, and rights work at cross purposes to justice. They surround the citizen with a fixed zone of inviolability, whereas each deed is particular, and it is more flexible to leave the broad view to a man of benevolence and virtue than to rely on rights. And yet to "improve" minds and bring them to a sense of virtue and duty *takes* time, because it requires education. Godwin never resolves the contradiction between constraints brought about by past vows and the time it takes to educate a free man. In any case, he opposes all social violence and all state violence.

Both Godwin and Mary Wollstonecraft reserve their harshest judgment for obedience, which they see as slavish, unlike Milton, whom they both hold as their great authority, who (in contrast to them) based his epic of original sin on "disobedience," which caused the Fall from Paradise. It should be remembered that at this time, slavery was not just figurative, but literal. The slave trade was at once the economic basis for English prosperity, and a hot topic for debate in parliament:

> In the discussions that took place a few years ago, in the English parliament and nation, respecting the slave-trade, the sentiment we are here combating was used as a topic of argument by some of those persons who, from certain deplorable prejudices, were able to prevail upon themselves to appear as advocates for this trade. (*Political Justice*, p. 392)

The fact of slavery gave reality to the fantasy of tyranny, which increased fiction's use of the paranoid fantasy of total surveillance. The image of pursuit by a person with absolute power was a good plot device used for very different purposes in both slave narratives and in detective novels—a nascent literary genre of which *Caleb Williams* constitutes the first influential historical example. Both genres—slave narratives and detective novels (mysteries or thrillers)—are predicated on the description of a pursuit:

> My master met me at every turn, reminding me that I belonged to him, and swearing by heaven and earth that he would compel me to submit to him. If I went out for a breath of fresh air, after a day of unwearied toil, his footsteps dogged me. If I knelt by my mother's grave, his dark shadow fell on me even there. ("Incidents in the Life of a Slave Girl," p. 362)[8]

> But the change of my name, the abruptness with which I removed from place to place, the remoteness and the obscurity which I proposed to myself in the choice of my abode, were all insufficient to elude the sagacity of Gines, or the unrelenting constancy with which Mr. Falkland incited my tormentor to pursue me. Whithersoever I removed myself, it was not long before I had occasion to perceive this detested adversary in my rear. . . . It was like what has been described of the eye of Omniscience pursuing the guilty sinner. . . . (*Caleb Williams*, p. 316)

In 1819, Mary Shelley wrote a story called *Matilda*, which she sent to her father. He neither sent it on for publication nor returned it. The story of *Matilda* concerns a father's incestuous love for his daughter and her consequent desire for death. William Godwin found the subject of father-daughter incest "disgusting and detestable," and sat on it. Consequently, this second novel of Mary Shelley remained unpublished until 1959.

Incest and suicide—the cornerstones of this novella—were, however, common themes in the writings and lives of the Romantics. As Janet Todd attests in her introductory remarks to *Matilda,*

> The theme of incest was a common one in Romanticism and it is probable that Shelley's own interest helped inspire his wife. In both Byron and Shelley's works, sibling incest can suggest an escape from stifling social conventions. In Byron's *Manfred* which Mary Shelley was copying in the summer of 1816, the hero feels a forbidden passion for his sister. . . .
>
>   But father-daughter incest appears the reverse of the sibling sort and is described in the play *The Cenci*, which Percy Shelley had just completed, with Mary's encouragement, at about the time of *Matilda's* composition. (Todd, p. xxii)[9]

To the list of literary sibling incest, we should, of course, add Byron's actual affair with his half-sister.

The psychology of the narrator—male only because non-female—which Mary learned from her father or her husband, was a psychology of narcissistic doubles. And I think these sibling incests fall under that category—heterosexual narcissistic doubles, enamored of their own reflection in their brotherly or sisterly love object. After all, the watchwords of the French Revolution, happening around this same time, were "*liberté, égalité, fraternité*": "liberty, equality, brotherhood." Brotherhood proclaimed as a political ideal could well encompass its potential for incestuous historical, biographical, narrative, and psychoanalytic connotations.

Father-daughter incest, on the other hand, brought into question the paternal principle, as the basis of authority and hierarchy in the West. As we have seen from Godwin's reaction, it was an unmentionable taboo. Shelley's play *The Cenci* met with the same unsurpassable, prohibitive taboo. "Shelley wished *The Cenci* to be acted," Mary Shelley narrates in the biographical notes she appends to her edition of the *Poetical Works* of her husband. "The play was accordingly sent to [an intermediary agent]. He pronounced the subject to be so objectionable that he could not even submit the part to Miss O'Neil for perusal. . . ."[10]

Paternal power, for Shelley, fed into the kind of political domination he detested and opposed. He flouted his father's authority in every way, and his "translation" of *Oedipus Rex* is, emphatically, politically, *Swellfoot the Tyrant*. In his play *The Cenci*, paternal tyranny is so extreme that the tyrannical father orders his sons killed and rapes his daughter, who then kills him. The last we see of that daughter, Beatrice, is when she is imprisoned for parricide.

Whether it be the beheading of the king or the questioning of "God the father," the overturning of patriarchal power was profoundly threatening to nineteenth-century culture. But what happens if, rather than rebelling against the father, one falls in love with the father?

Father-daughter incest was not just a taboo; it was the *norm* in the nineteenth century. I remember reading this for the first time in Phyllis Chesler's *Women and Madness* many years ago.[11] This is what Mary Shelley understood and what Godwin couldn't bear. If Mary was looking for a female psychology for a female narrator, she had found it. The other great problem brought up by *Matilda* was, of course, the preoccupation with suicide. Having detailed in his *Memoirs* of his dead wife Mary Wollstonecraft her two historical suicide attempts out of thwarted love for the unfaithful Gilbert Imlay, Godwin calls Mary Wollstonecraft "a female Werther."[12] As Janet Todd put it:

> The greatest of the romantic suicides was of course Werther, who made suicide into the act of a great soul insisting in dying for love and an indescribable "inner raging." (Todd, p. xxiii)

Significantly thus, in Mary Shelley's work, *The Sorrows of Young Werther* turns out to be one of the few books on the syllabus for Frankenstein's monster to read in his hovel, so as to become precisely human.

CHAPTER TWO

Mary Wollstonecraft

Mary Wollstonecraft, Mary Shelley's mother, is best known as a pioneering feminist, author of *A Vindication of the Rights of Woman*. In that
work, she writes as a woman, and when she died she was working on a
novel, *Maria, or The Wrongs of Woman*. This interplay between Rights
and Wrongs, this consciousness of women's oppression, was, however,
not her first impulse.

Before writing *A Vindication of the Rights of Woman* (1792), Mary had
written *A Vindication of the Rights of Men* (1790), in response to Edmund
Burke's *Reflections on the Revolution in France* (1790). This was one of the
first English responses to Burke's critique of the revolution, even before
Thomas Paine's more famous response, *The Rights of Man* (1791). Mary
discovered the inequality of women as she wrote the first *Vindication*, and
it fed into her thoughts on female education. It also made her confront
her rather negative feelings about what women had become with their
prevailing education, to the point where Susan Gubar can speak of the
paradox of Wollstonecraft's "feminist misogyny."[1]

Mary wrote *A Vindication of the Rights of Men* in answer to Burke's
response to the French Revolution, and particularly as a response to his
contestation of the National Assembly's declaration of "the rights of man
and citizen." Her response was that the Assembly's declaration was a passionate defense of equality and humanity, not the "leveling" operation
Burke said it was. But in her first *Vindication*, Mary, like everyone else,
took "man" as a synecdoche for "mankind," not as a gendered term. In
other words, as in the case of Frankenstein's narrator, the male-gendered

"man" was taken as a universal "human"; there was no real opposition in the idea of an "opposite sex":

> I war not with an individual when I contend for the *rights of men* and the liberty of reason. You see I do not condescend to cull my words to avoid the invidious phrase, nor shall I be prevented from giving a manly definition of it. . . . Reverencing the rights of humanity, I shall dare to assert them . . . (*Vindications*, p. 35)[2]

Despite her attempt to not view gender as an opposition, Mary was "outed" as a woman by writing the first *Vindication*. One of the reviewers said, sardonically and condescendingly:

> The *rights of men* asserted by a fair lady! The age of chivalry cannot be over, or the sexes have changed their ground. . . . We should be sorry to raise a horse-laugh against a fair lady; but we were always taught to suppose that the *rights of women* were the proper theme of the female sex. (*Vindications*, p. 11)

Instead of a synecdoche, sexual difference created an antagonistic opposition within the very concept of the rights of man.

The same kind of difference—the same oppressive hierarchy—is documented between tyranny and slavery in the contemporary slave narratives by women:

> If God has bestowed beauty upon her, it will prove her greatest curse. That which commands admiration in the white woman only hastens the degradation of the female slave. (*Classic Slave Narratives*, pp. 361–362)

In other words, the white woman exemplified society's ideal of femininity, while the female slave—even through her beauty—exemplified only femininity's and beauty's dark side:

> Mrs. Flint [the mistress], like many southern women, was totally deficient in energy. She had not strength to superintend her household affairs; but her nerves were so strong, that she could sit in her easy chair and see a woman whipped, till the blood trickled from every stroke of the lash. (*Classic Slave Narratives*, p. 347)

Mary Wollstonecraft discovered not only the politically antagonistic reality of sexual difference, but also the fact that the moment any gender question was raised, the difference was consigned to the *purely* sexual. Thus, one of the impediments to women's equality was that a woman was *always* sexualized. It was for this reason that Mary, in her second vindication—*A Vindication of the Rights of Woman*—tried to see what the significance would be of feminine values without their sexual connotations: "Modesty—Comprehensively considered, and not as a sexual virtue," "Morality undermined by sexual notions of the importance of a good reputation," etc.[3]

Mary begins her treatise on women with two quotations from the most authoritative author of the time, to show the contradictory messages addressed to women:

> Milton . . . only bends to the indefeasible right of beauty, though it would be difficult to render two passages which I now mean to contrast, consistent. . . .

> > "To whom thus Eve with *perfect beauty* adorn'd,
> > My Author and Disposer, what thou bidst
> > *Unargued* I obey; so God ordains;
> > God is *thy law, thou mine*: to know no more
> > Is Woman's *happiest* knowledge and her *praise*."

> . . . . Yet in the following lines Milton seems to coincide with me; when he makes Adam thus expostulate with his Maker.

> > "Hast thou not made me here thy substitute,
> > And these inferior far beneath me set?
> > Among *unequals* what society
> > Can sort, what harmony or true delight?
> > Which must be mutual, in proportion due
> > Giv'n and receiv'd; but in *disparity*
> > The one intense, the other still remiss
> > Cannot well suit with either, but soon prove
> > Tedious alike: of *fellowship* I speak
> > Such as I seek, fit to participate
> > All rational delight . . ."

> (*Vindications*, pp. 127–128; Wollstonecraft's italics)

Mary thus finds that femininity is founded on a contradiction, yet, in her *Vindication of the Rights of Woman*, she does everything she can to minimize the conflict between men and women:

> Yet, because I am a woman, I would not lead my readers to suppose that I mean violently to agitate the contested question respecting the equality or inferiority of the sex. . . . A degree of physical superiority cannot . . . be denied . . . (*Vindications*, p. 110)

Which does not prevent critics like Horace Walpole from calling Mary a "hyena in petticoats."[4]   In fact, so insistent is Mary that the answer to the question "what's wrong with women?" has nothing to do with sexual difference, that she cites an example of men falling into the same error of manifesting women-like behaviors: "politeness" and an erroneously excessive preoccupation with their own appearance:

> As a proof that education gives this appearance of weakness to females, we may instance the example of military men. . . . Soldiers, as well as women, practise the minor virtues with punctilious politeness. Where is then the sexual difference, when the education has been the same? . . .
> It may be further observed, that officers are also particularly attentive to their persons, fond of dancing, crowded rooms, adventures, and ridicule. . . . [They manifest the same] fondness for dress . . . (*Vindications*, pp. 131, 132, 137)

Soldiers, like women, obey a strict chain of command, do not think for themselves, and are valued for their appearance. Who can forget the ostentatious red coats of the regiment stationed nearby in *Pride and Prejudice*?

Mary was one of the first truly independent women—one of the first writers to try to live by her pen. She was not supported by father or husband, but was mentored by a series of father figures, including Richard Price, a dissenting minister she knew when she tried to run a school in Newington Green, and Joseph Johnson, her London publisher, who aligned himself with the supporters of the French Revolution.

She was a true child of the Enlightenment who thought that there were three faculties in mankind—reason, the senses, and the emotions. While the "man of feeling" was ever more prominent on the literary scene, Mary urged women to be governed by "reason." What did Mary mean by "reason"? The term is vague, but may perhaps be understood in the Kantian sense of the mind not subject to natural law—mental activity not affected by emotions ("sensibility") or senses.

The French Revolution seemed to usher in a new era of equality for all. At first, many English writers hailed it as a new era of freedom:

> O pleasant exercise of hope and joy!
> For mighty were the auxiliars which then stood
> Upon our side, us who were strong in love!
> Bliss was it in that dawn to be alive . . .
>   (*The Prelude*, Book XI, ll. 105–8)[5]

as William Wordsworth would later describe the sentiments of that time. The events of the forthcoming Terror were still invisible: they soured many months later.

But it was not the "new dawn" inaugurated by the French Revolution that impelled Mary Wollstonecraft to argue for the rights of women. No one, including Mary, was arguing at that point for women's right to vote. It was Mary's ongoing plea for women's education, begun in her *Thoughts on the Education of Daughters* (1787) and other works, that she pursued. *A Vindication of the Rights of Woman* was dedicated to Talleyrand, who had argued for women's education. Even Wollstonecraft's beloved Rousseau, whose *Emile* had offered a system of education she approved of, had portrayed his vision of women's education as rendering them "pleasing" to men:

> Consequently, the most perfect education, in my opinion, [Mary writes,] is such an exercise of the understanding as is best calculated to strengthen the body and form the heart. Or, in other words, to enable the individual to attain such habits of virtue as will render it independent. In fact, it is a farce to call any being virtuous whose virtues do not result from the exercise of its own reason. This was Rousseau's opinion respecting men: I extend it to women, and confidently assert that they have been drawn out of their sphere by false refinement, and not by an endeavor to acquire masculine qualities. (*Vindications*, p. 129)

Contrary to what one might expect from an admirer of the French Revolution, Mary's argument in support of the rights of women is based not on the new civic principle of equality, but rather, on a secular consideration of humanity as mortal: women should not waste their lives, as though they had the luxuries of *immortality*:

> How grossly do they insult us who thus advise us only to render ourselves gentle, domestic brutes! . . . [A]nd how insignificant is the being—can it be an immortal one? who will condescend to govern by such sinister methods! . . . I see not the shadow of a reason to conclude that [the] virtues [of women and men] should differ in respect to their nature. In fact, how can they, if virtue has only one eternal standard? . . . It follows then that cunning should not be opposed to wisdom, little cares to great exertions, or insipid softness . . . to that fortitude which grand views alone can inspire. . . . Women ought to endeavor to purify their heart; but can they do so when . . . no noble pursuit sets them above the little vanities of the day . . . ? Surely she has not an immortal soul who can loiter life away merely employed to adorn her person . . . (*Vindications*, pp. 127, 135, 138)

The term "immortality" was not used primarily for religious reasons, but to ensure that women were understood to be of the same species as men.

Here as elsewhere Mary's contrasting foil is the East: Western Christianity is compared to Eastern religious beliefs and to Eastern perceptions concerning women:

> [I]n the true style of Mahometanism, they are treated as a kind of subordinate beings, and not as a part of the human species, when improveable reason is allowed to be the dignified distinction which raises men above the brute creation, and puts a natural sceptre in a feeble hand . . .
>
> [Women] dress; they paint, and nickname God's creatures. –Surely these weak beings are only fit for a seraglio! (*Vindications*, pp. 109–110, 113).

Adam's task was to *name* the animals; women's belittling, subaltern task is to *nickname* them. Like many others of her age, Mary thought Islam did not believe women had souls. But it wasn't clear that Christianity did either. This missed confrontation between East and West is similar to the missed encounter in Constantinople described by Mary Shelley in her novel *The Last Man*. Where the West prepares to triumph over the East, it is the plague that triumphs over Constantinople.

The allusion to Hamlet's view of Ophelia as a classic male perception, which Mary Wollstonecraft cites often, is indicative of what Mary thinks is wrong with female education:

> The education of women has, of late, been more attended to than formerly; yet they are still reckoned a frivolous sex, and ridiculed or pitied by the writers who endeavour by satire or instruction to improve them. It is acknowledged that they spend many of the first years of their lives in acquiring a smattering of accomplishments; meanwhile strength of body and mind are sacrificed to libertine notions of beauty, to the desire of establishing themselves,—the only way women can rise in the world,—by marriage. (*Vindications*, p. 112)

According to Mary, education needed to address three faculties: reason, the emotions, and the senses. Current arrangements confined and restricted women's reason (the only faculty that could lead to true freedom and independence), over-refined women's emotions, and developed their senses without anchoring them through the other faculties. Wollstonecraft's first novel, *Mary*, was said to create a fictional image of "the mind of a woman, who has thinking powers."[6] Current women's training developed the senses and the emotions, but not the mind:

> In nurseries, and boarding-schools, I fear, girls are first spoiled . . . A number of girls sleep in the same room, and wash together. And, though I should be sorry to contaminate an innocent creature's mind by instilling false delicacy, or those indecent prudish notions, which early cautions respecting the other sex naturally engender, I should be very anxious to prevent their acquiring nasty, or immodest habits; and as many girls have learned very nasty tricks, from ignorant servants, the mixing them thus indiscriminately together, is very improper.
>
> To say the truth women are, in general, too familiar with each other, which leads to that gross degree of familiarity that so frequently renders the marriage state unhappy. (*Vindications*, p. 259)

Mary is clearly uncomfortable letting the senses lead, uncomfortable with the body *per se*, but she sees how the marriage laws disadvantage women by enforcing their need for a "protector" (i.e., tyrant). In the game of chicken of sexual difference, woman is a beautiful object (i.e., someone's possession, someone's dependent, passed from father to husband) on condition that she always blink first.

One of the most pernicious influences on women, according to Mary Wollstonecraft, was the reading of novels. But she died writing one herself (*Maria, or The Wrongs of Woman*, 1798) and had earlier written another one (*Mary: A Fiction*, 1788). In the one she was writing on her deathbed, she discovered the injustice of the marriage laws:

> Was not the world a vast prison, and women born slaves. . . . "Marriage had bastilled me for life." (*Maria*, pp. 64, 115)[7]

The prison imagery was a staple of popular novels of the period. Even *Caleb Williams* turned on several prison breaks.

Popular women's novels are still called "gothic romances," even though the name comes from a Germanic tribe and a vernacular literature. The popular sense of "romance" is a mistake—a mistake that has been there from the beginning. It is the same mistake that made the word "romantic" precede and outlast the content of the movement known as Romanticism.

The gothic novel, which was in fashion in the late eighteenth and nineteenth centuries in England, was so called because of Gothic architecture. It combined the fantasy of chivalry with a craze for medieval castles and convents, for secret passageways and subterranean spaces, for dungeons and dragons. Indeed, it started a craze for medievalism that only grew greater with the excesses of the French Revolution. It tried to combine the Enlightenment with the magic of ghost stories and fairy tales. Shakespeare was the model throughout: *Hamlet, A Midsummer Night's Dream, Macbeth*.

From the first "romances," tales of knights-errant were combined with courtly love. The term "romance," which could simply have been a reference to a genre in French, took on a meaning of "fantasy" or wish-fulfillment. But the French term "*roman*" simply means "novel," while in English, "romance" designates a specific genre. Here, too, Shakespeare is the admired precursor: *The Tempest* is often cited, and Prospero's relation to Miranda is often taken as a model for father-daughter relations. Mary Shelley called her early works "romances" and then her last, contemporary work, "a novel." The disparagement of women for their emotionalism is what novels exploited, and why novel-reading was condemned. And "romantic" was initially used when women's fantasies were out of control. Percy Shelley critically spoke of his wife's "excessive & romantic attachment to [her] Father."[8] Sometimes the word "romantic" is used to discredit female characters; this label in itself is sufficient to depict women's feelings as conventional and trite. In Mary Wollstonecraft's first novel, *Mary*, when Mary's indifferent husband calls her feelings for Ann a "romantic friendship," we know that he means it is not to be taken seriously and that we consequently should.

The gothic novel in English had three sources of interest: the features of medieval architecture (massive castles and cathedrals), the abolished institutions of Catholicism, and the attempt to reconcile supernatural beliefs with Enlightenment beliefs.[9] The medieval was made to assume a cruelty and a superstition considered passé. Still today, much of the paraphernalia of sadomasochism is inspired by medieval instruments of torture. In the film *Pulp Fiction*, punishing a rapist, a mobster instructs his goons to "get medieval" in torturing him.

Given that the gothic novel was mainly inspired by Gothic architecture, it is interesting that the United States, not having a medieval past, but still having a repressed historical inheritance of a European medieval past, should take Victorian architecture as an equivalent. The Bates Motel, in the film *Psycho*, is a spooky old Victorian mansion complete with a corpse in the basement and with a shower curtain in the place of a veil. Similarly, on television, the Addams family's mansion in *The Addams Family* is Victorian.

The French Revolution involved the destruction of much church property—the beheading of statues of saints, etc., to stamp out superstition and religion. The gothic novel in English had several ways to achieve this without upsetting dominant ideology. Henry VIII, in instituting Protestantism against "Popery," had closed Catholic institutions in England, the result of which was the growing popularity of ruined abbeys and monasteries. Gothic novels were often also set in Catholic countries. Horace Walpole, whose novel *The Castle of Otranto* (1764) started the genre, wrote in a brisk, well-researched, satirical style, similar to Jane Austen's first novel, *Northanger Abbey* (published posthumously, 1818). *The Castle of Otranto* resembled *Don Quixote* (1605, 1615) for the credulity of its characters—it even opened with a giant helmet falling from the sky and killing the villain's son (a major episode in *Don Quixote* has the hero mistake a barber's basin for a knight's helmet). The British author Ann Radcliffe, whose gothic novel *The Mysteries of Udolpho* (1794) was read all over Europe, set her novel in the south of France and Italy. She used servants' stories to represent superstition, and the heroine's perspective to stand as Enlightenment "reason."

Mary Wollstonecraft, too, in her final work, *Maria, or The Wrongs of Woman*, made a woman of the serving class tell her story at length, but far from vindicating Enlightenment reason over superstition, she showed the similarities of woman's condition in any class. The "wrongs of women" inhere in the injustice of the marriage laws and in the fact that if a woman is sexualized, even involuntarily, and unmarried, she is "ruined." Men have the power to control women's destiny.

Mary's *Vindication of the Rights of Men* was written as a response to Burke's very long, polemical *Reflections on the Revolution in France* (1790), which itself is written to a (perhaps fictional) French correspondent. It was occasioned by a sermon by British moral philosopher and preacher Richard Price on the "Love of Our Country," delivered on the anniversary of the "Glorious Revolution" to express happiness about the French Revolution, which had just begun. Price's sermon ignited the war of pamphlets known as "the Revolution Controversy" by giving birth to Burke's acerbic rebuttal. Perhaps because Price had been a notorious supporter of American independence and of the American Revolution, Burke acted as if England had been again attacked: he set out to judge the efficacy and necessity of revolution rather than reform. He asked three questions: were the targets deserving of revolutionary violence? Was the confiscation of church property going to solve the French budget problem? Had they tried reform? The ideology of equality, Burke claimed, meant that citizens henceforth had only a numerical, not a rhetorical, existence:

> [T]he age of chivalry is gone.—That of sophisters, economists, and calcula- tors, has succeeded; and the glory of Europe is extinguished for ever. Never, never more, shall we behold that generous loyalty to rank and sex. . . . (Burke, *Reflections*, p. 170)[10]

Mary Wollstonecraft's first *Vindication* taxes Burke with arguing for the inequality of rank against the National Assembly's statement of equality: "You have shewn, Sir, . . . that your respect for rank has swallowed up the common feelings of humanity; you seem to consider the poor as only the live stock of an estate, the feather of hereditary nobility" (*Vindications*, p. 47).

One of the most eloquent passages in Burke's *Reflection*—which em- bodies the "chivalry" he says is dead—is his description of Marie Antoi- nette besieged by a brutal mob. Mary sees this as an example of a knight coming to the defense of a damsel in distress; Burke plays out, unwit- tingly, the whole part of the code of knights-errant, and demonstrates the over-refined feelings cultivated by literature. After all, the word "chivalry" comes from *cheval* ["horse"]. A knight was supposed first and foremost to be daring in feats of arms. The feelings aroused by the sufferings of the beset queen were part of courtly love's cult of sexual difference, which Burke feared would be "leveled" by the operations of equality. "Sensibility" was an emotional response to sexual difference. "Sensibility is the *manie* [mania] of the day," writes Wollstonecraft, "and compassion the virtue which is to cover a multitude of vices . . . " (*Vindications*, p. 36). But, as Claudia Johnson points out,[11] this is *male* sensibility, promoted by Burke and Rousseau. The man capable of tears and blushes (like Rousseau) had already set a new standard of masculinity. But this had not changed the role of sexual difference. It had only given men the emotional expressions once reserved for women.

> I perceive [—says Wollstonecraft to Burke—], from the whole tenor of your Reflections, that you have a mortal antipathy to reason. . . . These are gothic notions of beauty . . . (*Vindications*, p. 38)

What does Mary mean by "gothic notions of beauty"? She implies that Burke's text catered to readers of gothic novels, in that it put the senses and the emotions ahead of reason as a motive for human—*a fortiori* women's—action.

But Mary had her own problems with emotion. That may be why she also wrote novels. After lambasting over-cultivated sensibility in her treatise, she sings its praises in her novels:

> "Sensibility is the most exquisite feeling of which the human soul is susceptible: when it pervades us, we feel happy; and could it last unmixed, we might form some conjecture of the bliss of those paradisiacal days, when the obedient passions were under the dominion of reason, and the impulses of the heart did not need correction." (*Mary*, p. 43)

Ann Radcliffe—the female pioneer of the gothic novel—wrote women's novels with Gothic architecture: the *Mysteries of Udolpho* involved gushing tears from a daughter for a father, and a painstaking marriage plot. The great length of the novel is spent on arguing away the sins of the man the heroine loves so that she can marry him. It is easy to see how the modern "mystery" novel might grow out of it: it often involves solving a murder or getting in or out of a locked room. The Gothic castle with its secret passageways and concealed doors was a perfect setting. Walter Scott, another enthusiast of the medieval Gothic revival, wrote, in his introduction to *The Castle of Otranto*:

> *The Castle of Otranto* is remarkable not only for the wild interest of the story, but as the first modern attempt to found a tale of amusing fiction upon the basis of the ancient romances of chivalry.[12]

The literary motive of chivalry brings us back to the politics of Burke, as well as to the juncture between politics and literature in Mary's Wollstonecraft's own writing.

Mary's reply to Burke was not only a political expression of her conviction: it was part of her political and personal attempt to earn a living as a writer. Her publisher, Joseph Johnson, printed each sheet as soon as she had written it. It is not surprising that in her novel *Maria* the heroine should fall in love with the hero when he in turn addresses her through his writing—through the marginalia he inscribes within the books he lends her. When he lends her *La Nouvelle Héloïse*—another epistolary novel which Percy Shelley read when in the company of Lord Byron on Lake Geneva, where the novel is set—he writes in the margin of the book:

> "Rousseau alone, the true Prometheus of sentiment, possessed the fire of genius necessary to pourtray the passion, the truth of which goes so directly to the heart." (*Maria*, p. 71)

There was a profound disconnect between reason and the emotions in Mary Wollstonecraft's work—and her life. Her contemporary Ann Radcliffe solved such disconnect by shifting the disjunction onto the class difference between servant girls and ladies. Radcliffe was criticized for giving at the end a rational explanation for everything: but what is in reality at stake, in my view, is her hasty attempt to have the heroine's Enlightenment beliefs dominate over the servants' superstition.

Mary Wollstonecraft, contrasting with and yet paralleling Radcliffe, set up her last novel to *resist* Enlightenment ideas and to give center stage to female feelings, but everything seems attributable to an identifiable gender rationale: the injustice of the marriage laws. *Maria* begins with the heroine confined to a mental institution. Insanity is the very opposite of reason, but she is "locked up" because she is under the control of her husband. Like many other novelistic plots, this one ends with a trial designed to show the injustice of the justice system.

> The judge, in summing up the evidence, alluded to "the fallacy of letting women plead their feelings, as an excuse for the violation of the marriage-vow. For his part, he had always determined to oppose all innovation, and the new-fangled notions which incroached on the good old rules of conduct. We did not want French principles in public or private life—and, if women were allowed to plead their feelings, as an excuse or palliation of infidelity, it was opening a flood-gate for immorality. What virtuous woman thought of her feelings?" (*Maria*, p. 145)

The injustice of the marriage system for women inheres in the fact that men have total control and in the fact that women's feelings are irrelevant. But Mary Wollstonecraft's last novel is unfinished. In at least one sketch of an ending, she depicts the hero as unfaithful. It is clear that however unjust a justice system is that disregards women's feelings, feelings aren't necessarily the answer, either. But Mary realized that she couldn't leave them out.

Trying to behave as a professional writer, there was at first no correspondence between Mary's life and her work. She replied to Burke, and then went to France to report on the revolution. The disconnect between her private life and her life as a writer was an indication, either that she was not allowing a sufficient place for emotion in a life she wished to mold out of pure reason, or that her conception of enlightened reason left no room for a corresponding theory, or understanding, of emotion. Either because women's reason (as she had claimed) was repressed, or because her own emotions were overwhelmingly gushy, Mary Wollstonecraft was in practice a walking contradiction. Who would have guessed that the author of *A Vindication of the Rights of Woman* had fallen so deeply in love with Henry Fuseli that she proposed to his wife that the three of them live in a *ménage à trois*? That when Fuseli's wife refused with indignation, Mary went to Paris? That she met there a dashing American named Gilbert Imlay, with whom she had a passionate affair? That when British citizens were in danger in France, she was registered as his wife? That when she discovered Imlay's infidelity, Mary twice attempted suicide? It was in a last-ditch effort to get Imlay back that she offered to be his business agent in Scandinavia. But it was there that her writing life and her emotional life finally came together.

She published, in a work entitled *Letters Written During a Short Residence in Sweden, Norway, and Denmark* (the last work published in her lifetime, 1796), a series of letters to Imlay from Scandinavia (not so much her real letters as excerpts from her journal). This was in the style of a new genre, a sort of travel diary combined with an autobiographical memoir, a combination of a tour guide, a philosophical commentary, and an epistolary novel, a genre that became extremely influential on, and popular with, the Romantic poets. Wollstonecraft's future husband, William Godwin, wrote upon reading this work: "If ever there was a book calculated to make a man in love with its author, this appears to me to be the book."[13] The first published work of Mary Shelley, Wollstonecraft's daughter with Godwin, would also be this kind of travel diary, done by Mary in collaboration with her husband: *History of a Six-Weeks' Tour through a Part of France, Switzerland, Germany, and Holland: With Letters Descriptive of a Sail round the Lake of Geneva, and of the Glaciers of Chamouni* (1817), written during the same summer as *Frankenstein* (1816). *Childe Harold's Pilgrimage*, the work that made Byron famous overnight, was a similar poetic account of his grand tour (published between 1812 and 1818). In the absence of today's extensive travel literature, no writer worth his salt could go anywhere without writing about it. And the epistolary genre was so entrenched that at first Mary Shelley's novel *Frankenstein* (1818) acts like one (in Walton's letters to his sister). But it gave way to a new genre that was just getting its start, autobiography, also inaugurated by Rousseau. Rousseau's *Confessions* begins "Je suis né à Genève en 1712," and Frankenstein's long account of himself begins "I am by birth a Genevese." It is near Chamouni (Mont Blanc, about which Percy wrote a famous poem at the same time) that the monster tells his story.

In Mary Wollstonecraft's author advertisement to her *Letters Written During a Short Residence in Sweden, Norway, and Denmark*, she wrote, unwittingly reflecting on the rare genre of female autobiography: "In writing these desultory letters, I found I could not avoid being continually the first person—'the little hero of each tale.'"[14] Mary finally learned to use the first person in her writing. By combining autobiography and tale-telling, she spoke of herself as a literary character. This is in marked contrast to what her daughter tells us, in her 1831 Preface to *Frankenstein*, about her creative imaginings, where the fiction-making activity goes on almost without her: "My imagination . . . possessed and guided me." "I did not make myself the heroine of my tales" (*Frankenstein*, pp. x, viii).

With all the prison imagery of the gothic novel and the marriage laws, with the efforts to find a place for unruly emotions, there is one thing Mary Wollstonecraft left out, and that was the thing that, in the end, she died from. In the gothic novel, women are often confined: in dungeons or in their own apartments. For their protection, they are confined to a convent if they are unmarried or want to retire from the world. Witness how often Jane Austen, to get a sexual ball rolling, has a woman confined to bed for disease. But the most telling instance of "confinement to bed," the most indicative of sexual difference, was childbearing. If a woman threw herself at a man or ran off with him without being married, an illicit pregnancy was bound to occur. When Mary Wollstonecraft found herself pregnant by William Godwin, the staunch feminist marriage resister got married so that the child would not be born illegitimate. In his play *The Winter's Tale*, Shakespeare plays on two senses of "confinement" when he has his pregnant heroine imprisoned. When the child is born, the "delivery" is very like a liberation from prison:

> This child was prisoner to the womb, and is
> By law and process of great nature thence
> Freed and enfranchised . . . (*The Winter's Tale*, II:2)[15]

Having a baby changed everything for Mary, but she did not let that get in the way of her activity, nor did she subscribe to the cult of motherhood that many other women endorsed. She treated pregnancy as an inevitable part of her life, not as an occasion for emotion. She did not consider it a solution to the problem of women's emotions, although her last novel is written fictionally to her (dead) daughter. In other words, Mary Wollstonecraft did not solve the question of women's emotion, but she did see motherhood as women's destiny. For Mary, this was certainly the case. She traveled to Scandinavia with a toddler from Gilbert Imlay, and she died of complications from giving birth to the future Mary Shelley.

CHAPTER THREE

Percy Bysshe Shelley

Percy Bysshe Shelley grew up surrounded by adoring sisters, and he took female admiration as his normal state. Indeed, there was much to admire. He was handsome in an androgynous way that appealed to both men and women: tall, slim, and very intense about his ideas. He was the author of two gothic novels by the age of eighteen. He often had intellectual friends along with his love objects, although sometimes they fell in love with him. There was Elizabeth Hitchener alongside his first wife, Harriet, and the friend (and perhaps co-author) Thomas Jefferson Hogg, with whom he was expelled from Oxford for circulating his pamphlet *The Necessity of Atheism*, and with whom he tried to share both his wives. Elizabeth Hitchener was a schoolteacher and intellectual correspondent; she unwisely quit her job and followed Shelley, but never shared life with him. Hogg probably loved Shelley through the women they shared (and vice versa). Shelley eloped twice and married twice. He was both less transgressive and less benevolent than he wished to appear: the authorities were at first reluctant to expel him from Oxford, and, although he was always giving coins from his pockets to the poor, he always possessed a carriage and good clothes. He was a vegetarian, but was trained as a skilled huntsman and harbored murderous feelings; he had cut off relations with his own father, Timothy, but faithfully paid William Godwin's debts. Godwin's political ideas very much impressed and formed him; he was perhaps the kind of son-in-law that was really in love with the father. He both sought and spurned his inheritance. He agreed with Godwin that wealth was unequally distributed, but he wanted to have some to give away. That may be why he gave so much to Godwin, and why he was always harassed by debts. It was more fitting to his self-esteem to be an aristocrat who lacked money than to be a poor man. He had small regard for poor or working men; he left debts to carriage-makers and upholsterers.

For someone who opposed marriage, he was surprisingly often married. He agreed with Godwin's critique of any fettering promise:

> [W]e abridge . . . the time of gaining information, if we bind ourselves today to the conduct we will observe two months hence. (Godwin, *Political Justice*, p. 220)[1]

> Love is free: to promise for ever to love the same woman is not less absurd than to promise to believe the same creed: such a vow, in both cases, excludes us from all inquiry. (Shelley, *Poetical Works*, p. 807)[2]

In Shelley's early novel *Zastrozzi*, the hero, Verezzi, is tricked into marriage by the evil Matilda, who tells him that the woman he loves, Julia, is dead. When he sees her unexpectedly, he tells her "I am—I am—married to Matilda"[3] before killing himself. Men, too, felt confined by marriage, but Percy recognized that what Godwin called the "sexual monopoly" was more unfair to women. He was always surrounded by admiring women (in fact, he needed to be), but he was never free because always married (his relation to women was something like today's relations between celebrities and paparazzi). Percy had a knack for making people fall in love with him, which left a lot of collateral damage in his wake. Either he did not notice some of these adoring women (Fanny Imlay, Mary Wollstonecraft's illegitimate daughter, quietly in love with him and in despair at not being wanted anywhere, committed suicide) or he left them (his first wife, Harriet, far advanced in pregnancy by no one knows who, also committed suicide, enabling him to marry Mary Godwin at the end of 1816).

At least, unlike the legal system, he did think of marriage as an affair of feelings—Wordsworth had defined the new style of poetry as "the spontaneous overflow of powerful feelings," which "takes its origin from emotion recollected in tranquility"[4]—except that for Percy there was no recollection, no tranquility. For Percy, indeed, romantic love was the driving force of life, but the objects of romantic love kept changing:

> Thy look of love has power to calm
> The stormiest passion of my soul . . . ("To Harriet")[5]

My baffled looks did fear yet dread
To meet thy looks—I could not know
How anxiously they sought to shine
With soothing pity upon mine . . . ("To Mary")[6]

Yet look on me—take not thine eyes away . . . ("To——")[7]

As the dash indicates, the women to whom he addressed himself were interchangeable.

Like the protagonist in Thomas Hardy's *The Well-Beloved*, Percy's ideal inhabited first one person, then another. He was always faithful to it, but never found it for long in a real woman; his women often felt forsaken as he pursued his ideal. In a variation on the invocation to the muse or the epistolary novel, Percy sought an addressee; for that reason there are many poems entitled "To Harriet," "To Mary," "To Constanza" (Claire Clairmont, Mary's stepsister), "To Jane" (Jane Williams, whose husband, Edward, went with Percy on his ill-fated voyage in his boat, the *Ariel*), "To——." Of course, odes to everything were common in literature, and Percy was no exception: "To William Shelley" (his dead son), "To Liberty," "To a Skylark," "To the West Wind," "Hymn to Intellectual Beauty."

He dedicated his first long poem, *Queen Mab*, to his first wife, and his second, *The Revolt of Islam*, to his second wife. And he wrote *Epipsychidion* for an Italian girl confined in a convent until her wedding day. But even if it was conventional, Percy seems to take this use of the vocative to extremes. It was as if the vocative was the way to bring something into poetic language.[8]

The other great discourse where a speaker speaks to an audience is of course political discourse. Percy, in fact, was equally interested in politics. His initial admiration for William Godwin was for a political thinker capable of applying reason to political problems and capable of sharing his vision of a rosy future. Shelley wrote at least as much prose as verse, most of it political, not fictional. Sometimes it was an essay on a religious, moral, poetic, or political subject. But it nevertheless often involved the vocative: "An Address to the Irish People," "A Letter to Lord Ellenborough," "An Address to the People on the Death of the Princess Charlotte." But the distinction between verse and prose is misleading because *both* kinds of writings are, in Shelley's case, about a world in which liberty instead of tyranny would reign. He was criticized for advocating free love, which he would not have known how to practice, but for him, ideal love had to be free.

Another look, however, at the poems Percy adoringly addressed to women tells us they are all about *being looked at*. The object addressed, in other words, turns out to be his own idealized self, as an idealizing woman believes it to be. This is also true when the entity addressed is omnipotent. Percy addresses two kinds of objects: a woman who complements him, a yin for his yang, and an all-powerful agent capable of carrying him away. As he says to the West Wind, "lift me as a wave, a leaf, a cloud." In both cases, he says to the image, "Be thou me!"

This relationship, which is always to the self, has been analyzed as narcissistic:

> [I]n his relations with women [—one critic writes—] Shelley sought not harmony but narcissistic unison . . . [He] sought himself or his own likeness in a woman.[9]

Handsome and androgynous as he was, he was the very image of Narcissus, staring at his image in the water (it is fitting that he died by drowning):

> Two anglers saw Shelley on the river at Marlow in 1817, as they punted slowly past. The poet was crouching in the bow of his boat, alone, and transfixed by something in the water. His look was so piteous and horror-struck that one fisherman supposed he wished to drown himself. His friend thought he had probably dropped his brandy flask in the river.

What Shelley was gazing at was his own reflection—"the thing in the water," as he mildly told them. In *The Revolt of Islam*, which he had broken off from writing, he described, as it seemed, what he had seen that day.

> I saw my countenance reflected there;—
> And then my youth fell on me like a wind
> Descending on still waters—my thin hair
> Was prematurely gray, my face was lined
> With channels, such as suffering leaves behind,
> Not age . . .

In *Alastor*, too, the Poet came to a well among the trees and lingered, looking.

> His eyes beheld
> Their own wan light through the reflected lines
> Of his thin hair, distinct in the dark depth
> Of that still fountain; as the human heart,

> Gazing in dreams over the gloomy grave,
> Sees its own treacherous likeness there.[10]

This is a story very much like that of Narcissus, who ends up dying in the water in trying to embrace his own reflection.

Indeed Percy often walked on the edges of cliffs, and was much more likely to kill himself than William Godwin, despite the fact that in Mary Shelley's story *Matilda* (written 1918–19), it is the fictional father who has committed incest with his daughter who kills himself. For a while, Percy slept with pistols and poison. Like his hero Werther, who gave the tone to (German) Romanticism, Percy was ready to die for love. In *Matilda*, there is a great deal of Percy in the father.

But there is one difference, at least from the traditional story of Narcissus (although the etymological pun behind the genre of *vanitas* may be a hint—i.e., emptiness and self-love). Instead of a substance in love with an image, this Narcissus seeks in the love object the substance he lacks. He is an empty form, a blank,[11] or as he puts it in his *Defence of Poetry*, using a very common figure the period, an Aeolian harp:

> Poetry, in a general sense, may be defined to be "the expression of the imagination," and poetry is connate with the origin of man. Man is an instrument over which a series of external and internal impressions are driven like the alternations of an ever-changing wind over an Aeolian lyre, which move it by their motion to ever-changing melody. (*Shelley's Prose*, p. 277)[12]

In other words, the Poet is that through which the universe sounds. This may not be self-love, but neither is it concern about the love-object.

Mary was madly in love with Percy, declared her love for him on her mother's grave, and eloped with him to the continent in 1814. Percy, still bound in marriage to Harriet, was unable to marry at the time, but Mary should have been able to see the danger signs. Her stepsister, Claire Clairmont, accompanied them—Claire having talked until late at night with Percy. Mary was at first enchanted with Percy's preoccupations, to which she was for many years an empathic and attentive listener. In his Notes to *Queen Mab*, Percy writes of the cosmos:

> Beyond our atmosphere the sun would appear a rayless orb of fire in the midst of a black concave. The equal diffusion of its light on earth is owing to the refraction of the rays by the atmosphere, and their reflection from

other bodies. Light consists either of vibrations propagated through a subtle medium, or of numerous minute particles repelled in all directions from the luminous body . . . (*Poetical Works*, p. 800)

Shelley's intellectual passion for cosmic and celestial phenomena has left its mark on Mary's own cosmic imagination, as can be seen in the following passage from Mary's novel *The Last Man*:

A strange story was brought to us from the East, to which little credit would have been given, had not the fact been attested by a multitude of witnesses, in various parts of the world. On the twenty-first of June, it was said that an hour before noon, a black sun arose: an orb, the size of that luminary, but dark, defined, whose beams were shadows, ascended from the west; in about an hour it had reached the meridian, and eclipsed the bright parent of day . . . (*The Last Man*, p. 162)[13]

Writing in the flush of grief for the unanticipated, premature death of her husband, Mary described a devastated world in which she felt as alone as the last person on earth. She nevertheless put as a minor character— in a novel with few minor characters—an astronomer, Merrival, whose death from the plague cannot be prevented despite all his astronomic knowledge.

The Last Man contains a semi-fictional "Author's Introduction" which, like the 1831 introduction to *Frankenstein*, talks about Mary's own subjectivity as author, and about her own loss. In this novel the author and her companion are wandering in the Sybil's cave and find fragmentary leaves in ancient and modern languages lying about. "For awhile my labours were not solitary; but that time is gone; and, with the selected and matchless companion of my toils, their dearest reward is also lost to me" (*The Last Man*, p. 3). Mary describes her role as that of a solitary translator and editor of the leaves.

Frankenstein, written eight years earlier, was, however, a critique of Percy's obsessive quest for knowledge. Percy's erotic infidelity was only to increase later, as was his neglect of his children. But already Mary, though still infatuated, was mad at him. Like Frankenstein, Percy was known for his unreliable chemistry experiments, and for his disregard for the life around him.

In addition, Mary's novel expressed a new appreciation for Alpine landscapes, for their metaphorical conveyance of a sense of the sublime embodied in Nature. In this new appreciation for the scenes of nature, as well as in the new generic combination of majestic nature with the supernatural, Mary's novel continued and developed (the female brand of) the gothic tradition inaugurated by Ann Radcliffe. Radcliffe's novels of gothic and romantic terror, most notably her most popular novel, *The Mysteries of Udolpho*, innovatively inscribed scenic descriptions of sublime (majestic, overpowering, unconsciously exciting, taunting) natural surroundings, as the natural stage for human plots of equally grand, equally obscure, and ravishing passions and emotions:

> On the pleasant banks of the Garonne, in the province of Gascony, stood, in the year 1584, the chateau of Monsieur St. Aubert. From its windows were seen the pastoral landscapes of Guienne and Gascony, . . . To the south, the view was bounded by the majestic Pyrenées, whose summits, veiled in clouds, or exhibiting awful forms, seen, and lost again, as the partial vapours rolled along, were sometimes barren, and gleamed through the blue tinge of air, and sometimes frowned with forests of gloomy pine, that swept downward to their base . . .
>
> From this sublime scene the travellers continued to ascend among the pines, till they entered a narrow pass of the mountains . . . This pass, which led into the heart of the Apennine, at length opened to day, and a scene of mountains stretched in long perspective, as wild as any the travellers had yet passed . . .
>
> Wild and romantic as were these scenes, their character had far less of the sublime, than had those of the Alps, which guard the entrance of Italy . . . [The setting sun] streamed in full splendour upon the towers and battlements of a castle, that spread its extensive ramparts along the brow of a precipice above . . .
>
> "There," said Montoni . . . "is Udolpho."
>
> Emily gazed with melancholy awe upon the castle, which she understood to be Montoni's; for . . . the gothic greatness of its features, and its mouldering walls of dark grey stone, rendered it a gloomy and sublime object. (*The Mysteries of Udolpho*, pp. 5, 215–216) [14]

The gothic novel instated the claims of the sublime, emphasizing as a point of departure the majestic, overpowering magnitude of its natural surroundings. Thus *Frankenstein's* creature tells his story on the Alps, and thus Percy Shelley writes his ode to Mont Blanc.

But there was yet another tradition of the gothic novel, one exemplified by "Monk" Lewis, one that shaped Percy's early novels: the irresistible fascination with evil. This tradition equally has left its mark on *Franken-*

stein. These novels usually involved torture, revenge, punishment, and forbidden sexuality. It should be remembered that physical torture was abolished during the French Revolution, abolition that was part of the ideology of liberty, based on the idea of sympathy, or identification with another's pain.[15] But gothic novels still continued to depict "medieval" torture, and had their own way of describing an obsessive, terrifying mental torture. *Frankenstein* was no exception.

In the novel Mary wrote before Percy died, *Valperga* (published in 1823, but edited by Mary's father, Godwin, between 1821 and 1823), there is a study of the psychology of infidelity, with which Mary must have struggled. Mary had given herself entirely to Percy when they eloped in 1814, but her father reacted more like a conventional father than like Percy's mentor when he condemned Percy for this illicit love affair and accused him of stealing his daughter, even when Shelley finally married Mary after Harriet's suicide, in 1816. Ironically enough, fifteen years before, Godwin, like Percy, had had his own run-in with convention, and had in turn scandalized traditional society, when people were outraged by his candid disclosure of wife's behavior in his posthumous memoir of her life and of her love affairs. This act of remembrance of his dead wife, which Godwin intended as a biographical record of her glory (*Memoirs of the Author of* A Vindication of the Rights of Woman) instead provoked public derision and shame.

1816, the eventful year of Percy Shelley's first wife's suicide and of his second marriage to Mary, was also, of course, the memorable year of the ghost-story writing contest that gave birth to *Frankenstein*. In the introduction to the new edition of *Frankenstein* in 1831, Mary gives an account of her initial creative inhibition, her initial inactivity and lack of productivity:

> Travelling, and the cares of a family, occupied my time . . . (*Frankenstein*, p. viii)

Mary had many children by Percy, in fact. She was pregnant five times by the age of twenty-five. After Harriet's death, Percy sought custody of their two children, but was not awarded it because of his atheism and his unorthodox lifestyle. Although Mary thought this unfair, she did not think Percy took parenthood as seriously as a mother needed to. When her daughter Clara Everina died after a rapid journey to Venice, where Percy, staying with Byron, had called them, Mary blamed Percy for their daughter's death. And when William, Percy's son and heir, died a few months later in the region of Italy the family had moved to partly for Percy's health, Mary was disconsolate. Percy thought she mourned too long, and she resented him for that, too. So she was mad at him for several things when he drowned in 1822. And though she was in deep mourning, his death had two empowering effects on her: she looked good in black, and, while a living husband could always be unfaithful, there could only be one official widow.

Percy had tried to combine, in Mary, the functions of love-object and friend, which had been separate before. With the friend he had discussed books, and to the companion-interlocutor he had given learning tasks and assignments. He liked to be the teacher, the "subject presumed to know."[16] Mary was more intellectual than others, but also an assiduous, good student. After his death, she set about editing his works conscientiously: first some posthumous poems, then the collected poems. With the humility common in fictions where the author claims merely to be an editor or translator, she listed the books he read each year and appended a note to every major poem. Editing Percy suddenly gave Mary power over him, a power she did not have in his lifetime; how he was remembered was entirely in her hands. The world did not know him as well as it ought to; she would fix that, but in the process she would package him—repackage him—as a public person. Even his personal life was henceforth public property. Thus Mary composed a myth of Shelley for posterity, in which she was the sufferer who had been blessed for a few years with his presence. As editor, in other words, Mary created a new public myth both of Percy's poetic genius and of her loss. This double narrative of Shelley's genius (and of her loss) inscribes itself already in 1831, in Mary's retrospective Introduction to *Frankenstein*:

> Travelling, and the cares of a family, occupied my time; and study, in the way of reading or improving my ideas in communication with his far more cultivated mind was all of literary employment that engaged my attention. (*Frankenstein*, p. viii)

Eight years later, in her Preface to Shelley's *Poetical Works* in 1839, Mary describes her work as editor as follows:

> . . . I hasten to fulfil [*sic*] an important duty,—that of giving the productions of a sublime genius to the world, with all the correctness possible, and of,

at the same time, detailing the history of those productions, as they sprang, living and warm, from his heart and brain. I abstain from any remark on the occurrences of his private life, except inasmuch as the passions which they engendered inspired his poetry. This is not the time to relate the truth. . . .

In the notes appended to the poems I have endeavoured to narrate the origin and history of each. The loss of nearly all letters and papers which refer to his early life renders the execution more imperfect than it would otherwise have been. I have, however, the liveliest recollection of all that was done and said during the period of my knowing him. (*Poetical Works*, pp. xxi, xxiii)

This editorial principle transforms anything written before Percy knew Mary, published or unpublished, into "Juvenilia." And gives everything written in Mary's time more authority. Given Percy's love for books and his classical learning, and given that the editor of his poems wanted to put forward their textual rather than personal ancestry, here is the testimony she records about the year 1816, commenting on the poems of that year:

This was an eventful year, and less time was given to study than usual. In the list of his reading I find, in Greek, Theocritus, the *Prometheus* of Aeschylus, several of Plutarch's *Lives*, and the works of Lucian. In Latin, Lucretius, Pliny's *Letters*, the *Annals* and *Germany* of Tacitus. In French, the *History of the French Revolution* by Lacretelle. He read for the first time, this year, Montaigne's *Essays*, and regarded them ever after as one of the most delightful and instructive books in the world. The list is scanty in English works: Locke's *Essay*, *Political Justice*, and Coleridge's *Lay Sermon*, form nearly the whole. It was his frequent habit to read aloud to me in the evening; in this way we read, this year, the New Testament, *Paradise Lost*, Spenser's *Faery Queen*, and *Don Quixote*. (*Poetical Works*, p. 536)

1816 was, importantly for Mary, the precise year of the ghost-story contest in which Shelley was a participant, and which was the origin of *Frankenstein*. It is noteworthy that although the editor of Shelley's *Poetical Works* does not (of course) so much as mention these events that gave rise to her own writing, *Frankenstein* itself contains another form of her notes on Shelley's works: some of the books the creature reads in his hovel are on this reading list.

Mary's mention of Aeschylus' *Prometheus* also brings up the whole question of intertextuality and of the impact of prior texts on both Mary's and Shelley's works. Education involved making explicit one's sources, displaying one's classical learning, depicting one's work as an updated version of Greek myth. Thus *Frankenstein* was explicitly subtitled *The Modern Prometheus*, and thus John Polidori, another participant in the ghost-story contest, wrote *Ernestus Berchtold, or The Modern Oedipus*. And Mary's edition of Percy's poetry gave a prominent place to translation. Percy wrote what he considered his masterpiece, *Prometheus Unbound*, after a lost play of Aeschylus. Byron, too, wrote a poem called *Prometheus*. But who is Prometheus? Ancient versions do not agree. Is he the being who stole fire from the gods, or is he a creator of man? Rebel or rival maker? There seems to be confusion everywhere. In addition, Mary seems to conflate—or to perceive synchronically—the Greeks with Milton. The title page of *Frankenstein* contains an epigraph quoted from *Paradise Lost*:

> Did I request thee, Maker, from my clay
> To mould me Man, did I solicit thee
> From darkness to promote me?
> (*Paradise Lost*, X, ll. 743–45)

It is easy to see the relevance of this sentiment to the novel, but harder to say whether the hero is Greek or Miltonic. Percy seemed to have the same confusion in a different form: he didn't believe in evil but was fascinated by it. He considered revolt against tyrants good, but wanted to replace revenge with forgiveness. He usually reveled in horrible punishments for his evil characters, and covertly considered Milton's Lucifer a romantic hero. The whole question revolved around God. Was he a tyrant or a creator? Both? Here is Mary's attempt at neutrality on this question in her notes to the poems:

> Shelley believed that mankind had only to will that there should be no evil, and there would be none. It is not my part in these Notes to notice the arguments that have been urged against this opinion, but to mention the fact that he entertained it . . . (*Poetical Works*, p. 271)

The daughter of Mary Wollstonecraft was indeed often chided for not having strong opinions and not serving a cause. In her journal of 1838, she implicitly answered those who urged her to take a more active role in endorsing liberal political causes:

> In the first place, with regard to "the good cause"—the cause of the advancement of freedom and knowledge, of the rights of women, &c.—I am not a person of opinions. I have said elsewhere that human beings differ greatly

in this. Some have a passion for reforming the world; others do not cling to
particular opinions. That my parents and Shelley were of the former class,
makes me respect it. . . . For myself, I earnestly desire the good and enlightenment of my fellow-creatures, and see all, in the present course, tending to the
same, and rejoice; but I am not for violent extremes which only bring on an
injurious reaction.[17]

Mary had witnessed such injurious reactions; not only did she share the
English horror at the bloody end of the French Revolution, but she saw
her father's loving memoir of her mother rejected as improper. Then her
father married not another independent woman, but a proponent of
rather conventional femininity. And Percy—in Mary's name—promoted
domesticity in the preface he wrote for his wife's novel:

> . . . [M]y chief concern in this respect has been limited to . . . avoiding the
> enervating effects of the novels of the present day, and to the exhibition of
> the amiableness of domestic affection, and the excellence of universal vir-
> tue. The opinions which naturally spring from the character and situation
> of the hero are by no means to be conceived as existing always in my own
> conviction; nor is any inference justly to be drawn from the following pages
> as prejudicing any philosophical doctrine of whatever kind. (*Frankenstein*,
> p. xiv)

Percy must have felt intuitively some hostility from his wife's novel, but
wasn't sure of its nature, so he denied the novel the capacity of making
any statement whatsoever. Although he seemed to want a wife who was
an equal, he associated women with the domestic sphere. In his poetic
dedication of *The Revolt of Islam* to Mary, he makes clear their respective
roles of knight-errant and hearth:

> So now my summer task is ended, Mary,
> And I return to thee, mine own heart's home;
> As to his Queen some victor Knight of Faëry . . .
>   (*Poetical Works*, p. 37)

For Percy, there was a huge difference between "the ideal person" (which
he tried to be) and "ideal woman" (which he sought). Mary Wollstonecraft was an equal, a mind, a philosopher, but not, for him, a woman. Her
daughter thus was in a double bind: she was under tremendous pressure
to be like her mother, but all around her the men she loved were choosing
conventional femininity. Two things made her choice of ideal femininity

easier: she was prettier than her mother, and her fantasies did not revolve around herself. As she said in her 1831 introduction to *Frankenstein*:

> It was beneath the trees of the grounds belonging to our house, or on the bleak sides of the woodless mountains near, that my true compositions, the airy flights of my imagination, were born and fostered. I did not make myself the heroine of my tales. . . . I could not figure to myself that romantic woes or wonderful events would ever be my lot . . . (*Frankenstein*, p. viii)

In other words, the fantasies of the "romantic" came to Mary from outside, from her culture, or perhaps from those "novels of the present day" that Percy reviled. Mary could not compete—did not try to compete—with her mother's independent will. In a fantasy world where women were beautiful and men were brave, Mary Wollstonecraft had no place. But in *Lodore*, one of Mary Shelley's last novels (written in 1830, long after Percy's death), a novel about a heroic and self-sacrificing mother, Mary Wollstonecraft made a final appearance in the character Fanny Derham:

> Such a woman as Fanny was more made to be loved by her own sex than by the opposite one. Superiority of intellect, joined to acquisitions beyond those usual even to men; and both announced with frankness, though without pretension, forms a kind of anomaly little in accord with masculine taste. Fanny could not be the rival of women, and, therefore, all her merits were appreciated by them. They love to look up to a superior being, to rest on a firmer support than their own minds can afford; and they are glad to find such in one of their own sex, and thus destitute of those dangers which usually attend any services conferred by men . . .
>
> Each [Ethel Fitzhenry and Fanny Derham] had been the favourite daughter of men of superior qualities of mind . . . Lord Lodore had formed his ideal of what a woman ought to be, of what he had wished to find his wife, and sought to mould his daughter accordingly. Mr. Derham contemplated the duties and objects befitting an immortal soul, and had educated his child for the performance of them . . . One only remains to be mentioned: but it is not in a few tame lines that we can revert to the varied fate of Fanny Derham . . . What the events are, that have already diversified her existence, cannot now be recounted . . . In after times these may be told, and the life of Fanny Derham be presented as a useful lesson . . . (*Lodore*, pp. 214, 218, 313)[18]

Mary Shelley had made peace with her mother. After years of rivalry, she accepted the fact that she and her mother were different types of women, and she bid her good-bye with this tribute. She realized that the narrative forms of her time were not ready for such an independent woman and that she had chosen a structure of fantasy instead. She knew by now that fantasy's promise of a happy ending was often false, but such a fantasy was nonetheless built into the very structure of narrative and storytelling.

Mary Wollstonecraft was a creature of reason, but Percy opened for her daughter something more: imagination. As he put it in his *Defence of Poetry*:

> According to one mode of regarding those two classes of mental action which are called reason and imagination, the former may be considered as mind contemplating the relations borne by one thought to another, however produced; and the latter, as mind acting upon those thoughts so as to colour them with its own light . . . Poetry, in a general sense, may be defined to be "the expression of the imagination," and poetry is connate with the origin of man. (*Shelley's Prose*, pp. 276–277)

There was one role Mary had no trouble seeing her husband in: the role of teacher. One similarity between her mother and her husband that Mary endorsed was an interest in education. One difference between men and women was the inequality of their educations. This meant that not only were women less learned, but men and women had different objects of attraction. Women sought in books what they sought in life, while men sought to be great—like the authors in the canon. When describing the nature of poetry, Percy always began with the Greeks. Men's works looked up to Shakespeare, Dante, and Milton; women sought to be loved by Superman. This female lack of classical education and this cultural focus on the "great books" was why women's books were denigrated.

Therefore, when Mary understood that her writing was not learned enough, she started to engage in diligent research. She read a history of Italy when the Shelleys were going to live there. Her first novel after *Frankenstein*, *Valperga* (1823), was full of research. But nevertheless she made it her own.

Valperga's protagonist, Castruccio, was a real historical figure from the fourteenth century, but Mary recognized in him a type of hero she was searching for. Her ears pricked up when she read in Sismondi's *History of the Italian Republics of the Middle Ages*:

> Castruccio was thirty-two years of age when he obtained the sovereignty of his country. He was tall, with an agreeable countenance; and his face, thin and surrounded with long fair hair, was remarkable for its paleness.[19]

In a history book that has little room for individuals, Mary found her romantic hero. The more she researched, the more research confirmed it. Machiavelli wrote at length about Castruccio, noting, for example:

> As we have seen then, Castruccio was a rare man not only for his own times, but also for those that had gone before. Physically, he was taller than average and well proportioned; and he was very handsome . . .[20]

In attempting to tailor her book to the popular female taste, Mary at first used Machiavelli's title and called her novel tentatively "The Life and Adventures of Castruccio, Prince of Lucca," but then, given the taste for gothic novels, particularly among women readers, she changed it to *Valperga*, which is the name not of a person but of a castle—the castle of one of the heroines—and which Castruccio ends up destroying. In fact, the love life of Castruccio occupies a prominent place in Mary's novel: Castruccio is torn between two women, one who has loved him all her life (for whom Mary invents the name Euthanasia) and an upstart Beatrice, by whom Castruccio is fascinated. The culminating scene is a meeting between the two women, clearly the emotional center of the book.

The novel takes place in Dante's time: the Guelphs and the Ghibellines are pitted against each other. This was also the time when vernacular literature began in the Italian language. As was the case with French at the same stage, Italian literature was interested in courtly love (see Petrarch) and Christianity (see Dante). Euthanasia is a Ghibelline whereas Castruccio fights for the Guelphs. Euthanasia and Castruccio try to keep politics out of their relationship, but finally Castruccio realizes that he will be thwarted in his ambitions if he does not attack the Ghibelline noblewoman's castle. The narrative voice sees military ambition as a difference between men and women, or at least between Castruccio and Euthanasia:

> Ambition, and the fixed desire to rule, smothered in his mind the voice of his better reason; and the path of tyranny was smoothed by his steady resolve to obtain the power, which under one form or other it had been the object of his life to seek. (*Valperga*, p. 173)[21]

Mary was probably still following Percy's advice when she conceived her fourth novel, *The Fortunes of Perkin Warbeck* (published in 1823). She researched it extensively and even asked her father for research help. "By January 1827," writes D. D. Fischer in his Introductory Note to the novel, "less than a year after publishing *The Last Man*, [Mary] had found her new subject: the pretender to the English throne who claimed to be the younger of the two princes allegedly murdered by Richard III . . . Many of the characters in her novel appear in the *Henry VI* trilogy and *Richard III* of Shakespeare [and others] . . . ”[22] In her own "Author's Preface," Mary writes that she recognized the survival of the prince in the tower as a subject for romance, i.e., fairy tale:

> The story of Perkin Warbeck was first suggested to me as a subject for historical detail. On studying it, I became aware of the romance which his story contains . . . (*Perkin Warbeck*, p. 5)

The name of the hero comes from the fact that the rescued prince was taken in by a Flemish moneylender, John Warbeck. Once again Mary did a lot of research. And once again she transformed the center of interest of the story. This time she invented whole scenes not to be found in the original sources. The original inspired her by its romantic knightly valor, but, trained by the gothic novel pioneered by women writers, she greatly expanded the role of the Tower of London's spooky architecture, mossy walls, and damp labyrinth, and gave more importance to the novel's women. The hero is again torn between two women: Monina de Faro, the half-Moorish daughter of John Warbeck's sister and a Spanish mariner, and Lady Katherine of Scotland, his wife. The tale takes place at the time of Columbus: Monina is supposed to sail off to America with her father. In fact America figures in all three of Mary's last three novels as a place where identity can be laundered and life begun anew. It functions as an allegorical "other place," a blank on which the imagination can at leisure write. But this time there is no question of infidelity (as in *Valperga*). The two women simply love the same man. When they meet, they stare out at the sea from the top of Mont Saint-Michel, in some ways the paradigm of Gothic architecture. They do not look at each other but are looked at as women:

> Nothing beautiful could be so unlike as these two fair ones. Katherine was the incarnate image of loveliness, such as it might have been conceived by an angelic nature; noble, soft, equable from her tender care not to displease others . . . Monina,—no, there was no evil in Monina; if too much self-devotion, too passionate an attachment to one dear idea, too enthusiastic an adoration of one exalted being, could be called aught but virtue. The full orbs of her dark eyes, once flashing bright, were now more serious, more melancholy . . . "He goes to conquer; God will give victory to the right: as a warrior he treads his native land; as a monarch he will rule over her." (*Perkin Warbeck*, p. 304)

Mary describes the same entrapment of women in marriage and poor education for women as her mother did before her, but she makes these very limitations into occasions for female virtue and other kinds of distinctively female knowledge:

> Then Lady Katherine . . . declared that she was nothing moved from her bridal vow . . . State and dignity, or their contraries, humiliation and disgrace, could only touch her through her husband; he was her exalter or debaser, even as he rose or fell . . . As a princess she was lost or redeemed by her husband's fortunes. As a woman, her glory and all her honour must consist in never deviating from the strait line of duty, which forbade her absence from his side. (*Perkin Warbeck*, pp. 269–270)

> "You are going to answer, perhaps to refute me—do not. Remember I am a woman, with a woman's tutelage in my early years, a woman's education in the world, which is that of the heart—alas! for us—not of the head. I have no school-learning, no logic—but simply the voice of my own soul which speaks within me." (*Perkin Warbeck*, p. 398)

This was neither the education Mary Wollstonecraft described, nor the one her daughter actually received. In *Perkin Warbeck*, Katherine's education is not a *lack* of training, but a sentimental education that Percy's wife probably felt she needed.

Meanwhile she dutifully researched her novel. In terms of genre, *Perkin Warbeck* resembles Shakespeare's history plays: dry, male, full of battles. Shakespeare was the model for all types of writing, and Walter Scott had popularized the historical novel. Yet in a note to her conclusion, Mary shows that, through the intermediary of her favorite heroine, she is also writing an apology—a vindication of the rights of widows:

> I do not know how far these concluding pages may be deemed superfluous: the character of the Lady Katherine Gordon is a favourite of mine, and yet many will be inclined to censure her abode in Henry the Seventh's court, and other acts of her after life. I desired therefore that she should speak for herself, and show how her conduct, subsequent to her husband's death, was in accordance with the devotion and fidelity with which she attended his fortunes during his life. (*Perkin Warbeck*, p. 395)

Through this novel, Mary was clearly arguing for her own right to a life after Percy. But Richard's widow would never have edited his poems.

At the heart of Mary's edition of her husband's poems and of the Shelley myth that she creates are two major works by Shelley, two verse dramas, that readers have always seen as very different, but that I propose to juxtapose and view together: *Prometheus Unbound* (1820) and *The Cenci* (1819). The first, after a lost drama of Aeschylus, is about the freeing of the liberator of mankind; the second concerns an incestuous rape. Incestuous rape was such a taboo subject that even Percy in his play never calls the act by name. In refraining thus from mentioning the act explicitly, Shelley taught his widow an important rhetorical lesson, as Mary Shelley's editorial note attests:

> In speaking of his mode of treating this main incident, Shelley said that it might be remarked that, in the course of the play, he had never mentioned expressly Cenci's worst crime. Every one knew what it must be, but it was never imaged in words—the nearest allusion to it being that portion of Cenci's curse beginning—'That, if she have a child,' etc. (*Poetical Works*, 336)

Mary thus learned to center a work around something not said; but therefore in this case the crime itself remains open to interpretation. Is it incest or rape? Sexual violence or sexuality itself? One thing is clear: one outcome of female sexuality is pregnancy. And one thing that makes a father is posterity. And this play is about paternal authority (and paternal tyranny): the authority (the tyranny) of the father, of the Pope, of God. Procreation makes a father; it ruins a woman (in this case, the daughter).

Cenci is an evil father who rapes his daughter. He who is supposed to be his daughter's protector is her violator. The play thus unmasks the potential evil of paternal authority and shows that if women are willing to defer to men, it is because they want protection from rape. But Percy the moral philosopher puts Beatrice Cenci in a bind: her father has done the unthinkable, but Percy doesn't approve of revenge. In weighing in his play the political evil of tyranny versus (female) victimhood, Percy promotes forgiveness over revenge. Percy was thus trying to solve not a personal but a political dilemma when he wrote *The Cenci*.

The story of Beatrice Cenci and her father was of course well known in Italy. It was the only drama Percy wrote on the basis of popular tradition. But using a popular tradition does not make one popular. Its taboo subject prevented it from being shown, not even to the actress Percy wanted to play Beatrice. But without taboo subjects, we would have very little classic drama. Anyhow, what is the taboo? Rape or the questioning of paternal authority?

In any case, Beatrice takes revenge on her victimizer by killing him, and the last act of the drama takes place in Beatrice's prison cell. To see why Beatrice's revenge posed a problem for Percy, let us look at the contrasting reaction in *Prometheus Unbound*:

> I speak in grief,
> Not exultation, for I hate no more . . .
> *(Poetical Works*, p. 209)

In other words, Percy took from Christianity one thing which fit his politics: the idea that forgiveness is better than revenge. For Percy, Jesus Christ was not a religious leader but a moral philosopher, one who had discovered the politically beneficial effects of turning the other cheek. In *Prometheus Unbound*, the victim (Prometheus), when faced with tyranny (Jove), forgives rather than seeking revenge.

So Prometheus forgives while Beatrice kills. What is the difference? One difference is sexual. In one drama the victim is male, and in the other the victim is female. Another difference is generic: *Prometheus Unbound* is called a lyrical drama, while *The Cenci* is called a tragedy. Here again Shakespeare is the model: *The Cenci* resembles Shakespearean tragedy (particularly *King Lear* and *Macbeth*), while *Prometheus Unbound* seems as if it were written by Ariel (Shakespeare's *Tempest*).

If the victim of tyranny in *Prometheus* is not female, that does not mean that women have no role in the play: on the contrary; but the heroine is very different from Beatrice Cenci. Prometheus loves and is loved by the beautiful Asia, from whom he has been separated since he was chained by Jove. The moment he is liberated, he rejoins her, and the play ends with rejoicing and universal harmony. Asia is Prometheus's perfect counterpart, the ideal love object, an adoring nonentity. Both Prometheus and Beatrice are sufferers, but while Beatrice remains a victim, Prometheus becomes a martyr (and in the end is liberated from his martyrdom). What then is the difference between a victim and a martyr? What is the role of sadism in Christianity? What is the relation between Prometheus on his rock and Christ on his cross? In any case, Prometheus is conflated with Christ in the vision of Panthea (one of Asia's sisters):

> *Ione.* What didst thou see?
> *Panthea.* A woful sight: a youth
> With patient looks nailed to a crucifix. . . .

Prometheus. Remit the anguish of that lighted stare;
Close those wan lips; let that thorn-wounded brow
Stream not with blood . . .

(*Prometheus Unbound,* I, *Poetical Works,* p. 221)

Shelley has often been called a visionary poet, but this does not mean he does not have an ambivalent relationship with seeing:

[T]he deep truth is imageless.

(*Prometheus Unbound,* II, iv; *Poetical Works,* p. 238)

Percy often has vivid descriptions of earthly sights:

[A]s lean dogs pursue
Through wood and lake some struck and sobbing fawn,
We track all things that weep, and bleed, and live . . .

(*Prometheus Unbound,* I, i; *Poetical Works,* p. 218)

Sometimes these visual sights are analogies for mental operations, which interest Percy more than perception:

. . . Hark! the rushing snow!
The sun-awakened avalanche! whose mass,
Thrice sifted by the storm, had gathered there
Flake after flake, in heaven-defying minds
As thought by thought is piled, till some great truth
Is loosened . . .

(*Prometheus Unbound,* II, iii; *Poetical Works,* p. 234)

This resembles the abstractions of allegory, which are not at all perceptible to the senses. Percy indeed loved abstractions, and filled his poetry with them:

The nations thronged around, and cried aloud,
As with one voice, Truth, liberty and love!

(*Prometheus Unbound,* I, i; *Poetical Works,* p. 222)

There was mingled many a cry—
Freedom! Hope! Death! Victory!

(*Prometheus Unbound,* I, i; *Poetical Works,* p. 223)

This is alone Life, Joy, Empire, and Victory.

(*Prometheus Unbound,* IV; *Poetical Works,* p. 268)

But Percy had other ways of obscuring sight. He often beheld shades, shadows, or blurs that make sight indefinite, and by using his favorite word for this, "shape," he conveys the idea that the poet is seeing something unidentified that cannot be represented for the reader. He also cancels out the reader's sight by using a sensual image with a negative suffix (especially "-less") or prefix (especially "un-"). But on the other hand, everything anyone has experienced—especially dreams and memories— remains readable in them.

Both in *The Cenci* and in *Prometheus Unbound* there is little physical action but a great deal of speech action. Prometheus's first wish concerns his curse:

> The curse
> Once breathed on thee I would recall.
>
> (*Prometheus Unbound*, I, i; *Poetical Works*, p. 209)

This curse to Jupiter is inscribed on all who heard it. Not only is action scarce, but much of the play consists of digging out the memory of what has already happened. But "recalling" here can be ambiguous: it can mean "remember" or "call back."

In *The Cenci,* which seems so different, we also read:

> Shall I revoke this curse?
> . . .
> I do not feel as if I were a man,
> But like a fiend appointed to chastise
> The offences of some unremembered world.
> My blood is running up and down my veins;
> A fearful pleasure makes it prick and tingle:
> I feel a giddy sickness of strange awe;
> My heart is beating with an expectation
> Of horrid joy.
>
> (*The Cenci*, IV, i; *Poetical Works*, p. 311)

But whereas the first curse was delivered from the victim to the tyrant, the second curse is from the tyrant to the victim, wishing her a hideous offspring.

"Blood" turns out to be an important word in *The Cenci*: referring to both kinship and wounds. And it was his blood's muscle that would outlive Percy in both senses. Percy's dead body was supposed to be completely burned on the beach where he washed up, but the heart remained unburned and was given to Mary. She spent the remainder of her life with it, living with and defending the rights of Percy Florence, her dead husband's only surviving child. When Mary died in 1851, the heart was buried with her.[23]

CHAPTER FOUR

Lord Byron

Byron was a commercial success and a famous figure in English Romanticism. But his fame as the "Byronic hero" was more biographical than textual, more mythical than literal. Here is how the *Reader's Encyclopedia* describes it:

> "Byronic hero"—a defiant, melancholy young man, brooding on some mysterious, unforgivable sin in his past. Whatever Byron's sin was, he never told, but neither did he deny the legends of wildness, evil, and debauchery that grew up about his name.[1]

It is hard to see how this image could be derived from the poem that made him famous, *Childe Harold's Pilgrimage*. In fact, it is hard to see why that poem made him famous in the first place. It is a somewhat ironic version of the grand tour that young men of means were expected to make before their entry into life. The idea of a journey as a setting for tales was exploited by many previous authors, most notably Chaucer. The poem is written in Spenserian stanzas, and, like that author, Byron uses self-conscious archaisms. One new feature in this poem is that there are two heroes: Childe Harold and the general narrator. At first Childe Harold seems to be a narrative tool, and he is presented rather mockingly. But as more cantos are added, there seems to be a rivalry between the two for narrative primacy, and, in the end, Childe Harold drops out. The narrator calls him "the wandering outlaw of his own dark mind" (III.iii),[2] but this characterizes neither Childe Harold nor the narrator, though it characterizes the Byronic hero they were both fighting to be.

Byron met Shelley at Lake Geneva in the summer of 1816. Byron had just separated from his wife of only a year. He and Shelley were introduced by Claire Clairmont, Mary's stepsister, who had been Byron's mistress in London and would soon give birth to his child. The two poets hit it off immediately and traveled to Chillon and Clarens together, leaving behind a jealous Mary, Claire, and John Polidori, Byron's accompanying physician. Byron later settled in Venice, where Shelley joined him. When Shelley died in 1822, Byron considered himself responsible for his widow, and gave her many of his works from which to make fair copies. He himself died only two years after Shelley, of a fever in Missolonghi, where he had gone to fight for Greek independence.

Byron and Shelley had much in common. Yet they were also very different. They had both been bullied in school. They both loved to read. They were both unusually sensitive. Byron favored a kind of eighteenth-century mock-heroic style while Shelley wrote in a romantic lyrical style; Byron was a misogynist and hated feminists and bluestockings; Shelley promoted the rights of women. They had both lost their first loves and never got over it—Byron a neighbor and distant relative named Mary Chaworth and Shelley his cousin Harriet Grove; Byron learned his Calvinism and his sexual sensitivity from his nurse May Gray; for Shelley love was purely or primarily emotional. Shelley was always married; Byron married only once, and it ended disastrously after only a year. Byron took seriously the theological doctrine of predestination: he believed he was predestined for evil. Shelley didn't believe in evil. Shelley went to the highest level of abstraction; Byron dealt concretely with what was in front of him. Shelley had sympathy for all mankind; Byron sympathized only with the suffering he could see. Shelley had bad relations with his father; Byron didn't have a father at all. Shelley had no sense of humor; Byron had a brilliant comic sense, and wittily mocked everything. Shelley tried to renounce his entails; Byron was very engaged in what can be called the "performance of lordship."[3]

Although the two poets were so different—Shelley so earnest an idealist and Byron so demystifying a satirist—Byron often spoke respectfully of Shelley after the latter's death. As he wrote to Thomas Moore in 1822:

> As to poor Shelley, who is another bugbear to you and the world, he is, to my knowledge, the *least* selfish and the mildest of men—a man who has made more sacrifices of his fortune and feelings for others than any I ever heard of. With his speculative opinions I have nothing in common, nor desire to have. (Byron, *Letters and Journals*, p. 283)[4]

But popular belief and the Shelley myth Mary was concocting saw the two men as opposites. In this perception, Shelley was a man of thought whereas Byron was a man of action. Shelley never learned to swim; Byron historically inaugurated open water swimming, when he swam from Europe to Asia across the Hellespont Strait. Shelley felt like an outsider; Byron actually had a clubfoot. Shelley wrote about incest; Byron had an actual incestuous affair with his half sister. Shelley worshipped ancient Greece; Byron fought for Greek independence. Shelley was androgynous; Byron had affairs with men.

Mary was committed to preferring Shelley, but in her novel *The Last Man* (written shortly after the deaths of both Shelley and Byron) she shows that she is very drawn to the Byronic figure, embodied in the character of Lord Raymond. While the Shelley figure, Adrian, however idealistic and idealized, remains in the novel without a partner, Lord Raymond is loved by two women. He is a swashbuckling romantic hero, the liberator of Greece about to conquer Constantinople. His role as epic hero is underscored by the similar circumstances surrounding the deaths of Lord Raymond's unnamed dog and Odysseus's dog Argos: each dog dies just after being reunited with its master:

> The poor animal recognized me, licked my hand, crept close to its lord, and died. (*The Last Man*, p. 149)[5]

> While he spoke
> an old hound, lying near, pricked up his ears
> and lifted up his muzzle. This was Argos,
> trained as a puppy by Odysseus . . .
> but he had grown old in his master's absence.
> Treated as rubbish now . . .
> Abandoned there . . . But when he knew he heard
> Odysseus' voice nearby, he did his best
> to wag his tail, nose down, with flattened ears,
> having no strength to move nearer his master.
> And the man looked away,
> Wiping a salt tear from his cheek . . .
> . . . death and darkness in that instant closed
> the eyes of Argos, who had seen his master,
> Odysseus, after twenty years.
>
> (*The Odyssey*, pp. 319–321)[6]

Mary, in her final two novels (*Lodore*, 1835, *Falkner*, 1837), shows that her idea of a romantic hero and of chivalry was influenced by Byron: Falkner fights for Greece and aristocracy, and this, in Mary's eyes, was a necessary kind of nobility for a good character. Byron had his nobility from both sides of his family: from his mother, Lady Catherine Gordon of Gight, who was a descendant of the Katherine Gordon about whose character in *Perkin Warbeck* Mary said that it was "a favorite of mine," and from his father, John Byron, whose ancestors came to England with William the Conqueror. John Byron had a gift for marrying rich heiresses and draining them of their money, before dying in 1791. In both *Falkner* and *Lodore* the title character that Mary imagines prefers to defend his honor in a duel, like an aristocrat, rather than to get justice in a court of law. Lodore dies and his daughter falls in love with his second, while Falkner never gets his duel but has to be judged by the law. The "performance of lordship" seems to have been as important to Mary as to Byron.

Byron loved large animals: he kept a tame bear in his rooms in Cambridge and he wrote a heartfelt epitaph on the elaborate tomb of his Newfoundland, Boatswain. In fact, Byron loved animals so much and identified so strongly with the victims of violence that it even got in the way of his own participation in aristocratic national blood-sports:

> The last bird I ever fired at was an *eaglet*, on the shore of the Gulf of Lepanto, near Vostitza. It was only wounded, and I tried to save it, the eye was so bright; but it pined, and died in a few days; and I never did since, and never will, attempt the death of another bird. (*Letters and Journals*, March 20, 1814)[7]

> Foil'd, bleeding, breathless, furious to the last,
> Full in the centre stands the bull at bay,
> Mid wounds, and clinging darts, and lances brast,
> And foes disabled in the brutal fray;
> And now the Matadores around him play,
> Shake the red cloak, and poise the ready brand:
> Once more through all he bursts his thundering way—
> Vain rage! the mantle quits the conynge hand,
> Wraps his fierce eye—'tis past—he sinks upon the sand!
>   (*Childe Harold*, canto I: LXXVIII)[8]

> And Harold stands upon this place of skulls,
> The grave of France, the deadly Waterloo!
> How in an hour the power which gave annuls

Its gifts, transferring fame as fleeting too!
In "pride of place" here last the eagle flew,
Then tore with bloody talon the rent plain,
Pierced by the shaft of banded nations through;
Ambition's life and labours all were vain;
He wears the shatter'd links of the world's broken chain.
       (*Childe Harold*, canto III:XVIII)[9]

The hunt, the bullfight, and the battlefield all reeked of bloodshed for Byron. Even though he admired individual valor (like that of Napoleon), he was repulsed by the sufferings inflicted by war. What was once an opportunity for individual valor became now an affair of numbers: modern war had no place in it for knights-errant. The victors at Waterloo (the British Duke of Wellington, the Anglo-allied Prussian field marshal von Blücher, and the restored Louis XVIII in France) were all mediocrities Byron abhorred.

When Byron came back to England after his grand tour, he prepared the first two cantos of *Childe Harold* for the publisher and took his place in the House of Lords. There, he became an advocate of social reform, and, notwithstanding his aristocratic origin and his adherence to his rank and privilege, revealed compassion for the plight of the workers when he had the opportunity to witness it firsthand. There was industrial unrest in Nottinghamshire in 1811, near his family estate at Newstead Abbey. The workers, increasingly losing jobs and wages through the introduction of machines and factories that competed with their work and demeaned the value of their learned skills, engaged in riots of machine-breaking as a form of industrial sabotage. Seeing the conditions of the workers, Byron sympathized with their predicament and their anxiety, sided with their right to struggle against capital (without abandoning his rank or privilege or loyalty to aristocracy), and in some ways identified with the literary symbolism of their rebellion. In a letter to Thomas Moore in 1816, Byron enjoyed improvising a "Song for the Luddites":

. . . Are you not near the Luddites? By the Lord! if there's a row, but I'll be among ye! How go on the weavers—the breakers of frames—the Lutherans of politics—the reformers?

As the Liberty lads o'er the sea
Bought their freedom, and cheaply, with blood,
      So we, boys, we
    Will *die* fighting, or *live* free,
And down with all kings but King Ludd!

When the web that we weave is complete,
And the shuttle exchanged for the sword,
   We will fling the winding-sheet,
   O'er the despot at our feet, . . .
           (*Letter* to Thomas Moore, December 24, 1816) [10]

The government persecuted the rebelling workers, and applied repressive measures against their anarchic form of working-class protest. In 1812, parliament passed the "Frame-Breaking Act," proposing that machine-breaking should henceforth become a capital offense. In his maiden speech in the House of Lords on February 27, 1812, Byron opposed the capital punishment proposed by this bill and made an impassioned plea against it, in defense of the workers. Speaking to his fellow landowners, he said:

> But suppose it [the bill] past, suppose one of these men, as I have seen them, meager with famine, sullen with despair, careless of a life—which your lord-ships are perhaps about to value at something less than the price of a stocking frame—suppose this man surrounded by the children for whom he is unable to procure bread at the hazard of his existence, about to be torn for ever from a family which he lately supported in peaceful industry, and which it is not his fault that he can no longer so support, suppose this man, and there are ten thousand such from whom you may select your victims, dragged into court, to be tried for this new offence, by this new law . . . [11]

The workers' machine-breaking Luddite movement, inspired by Ned Ludd—also known as Captain, General, or King Ludd (who may or may not have ever existed, but who by then was a folk hero)—was a movement of protest against larger stocking frames that cost workers jobs and increased capitalists' profits. Luddites have become known as against machines *per se*; but the industrial protesters directed their rage and violence against machines, attacking exclusively machines so as not to hurt life. And they perceived the new stocking frames as hurting life, because they cost workers jobs and decreased their wages. Lord Byron, in defending the workers and in trying to prohibit their capital punishment, was defending a feudal, more paternal relation between a lord and his vassals, as opposed to a relation of "trade." In capitalism, machines fit into production much better than people. After Newton, in effect, it was common to see mechanisms at the heart of the natural. Science was the discovery of mechanism, and the Enlightenment was an age of new machines. Switzerland was not only the land of liberty and Calvin but of watches and cuckoo clocks.

Capitalism had transformed people into machines of production. It had standardized time and made workers subject to the kingdom of "the clock." Modernization was symbolized by the railway—by the railway timetable. Wordsworth was known as an advocate of nature as opposed to machines, but this preference for nature did not prevent him from sometimes viewing women as machines—as objects rather than as subjects:

> She was a Phantom of delight
> When first she gleamed upon my sight. . . .
>
> And now I see with eye serene
> The very pulse of the machine . . .
>
> (Wordsworth, "She was a Phantom of Delight," ll. 1–2, 21–22)[12]

One author who combined Romanticism with this fascination for the machine was E. T. A. Hoffmann, a master of fantastic literature, who achieved surprisingly original effects by conflating in his turn natural women with machines. In his story "The Sandman" (written—in Germany—in 1816, the year of the ghost-story contest), a young poet falls in love with a woman of wood. Hoffmann combines science with superstition: the dreaded "Sandman" of folk belief who is said to steal and eat children's eyes is first described to the protagonist (the poet Nathanael) by his nurse, while the detested character of Coppola, whom Nathanael believes to be a reincarnation of the dreaded Coppelius of childhood, is in fact a dealer in scientific optical instruments; the new physics professor who is the doll's maker, the evil Spalanzani, is said to be her father. There *is* a real father in the story (Nathanael's father), who is killed by an explosion in the course of forbidden alchemical experiments he pursues with the hated Coppelius.

Hoffmann parodies Romantic writers, making the protagonist, Nathanael, a writer with his head in the clouds, thinking the "Ah! Ah!" of a doll a better response to his genius than the response of a real woman. In fact Hoffmann laughs at the Romantic writer's narcissism: the doll is a reflection of Nathanael's self. Nathanael prefers mechanical reproduction over sexual reproduction: every time he is about to marry his childhood sweetheart, the evil Coppelius appears and Nathanael faints.

Such elimination of sexual reproduction is why Mary Shelley has Victor Frankenstein destroy the female monster he is creating for his creature. It is also why Victor instantly applies the monster's warning, *"I will be with you on your wedding night,"* to himself. Thus, as one critic puts it, "the sentence against Victor as bridegroom is pronounced by Victor as monster."[13]

Hoffmann is parodying Romantic writers influenced by Goethe's novel *The Sorrows of Young Werther* (1774, revised 1787). Werther's sorrows are articulated in his letters; so too are Nathanael's feelings conveyed by letters. In terms of genre, *Werther*—an iconic *Sturm und Drang* novel—was a transformation of the epistolary novel. Because Werther commits suicide, the fictional editor framing the tale has to finish the novel after Werther dies. Werther kills himself out of obsessive love. Romantic love is, in its turn, the butt of Hoffmann's parody. *Werther* was the last gasp of courtly love. But the popularity of Goethe's novel showed that courtly love was not dead yet. In "The Sandman," the story begins with three letters, and exploits a potential technique of the epistolary style: misdirection. One of Nathanael's letters is sent to Clara by mistake. But it is not really a mistake, because Nathanael is actually addressing her unconsciously. Hoffmann, by using misdirection, is wandering into the terrain of the unconscious.

It is doubtless not by chance that Freud picked Hoffmann's "Sandman" in order to exemplify, to discuss, and to conceptualize the psychoanalytic notion of "The 'Uncanny.'" Freud's "uncanny" (*Das Unheimlich*, 1919) took over the Gothic tradition in an attempt to analyze and to explain what generates creepy effects. Freud was trying to refute Ernst Jentsch's theory, according to which uncanny effects are engendered by intellectual uncertainty about whether a thing is alive or not, in favor of his own interpretation, which explains uncanny feelings by the fear of castration. Therefore Freud's essay does not concentrate on the beloved doll Olimpia, but rather on Nathanael's fear of harm to the eyes. Freud neglects, thus, Hoffmann's critique of Romantic masculinity capable of loving only a reflection of itself, and (romantically, in turn) fixates rather on threats to masculinity. His essay begins with extracts from a dictionary showing that the German word *unheimlich* ends up meaning the same thing as its opposite, *heimlich*. This is because the "homey" can become the "secret." Shelley's preface to *Frankenstein* shows that there was indeed something uncanny about the "domestic affections."

But there was also something political in Freud's "uncanny": among the extracts Freud took from the dictionary to illustrate the usage of the term was the following example:

> The protestant land-owners do not feel . . . *heimlich* among their catholic inferiors. ("The 'Uncanny,'" p. 222)[14]

The example of "Protestant landowners" brings us back not just to Byron (and the Luddites), but to the same *unheimlich* relation between Protestantism and Catholicism that we saw in the gothic novels, many of which were set in Catholic countries. In this last example, it is clear that there is also an *unheimlich* class difference, and not just an *unheimlich* temporal difference, between Catholics and Protestants. As a matter of fact, Freud mentions many Gothic figures in his essay "The 'Uncanny'": ghosts, people buried alive, severed limbs that still live, doubles. When a narcissistic reflection takes on a life of its own, it is uncanny. And that is what ghost stories play on. It was a ghost-story contest, after all, that gave birth to *Frankenstein*. Indeed, that borderline between life and death seems to be the refuge of the supernatural. Psychoanalysis as the discovery of forces outside consciousness could be read, indeed, as one long gothic novel.

Of course, neither Byron nor Shelley finally contributed a text to the ghost-story contest. Mary in her *Preface* attributes their defection to their preference for poetry over narrative. And indeed poetry was considered more like real literature (more aristocratic) than prose. Both poets showed their virtuosity with versification in their early work, to the point where their early verse sounds like doggerel. But they matured in very different ways. Shelley pursued rhyme as a sign of substantive resemblance: he filled his verse with repetitions (especially "follow, follow" and "down, down" in *Prometheus Unbound*), while Echoes became characters, as in Ovid. Byron, on the other hand, stretched the properties of language: he played with language all the time, and that gave a flippancy to his work that enhanced its satirical power. In the dedication to *Don Juan*, he deflated pretension by using colloquial language ("Explaining metaphysics to the nation—/I wish he would explain his Explanation,"), or by using rhyming words from different lexicons ("muslin/puzzling"), or making acrobatic rhymes between long words and short ("intellectual/ hen-peck'd you all").[15] The comic or demystifying effects of these rhymes (which Noel Coward has skillfully exploited in our day) made people see his poetry as witty. Even in his letters, he couldn't resist using the same consciousness of language to undercut the literary profession ("pome," "literatoor") or even his own rhetoric ("followed close on the heels of his letters [by the bye I fear *heels* of letters is a very incorrect metaphor]").[16]

There is another strange similarity between Hoffmann's tale and the aspirations of the young Romantics—this time related not to Byron but to Shelley. The explosion that kills the hero's father in "The Sandman" was a secret alchemical experiment. Alchemy was suspect, as was all magic and superstition after the Enlightenment, but as late as Mallarmé and Rimbaud (the French Symbolists of the late nineteenth century), alchemy continued to be seen by poets as a precursor to poetry or a metaphoric analogue of poetry. Shelley, in his youth, read the major alchemists avidly before going on to more "reasonable" subjects. But neither he nor his admirers fully gave up the idea of Shelley the enchanter, the magician. In Mary's novel, Victor Frankenstein follows almost exactly the same path as Shelley before going on to study chemistry at the University of Ingolstadt:

> "The ancient teachers of this science," said he, "promised impossibilities and performed nothing. The modern masters promise very little; they know that metals cannot be transmuted and that the elixir of life is a chimera. But these philosophers, whose hands seem only made to dabble in dirt, and their eyes to pore over the microscope or crucible, have indeed performed miracles. They penetrate into the recesses of nature and show how she works in her hiding-places. They ascend into the heavens; they have discovered how the blood circulates, and the nature of the air we breathe. They have acquired new and almost unlimited powers; they can command the thunders of heaven, mimic the earthquake, and even mock the invisible world with its own shadows."
> (*Frankenstein*, p. 47)

These words in *Frankenstein* are uttered by Professor Waldman, a professor of chemistry who is addressing his class at the University of Ingolstadt. Professor Waldman is opposed to Professor Krempe. The first is handsome and refined, the second repulsive and coarse. These professors are among the many male doubles of Victor Frankenstein, perhaps harking back to the characters of Falkland and Tyrrel in Mary's father's novel, *Caleb Williams* (1794). William Godwin's second novel, *St. Leon* (1799), is equally relevant to the later novel of his daughter: the protagonist receives the secret of the elixir of life, but this elixir turns out to be a curse rather than a blessing. In any case, science seems to take up where alchemy leaves off, and to be just as supernatural—and as spooky—as what it replaced. The contrast between magic and reason no longer holds.

To return to Byron: unlike Shelley, he needed neither alchemy nor scientific learning to convince himself of his own superiority. Byron took for granted two forms of superiority: his nobility and his literary talent. He was the darling of worldly salons before 1816 and made a good marriage. When he left England for the second time he had just lost a lot of weight (thus achieving his ideal in bodily self-image, in his truly stunning physical beauty), but he was plagued by scandal and separated from his wife, who accused him of being insane. Byron still presumed upon his rank and literary gifts, but had no use for public opinion. His superiority was part of his self. Shelley's baronetcy was conferred for wealth, while Byron's lordship came from noble blood. Byron hated what he saw as the mediocrity of some capitalists and colonists. He was not opposed in principle to capitalism or colonialism: he benefited when his works sold well, and he admired Napoleon. But he detested mediocrity and never tired of mocking it. He enjoyed sex and other pleasures and opposed the tyranny and the self-righteousness of the morality based on mediocrity and opinion. Perhaps he was something of a frame-breaker after all.

CHAPTER FIVE

John Polidori

Polidori is known for one year of his life—1816, the year he spent traveling with Byron as his personal physician and participated in the ghost-story writing contest. And actually he had a very short life. He committed suicide in 1821. From the ghost-story contest he eventually wrote two works: a novel, in prose, vaguely about incest, called *Ernestus Berchtold, or the Modern Oedipus*, and a tale called *The Vampyre*, loosely based on a fragment by Byron. Without Frankenstein and vampires, the early cinema would look quite different. Of course, neither Mary Shelley nor Polidori was thinking of metaphors for cinematic "life" when they wrote their masterpieces: Mary was getting back at her husband for his interest in science and Polidori was getting back at his employer Byron for his noble blood.

How did it happen that Polidori became Byron's traveling companion in 1816? Byron had been under a doctor's care at home, he had just separated from his wife, who thought him evil or mad, and he had just lost a lot of weight after a brutal diet. He thought it prudent to travel with a doctor. Polidori had received his medical degree at the University of Edinburgh, the center of the Scottish Enlightenment, in 1815. But the school was so popular when Polidori went there, it became a victim of its own success:

> In 1750, there had been 158 students enrolled in the medical school; by 1800, there were some 650. This increase in enrolment [*sic*] led to a serious shortage of cadavers for anatomical demonstrations. (MacDonald, *Poor Polidori*, p. 15)[1]

Polidori was not only a doctor; he was also an aspiring writer, carrying around the manuscript of his first completed work, a drama called *Ximines, or The Modern Abraham*, which he thought Byron could help him publish. He was very much under his father's thumb, and his father had traveled with a literary man before settling in England as a man of letters and teacher of Italian. There was something compelling about traveling with the most famous writer of the day.

There was one other sort of talent—bodily talent—that Polidori discovered on the continent and hoped Byron would help him with: sexual prowess. As soon as they landed in Ostend, Polidori reports, Lord Byron "fell like a thunderbolt upon the chambermaid" (Macdonald, *Poor Polidori,* p. 62).[2] But Byron was not ready to be anybody's father or mentor, let alone role model. Byron thought of a personal physician as a domestic. His own sexual exploits were (mostly, though not only) with women of the serving class.

Polidori was good-looking, but accident-prone and unlucky. He sprained his ankle, dropped a book on the head of a girl in a bookstore, and had a carriage accident from which he perhaps never recovered. On April 1, 1819, the *New Monthly Magazine* published *The Vampyre: A Tale by Lord Byron.* Both Polidori and Byron were miffed because neither had sponsored it. Byron wrote to Kinnaird, " '*the Vampire,'*—what do I know of Vampires? it must be some bookselling imposture" (Byron, *Selected Letters and Journals,* p. 194). The naïveté that Byron professed was disingenuous, since his oriental ("Turkish") tale *The Giaour* was filled with vampirism, but it was quite true that he had nothing to do with the publication of *The Vampyre.* Byron had indeed started a tale about a death occurring in a Muslim cemetery—a tale that he initially intended to contribute to the famous ghost-story contest, but he soon abandoned it. And Polidori had tinkered with it and made it unrecognizable, developing it into a complete work. But neither had sent it for publication. Thus the publisher had used Byron's name and Polidori's work without permission. Polidori got just what he wanted in that his work was published with the aid of Byron's influence. But he resented the fact that Byron's name eclipsed his own in print no less than in life.

Polidori's official entry in the ghost-story contest was *Ernestus Berchtold.* In the edition he publishes in 1819, he reviews the ground rules of the writing contest:

> A tale that rests upon improbabilities, must generally disgust a rational mind; I am therefore afraid that, though I have thrown the superior agency into the background as much as was in my power, still, that many readers will think

the same moral, and the same colouring, might have been given to characters acting under the ordinary agencies of life; I believe it, but I had agreed to write a supernatural tale, and that does not allow of a completely every-day narrative. (Macdonald, *Poor Polidori*, pp. 221–222)

It is hard to see anything supernatural about incest, which, moreover, was a common topic among Romantics of the period.

The natural supernaturalism of life was at the two ends of it—birth and death. Ghost stories covered the uncanniness of death, but Mary Shelley's *Frankenstein* and Polidori's *Vampyre* were about what gave life. As Mary Shelley writes in her account of the novel:

Many and long were the conversations between Lord Byron and Shelley to which I was a devout but nearly silent listener. During one of these, various philosophical doctrines were discussed, and among others the nature of the principle of life. . . . They talked of the experiments of Dr. Darwin . . . who preserved a piece of vermicelli in a glass case till by some extraordinary means it began to move with voluntary motion. Not thus, after all, would life be given. Perhaps a corpse would be reanimated; galvanism had given token of such things: perhaps the component parts of a creature might be manufactured, brought together, and endued with vital warmth. (*Frankenstein*, p. x)

This famous conversation that Mary Shelley reports between the two poets most likely included Polidori as well. Polidori's medical thesis on nightmares and somnambulism was probably indebted to the British physician and scientist Erasmus Darwin—cited by Mary Shelley in the passage just quoted—who had scientifically conceptualized somnambulism as a disease. Erasmus Darwin (grandfather of the famous Charles Darwin) was a celebrated vitalist (holding the doctrine that life originates in a vital principle) rather than a mechanist. Interestingly, like Polidori, he too was a graduate of the University of Edinburgh. As a medical student at that university, Polidori probably had some firsthand experience in grave-robbing, since cadavers were in short supply at that time for students at Edinburgh; the scenes in which Frankenstein hangs around graveyards in search of body parts for his monster surely came from Polidori's narratives.

Since Byron had stopped dosing himself with laxatives in trying to lose weight, his health by the end of the summer of 1816 was robust, and he no longer needed the services of a physician. This gave him a chance to shake off a presence that had begun to weigh on him. Polidori, instead of serving him, somehow expected to be served by him; Polidori had become a dependent rather than a servant. In the meantime, Byron had made a new friend—Percy Shelley—with whom he often went off. This made everyone in that circle jealous: Mary over Percy, and Claire and Polidori over Byron. The two women, sexual partners of the poets, were probably enraged at being women; Polidori—equally neglected in an unrequited love, equally positioned as non-equal—took the brunt of Mary's and Claire's unspoken shared frustration, and soon became the butt of their mutual jokes.

One of Percy's favorite gothic writers was an American, Charles Brockden Brown, whose novel *Edgar Huntly* involved sleepwalking. He must have recommended it to Polidori, but actually the sleepwalker (who, it is implied, may be an inadvertent and unconscious murderer) is a red herring—the real murderer turns out to be a tribe of Indians. America is no longer a blank space of possibility; even though Brown is not on the side of the Indians, his gothic continent has become a space of conflict, of genocide.

Polidori and Byron parted relatively amicably at the end of the summer. As Byron wrote to Murray, his publisher, "his remaining with me was out of the question—I have enough to do to manage my own scrapes—& as precepts without example are not the most gracious homilies—I thought it better to give him his congé" (Macdonald, *Poor Polidori*, pp. 102–103). Polidori continued to write to Byron and to ask him for recommendations as he toured Italy and looked unsuccessfully for a medical practice, first in Italy, then in England (he was too young to practice in London). He then tried (equally unsuccessfully) to establish a career in publishing. He continued to write to his sister Frances, who married another expatriate Italian named Rossetti. The offspring of this marriage would end up forming another literary family with poetic aspirations (like Polidori, linking Italy with England) that, unlike Polidori, would reach great fame.[3] The reasons for Polidori's suicide are unclear. Some say he killed himself over gambling debts.

Polidori continued to work on his plagiarized *Vampyre*, but he never officially published it under his own name. Plagiarism is in fact like vampirism: it owes its existence to someone else's substance. In the latest version of the text, Polidori, like Hoffmann, puts the folk version of the monster in the mouth of the nurse: the vampire of folk legend is a subhuman creature who sucks the blood of anyone nearby. Polidori transformed the vampire in making him a portrait of Byron: an aristocrat, and a seducer. It is from this Byronic and iconic, biographical and mythical image, that the character of the modern gothic vampire would derive.

Epilogue

While both Mary and Polidori wrote out of suppressed anger and resentment, there was one aspect of their creatures that Byron and Shelley would have appreciated. Both creatures involved life springing from a single being. As we have seen, procreation involves two sexes, and the moment women are present, then pregnancy and motherhood ensue and are at issue. The only being that gives human existence from a single source is the Creator. The creative writer tries to equal that act: Mary, in her annotated posthumous edition of Percy's poems, treated the poems like living offspring:

> I hasten to fulfill an important duty,—that of giving the productions of a sublime genius to the world, with all the correctness possible, and of, at the same time, detailing the history of those productions, as they sprang, *living and warm*, from his heart and brain. (*Poetical Works*, p. xxi; Johnson's emphasis)

For the Romantics, writers were like gods: they produced all by themselves. Even Mary, representative of two-sex reproduction, as a writer became a creator: "And now, once again, I bid my hideous progeny go forth and prosper . . . ," she declared, in introducing the re-publication of the novel that was born out of the famous writing competition (*Frankenstein*, p. xii). This monstrous creature whose success surprised her, whose very hideousness was her creation, was her own progeny, as though part of her own flesh and her own body, and she was fond of it, no less than of a real child.

> At first I thought but of a few pages, of a short tale, but Shelley urged me to develop the idea at greater length. I certainly did not owe the suggestion of one incident, nor scarcely of one train of feeling, to my husband, and yet but for his incitement it would never have taken the form in which it was presented to the world. From this declaration I must except the preface. As far as I can recollect, it was entirely written by him.
> And now, once again, I bid my hideous progeny go forth and prosper. I have an affection for it . . . (*Frankenstein*, p. xii)

A writer was someone capable of having progeny alone. That, in sum, was the Romantic ideal. And that was the myth of creation that Mary—in her fiction and in her role as editor of Shelley—forcefully promoted, but which she also inadvertently contested, and with which she also struggled, in entering the writing competition with all her literary talents, with all her vital energies, and with all her (semi-conscious) critical perceptions, in inscribing through and out of this ghost-story contest, her own living performance as a woman, and her own gradually discovered (self-effaced and self-asserted) living signature as woman writer.

Shoshana Felman

Afterword
Barbara Johnson's Last Book

At various landmark moments of her own career, Johnson was discussing Mary Shelley, whose life and work became at once a vessel for her pioneering feminist critique and a touchstone for her literary ingenuity and theoretical inventiveness. "Mary Shelley" (as at once a mother, woman writer, and an autobiographer) was a topic Johnson in effect "invented" and created—for the first time in a keynote lecture in a course on narrative at Yale in the fall of 1980, when (on October 13) she was supposed to illustrate—before a team of teachers and the crowd of students of that course—the category of "Autobiography." Traditionally, this category was exemplified by Rousseau's *Confessions* (as well as, later on, by Dickens, Freud, and Sartre), and in the previous year (1979), Johnson had indeed presented Rousseau's text as the classical inaugural example of "Life Stories" in that course (known at Yale as "Literature X": "Man and His Fictions"). But in the fall of 1980, in implicitly rebelling against the fact that in the long tradition of this course very few women writers were included and "life stories" had always been presented as a male domain (deemed universal), Johnson daringly, inventively, surprisingly presents a reading of Mary Shelley's *Frankenstein* (a reading of the "confessions" of the monster, in lieu of Rousseau's *Confessions*), as a paradigmatic, autobiographical, specimen story of a woman writer (as a fictional dramatization of Mary Shelley's own disguised, repressed autobiography), dramatizing thus an alternative theoretical model of a woman writer's life (with its typically female problems of pregnancy and motherhood, and its typically female, hidden problematic of how to be a woman who, despite her female avocation, impinges on a male domain in venturing to

write). Johnson thus articulates a spectacular paradigm shift, an innovative theory of female autobiography. Two years later, in 1982, the class
on Frankenstein appears in print in *diacritics*, as Johnson's groundbreaking, influential essay, "My Monster/My Self."[1] Mary Shelley reappears
in Johnson's work at several other moments, some of which are seriously
and subtly literary, philosophical, and analytical (chronologically: "Le
dernier homme," 1980,[2] "My Monster/My Self," 1982, and finally, *Persons and Things*'s "Prologue," "Artificial Life," and "Animation," 2008),[3]
while other essays, meant to trigger laughter and to foster cultural change
through humor, expose prejudice and unself-conscious bias (linguistic,
structural, and institutional), and are hilariously witty, ironic, and satirical ("Gender Theory and the Yale School," 1984).[4] In this last piece,
which here concludes the "early essays," and which marks Johnson's tran-
sition from discipleship to intellectual independence, Johnson's emerging
leadership takes on the unexpected role of "the coryphaeus," the leader
of the chorus of laughter in ancient Greek comedy: Johnson's creative
daring and her dazzlingly ingenious sense of humor come to embody, in
this piece, not just an unanticipated call for a self-critical, communal self-
reflection, but also (in a different sense, perhaps, than the philosopher
intended) what Hegel hailed in womanhood and woman: "the eternal
irony of the community."[5]

Now in her last manuscript, entitled *Mary Shelley and Her Circle*, written in the last year of her life (2009), Johnson returns to Mary Shelley, and
to her own persevering feminist interrogation of the relationship between
literature and gender. What relentless, buried questions still remained un-
solved, and beckoned yet again from Mary Shelley's life? What is there in
Mary Shelley—and in the concept of a circle—that fascinated Barbara
Johnson and that moved her also, at the end of her own life, to trace a
circle in her own work, to circle back to the pathbreaking insights of the
start of her career, in order to rethink them in a broader, vaster context?
The present essay will address these questions from two vantage points:
What is the meaning of *Mary Shelley and Her Circle*? What is the meaning of Johnson's act of circling back? What, specifically, is the significance
for Johnson of her recapitulation of the life of Mary Shelley in the margin—at the ultimate frontier—of her own life?

PART ONE

I

Decentering Romanticism:
A Shadow Story, or The Unconscious of the Circle

In her introduction to *Mary Shelley and Her Circle*, Johnson refers to the notoriously canonical collection of manuscripts entitled "Shelley and His Circle" (originally purchased by the German financier Carl Pforzheimer, today archived in the New York Public Library), a collection managed by established Shelley scholars and considered academically foundational for any study of Romanticism. By an understatement whose ironic impulse is barely perceptible, Johnson declares that her intention is to talk about another, "more restricted" and more modest circle: "Mary Shelley and Her Circle." Her title, therefore, at once echoes the idea of a circle, and displaces this idea, decenters its collective meaning, in introducing gender as an interruption, an estrangement, in our customary ways of thinking and of naming things ("Persons and Things" belonging to Romanticism). In whatever way Johnson will define her more restricted circle, her very title is disjunctive to received assumptions, being ironically and quietly set against the official academic definition of Romanticism as a naturally male-centered (and for many authors of anthologies, still today exclusively male) literary circle.

But in bringing Mary Shelley to the fore of the Romantic picture as its doubling *shadow story*, Johnson does not simply (nor does she in actuality) shift from male-centered plots to a female-centered story. Rather, as a student of Freud (whose "Copernican revolution" had dislodged man once more from the center of the universe), Johnson knows that there is no direct path to what is central (in the circle, in its human story): consciousness is always prey to the decentering effects of language and of the unconscious. Texts, like dreams, are (as Freud puts it) always "otherwise centered"[6] than what they appear to be. What is seemingly peripheral may always turn out to be the story's nucleus, its true locus of significance. Mary Shelley might well be—as she is indeed in Johnson's reading—an embodiment of the unconscious of Romanticism, a portrait, and a narrative, of the unheeded textual and factual unconscious of the circle.

Between the Inside and the Outside:
Shifting Centrality and Marginality

What is more, the shifting question of the meaning of centrality and marginality, the question of what is inside or outside the circle, is not merely rhetorical and psychoanalytical, it is also, fundamentally and crucially, political. The question of what is included or excluded from the circle, of who (or what) is inside and what (or who) remains outside (or on the fringe), pertains not merely to a tropological or topological analysis, but requires a political interrogation, a politically perceptive (and ethically sensitized) analysis of *power structures* and of their built-in inequalities and hierarchies, foregrounded by various cultural systems of subordination and marginalization.

In this sense, Johnson's reading of the figure of the circle pursues the focal theoretical concern prevalent in all her work: the questioning and contestation of established boundary lines, whose claim is to define and to divide an inside and an outside; the radical interrogation—and recasting—of the very theoretical status of these boundaries, insofar as they establish institutions which repress outsiders and legitimize exclusions, under an untenable belief in (and claim to) their own universality. This is the case of the selective set of literary works known as "the Western Canon," an official canon (including the Romantic canon) whose institutional, restrictive boundaries Johnson keeps challenging, exploding, and expanding, by bringing the humanity of its outside inside, into the center of her teaching and her studies. She systematically protects and emphatically includes all groups that are implicitly, politically excluded from the (pseudo-universal) definitions of civilization (by virtue of their race, class, sexuality, or gender). It is thus not surprising that, in her last work as well, she brings inside the outside of Romanticism, insofar as she gives focus to what, within the structure of Romanticism, appears to be precisely (structurally) overlooked and overshadowed, discredited as minor and thus rendered invisible, skipped over and erased by the prevailing critical tradition, and by its hegemonic definitions (its canonical perceptions) of "Shelley and His Circle." In this Johnsonian reorganization and reconfiguration of the inside and the outside of the circle, rhetorical, linguistic, psychoanalytic, and political structures are inextricably tied up together, and are constantly shown to be profoundly implicated in one another.

The Revolutionary Implications of the Circle

Johnson's intuition of the revolutionary implications of the circle (revolution in both senses: ruptured space and endless circularity of motion), was born early. Remarkably, in her first published work on Mary Shelley—her 1980 lecture at Cerisy (published that year in France), "The Last Man"—Johnson articulates already the gist of the conceptual innovation of her reading:

> [I]t was precisely . . . [Mary's] marginality that has always earned her a certain celebrity. That marginality was of two kinds: one, she lived surrounded by writers whose works strongly marked the thought and literature of the epoch: her father . . . her mother . . . her husband; and the many friends of Shelley . . . *Aside from this marginality in the very center of the Romantic circle*, Mary Shelley knew *a second source of famous nonexistence* as the *anonymous author* of *Frankenstein*, a novel that she wrote at the age of nineteen and whose mythic power has only increased since, independently of the name and even the notion of the author. *In the shadow* of her parents, her husband, and her own work, Mary Shelley thus lived the Romantic period through its folds and margins.[7]

In Johnson's last work, *Mary Shelley and Her Circle*, it is no longer a particular text of Mary Shelley's but the broader historical fresco of the second generation of Romanticism that "agitates the question of marginality and is re-inscribed by it." In refracting her historical narrative of the late Romantic circle through Mary Shelley's texts and through her life (in its intersection with the texts and lives of others), Johnson offers an ironic and subversive *counter-narrative* to the prevailing literary critical Romantic story, as well as an implicit cultural critique of the taken-for-granted circle of critical assumptions informing the official academic picture of Romanticism. *Mary Shelley and Her Circle* offers a fresh global vision, in that it enables and affords a view of history *precisely from the margins*; a view from outside the canonic center, yet from inside Romanticism; a view enabled by a gaze that is located neither properly outside nor properly inside the circle, yet paradoxically both inside and outside it; a textual and contextual, testimonial double view; a crucially *off-centered* view, showing in addition how the literary and the nonliterary alike can be made to read and to rework each other.

This last book contains, therefore, a re-conceptualization of the notion, of the content, and of the collective meaning, of the circle.

II

Circling Back to Mary Shelley: An Act of Affirmation

I will suggest that this last book can be read, in Johnson's work, as a point of arrival which, beyond *Persons and Things* (and beyond *A World of Difference*), reflects on the traversed writing itinerary, in offering a panoramic recapitulation of the stakes of Johnson's whole work. As the figure of "a real woman" whose meaning Barbara Johnson had discovered in the world, in history, in literature, and through which she tested and attested for the first time her own singular interpretive capacity, Mary Shelley has become (as I have mentioned) a cornerstone in Johnson's own unique literary critical vocabulary. Mary Shelley names a pivot or an axis— both theoretical and narrative—around which the thinking processes of Barbara Johnson as a literary reader, as a feminist, and as a cultural critic, came into being and continued to historically, suggestively revolve. Over time, Mary Shelley's role in Johnson's work evolves, as it traverses and outlives all the historical vicissitudes of feminism. At the end of her career, Johnson is aware that the developing inner divisions within feminism[8] have introduced an inner fissure, between 'woman' as a concept that can never henceforth name all women, and "feminism as a movement that must—but *cannot*—consider 'woman' as a common epistemological ground for action" and for change (*Feminist Difference*, p. 7). And yet, despite this fissure, in placing her last work again under the sign of Mary Shelley, Johnson's final message is still obstinately feminist, still understatedly affirmative of a struggle toward a greater justice and a greater freedom. Johnson as the narrator of *Mary Shelley and Her Circle*—and her questioning—are inhabited by a sense of contradiction, a sense of radical impossibility, yet are also driven by a passion for the impossible. Johnson claims (for Mary Shelley, for herself, for feminists, for humans) a right to contradiction, a "right to ambivalence." The writing's act of affirmation—*countering the contradiction*—is enabled thanks to literature, whose promise and desire is to liberate, to set us free.

"In the final analysis," Johnson writes, "literature is important for feminism because literature can best be understood as the place where impasses can be kept and opened for examination, where questions can be guarded and not forced into a premature validation of the available paradigms" (*Feminist Difference*, p. 13). "Literature, that is, is not to be understood as a set of predetermined works, but as a mode of cultural work, the work of giving-to-read those impossible contradictions that cannot yet be spoken" (*Feminist Difference*, p. 13). *Mary Shelley and Her Circle* engages quite precisely, I would argue, in the work of "giving-to-read those impossible contradictions that cannot yet be spoken."

The circularity in Johnson's work around Mary Shelley is thus not a static but a creatively dynamic, progressive circularity; perhaps we might regard it as a circularity around the impossible, as well. But Johnson's work does not simply return to Mary Shelley: Mary Shelley represents what Johnson wants to say each time *at a specific given moment*. Mary Shelley keeps returning like a leitmotiv in Johnson's score, but the music of the leitmotiv always returns with a difference. Looking back at Johnson's work from this last book, I submit that Mary Shelley represents for Johnson both this central pivot (of the revolution in both senses) of her thought, and the existential boundary of her theoretical development and of her historicity at this frontier of life. Mary Shelley, at this limit, stands both for Johnson's biographical and literary anchor, and for the biographical and literary distance Johnson has traversed in her own lifetime diachronic and historic evolution.

A Circle of Relationships: A Collective Biography

Mary Shelley and Her Circle is at once a piece of literary criticism whose unfolding narrative reads like a novel, and an ambitious, infinitely multilayered work of intellectual and intertexual history, that is unique in Johnson's work, in being organized as a collective, multiple biography of a circle of Romantic writers whose lives converged, whose worlds intersected, and whose creative output, shaped by their shared history, was influenced by their reciprocal desires, as well as by their dialogues with one another. Johnson's narrative revolves around Mary Shelley's story, but Mary's story does not proceed according to the rules of linearity. Mary is defined by and within her (social, psychological, and literary) circle of relationships: her story is narrated circularly through the successive circles (the widening, expanding spiral narrative) of the surrounding lives and works of her significant others, insofar as these significant relationships with other writers (her parents, Shelley, Byron, among others; her love affairs, her friendships, her griefs, her literary heritage) have sparked and stimulated her own writing, and insofar as the intersecting dramas of their lives—and of their unexpected early deaths—registered their shocks in her work.

An Art of Juxtaposition: Life-Portraits, Texts,
and "the Surprise of Otherness"

Johnson's unique methodology—contingent on the weaving of this web of stories and on her own capacity to be surprised, and to receive the shocks of death, of life, of other lives, of other texts—creates in this last book an innovative genre of literary criticism: not only does she filter one life-story (one living literary story) through a multiplicity of other stories, thus always narrating *simultaneously* more than one story at a time. But also, she narrates the various life-and-literature biographies *in counterpoint* to one another, reading their stories and their texts through one another and against each other, thus creating a dynamic play of resonances—within an imaginative and insightfully synthetic global vision of dynamic intertextuality among the different lives, and among the different texts these writers have engendered through the intersections of their lives, under each other's mutual influence. Throughout the chapters, Johnson unexpectedly compares and sets alongside one another, in surprisingly illuminating ways, fragments of texts extracted from heterogeneous sources that nonetheless, despite their difference, are unpredictably combined, and made to resonate together. In this way, Johnson as storyteller builds uniquely and progressively (within each chapter, and from one chapter to another) a multilayered *textual architecture*, which orchestrates a colorful plurality of sensitivities, by juxtaposing and highlighting one against the other not simply the biographies and the life portraits of the different writers, but their different genres, different rhetorics, the different sorts of texts that link the writers to their language, and make the heterogeneity of the citations and the diversity of utterances powerfully resonate and *speak together*. This striking art of unexpected, bold juxtaposition has always been a salient and distinguishing characteristic of Johnson's interpretive technique and of her literary insight. Her last work differs only in the wide historical scope and in the panoramic and ambitious number of the texts and of the genres viewed and grasped together and against each other, thus pushing to its limit the interpretive technique of "the surprise of otherness"[9]—the power of illumination derived from the surprise and from the *shock* of the juxtapositions, which estrange the texts from their familiar, clichéd meanings and make them speak and resonate in fresh and innovative ways.

III

A Central Paradox: The Missing Name

What, then, is the difference between "Shelley and His Circle" and "Mary Shelley and Her Circle," since in many ways the characters of the two circles might be said to overlap? How does Johnson herself articulate, frame, and define this crucial difference, which is the topic—and the motivation—of her book?

The first thing we should notice with respect to Johnson's circle is the way in which her book—and Mary's circle—are built upon a central paradox. While the "surprise of otherness" in the defining title of the book consists in Johnson's unexpected act of *naming*—of reinscribing and *renaming* Mary Shelley (in the place of Percy Shelley) at the heart of the Romantic circle, in the remainder of the book, in contrast, Mary's name does not entitle and *does not name* any chapter. Following the Introduction, in which Mary—named as central—is explicitly announced as the book's protagonist, the five consecutive chapters of the book are respectively entitled: (1) William Godwin, (2) Mary Wollstonecraft, (3) Percy Bysshe Shelley, (4) Lord Byron, (5) John Polidori. Mary's name is missing from this list. Each chapter draws a portrait of a participant, a co-protagonist of the Romantic circle. But (contrary to our expectations), no chapter is called "Mary Shelley," no chapter brings in the totality of Mary's story *at its center*, as the chapter's central (and completed) plot. It is as though the structure of the book belied the focus of its title, as though Mary were not *the* protagonist or one of the protagonists of the Romantic circle, but in some ways the *absent center of the book*, an embodiment of the elusiveness or the empty space, the lack *within* the center of the circle; or else a sign for Johnson's project of perpetual critical displacement of the center.

The Absent Center: The Recurrence of a Leitmotiv

Mary's writings and her life are in effect narrated, analyzed (piecemeal), and made to resonate in each one of these chapters, but only insofar as they relate to, interact with, are influenced by, or novelistically inscribe, describe, the character who names the chapter (Godwin, Wollstonecraft, Shelley, Byron, Polidori). Mary's life and writing are, therefore, the central link that ties and holds together this concentric and eccentric multiplicity of portraits. "You talk about pearls," Flaubert wrote to Louise Colet. "But it's not the pearls that make the necklace: it's the thread."[10] Mary is [what makes] the necklace: the connecting thread between the chapters. But in each one of these chapters she is present only secondarily and marginally, as a doubling shadow story, as a subplot, or as a (sexual and textual) *subtext*.[11] Johnson knew what she was doing: "If I put the accent in this way on her marginality"—she had written—"it's not in order to discover for her a new centrality, but in order to analyze the new manner in which the question of marginality is inscribed in and agitates her work."[12]

Structurally, then, this is a book without a center, a book whose very structure illustrates the struggle between Johnson's vindication of the rights of Mary's name in the very center of her title, and Mary's famous anonymity and namelessness,[13] as the symbolically anonymous writer of *Frankenstein*, which rumor and persistent critical belief attributed to Percy Shelley, who, in writing the first preface to the novel, grammatically appropriated the first person of the author and thus assimilated to his own voice the authority and authorship of his wife's novel.

It is a tour de force of Johnson's storytelling and of the book's structure and design, to show how Mary Shelley's proper name is re-inscribed and reasserted at the heart of the Romantic circle, and yet cannot come fully to appropriate itself, and thus remains dramatically unspeakable, unnamable, or naming only an impossibility (its own impossibility). This radical impossibility of Mary's proper name to own itself, to claim self-presence and centrality in her own story, and fully to appropriate her own singular (female) experience and her own (unnamable) autobiography, is part of what the book reflects about and dramatizes.

IV

Johnson's Theoretical Conception

Barbara Johnson's explanation of her project, her elucidation of the difference she perceives and wishes to bring out between what critics customarily call "Shelley and His Circle" and what she contrapuntally calls "Mary Shelley and Her Circle," is condensed, summed up, and analyzed elliptically, in her Introduction. Since the book was written in physical conditions of advanced disease, across and in defiance of progressive bodily decline, it was written in a literal, and literally critical, race against time. Johnson always knew that "brevity is the soul of wit." But this book in particular had to be written speedily and briefly, in a minimalist style, if it aspired to be finished—to defeat time. There was no spare time for stylistic polish or for flourishing revisions. Thus, the Introduction hinges on the sharpness and the brevity of its condensation—on its density of insights. In this brevity resides "the soul of Johnson's wit"—the original theoretical conception and the imaginative conceptualization of her book. But the theory reads like a shorthand. Its stenographic density of insights needs to be unpacked.

As distinct from the traditional male-centered conception of "Shelley and His circle," Johnson's contrapuntal circle—"Mary's circle"—is inclusive of the feminine, but unsure where the center is. This circle is defined in Johnson's Introduction by three predominating features, three concepts which distinguish it from Percy Shelley's circle: (1) Johnson's circle— Mary's circle—is distinguished (Johnson says) by its emphasis on *listening* as the origin of its narrative desire, and as the driving force of its (female) storytelling. (2) Mary's circle—Johnson's circle—is distinguished by its positive assumption of its negative status as "minor" (it affirms itself as "minor," Johnson says, i.e., it is written *in the margin of the major*, written through its positive assumption of its marginality of *gender* and of *genre*, both), and through the transformation of its own minority (its negativity) into a source of literary and semantic power. (3) Johnson's circle—Mary's circle (Johnson says)—is a circle that proceeds from an engagement in an *autobiographical writing competition* that plays itself out, incessantly and allegorically, as a simultaneously aesthetic and erotic contest: Mary is competing with all other women (as well as with her parents, and with all surrounding men) for Shelley's intellectual and libidinal attention, at the same time she competes with all writers of the circle for an equal status as a (female) writer. This writing competition, both literal and figurative, finally ends up subsuming the entirety of Mary's life and of her literary writing: the whole of life, the whole of writing—and autobiography itself—is comprehended and experienced in this book (in the visionary theory of its introduction) as a literal and metaphorical, interminable *ghost-story contest*.

I will now try to unpack this re-definition of Romanticism, and to elaborate, more largely, on its totalizing theoretical and narratorial vision of the human condition and on its relationship with literature, insofar as this relationship reflects not just on Mary's life and writing, but also on Johnson's own book and on Johnson's own autobiography: an autobi-

ography which, in a Proustian manner, she was also writing in these last
months of her life, but which she did not have the time to finish, when
her writing suddenly was interrupted by her death.

∼

1. A Circle of Listening

In "Shelley and His Circle," Shelley is presumed to be the natural center
of attraction and of gravitation of the circle, the solar figure around which
all others orbit. In the central chapter of her book (Chapter 3) which
draws Shelley's poetical and human portrait, later inmixed with Mary's
contrapuntal portrait —through the double story of Mary's long relationship with Percy (before his death, and after it), Johnson discusses (at the
center of this double portrait) the irresistible seductiveness of Shelley's
vital narcissism, whose underside or counter-story is his totally oblivious,
narcissistically self-absorbed self-centeredness from which Mary—often
pregnant—suffers deeply and repeatedly: his blatant infidelity, his neglect
of his own children, his impatience with his wife's excessive, and (for him)
too lengthy grief over the deaths of several of their children. Even in his
poetry, Johnson notes, Shelley's relationship is always to himself: "Be thou
me," he famously says to the West Wind. In nature as in other human
beings, Shelley seeks his own mirror, his own (idealized) reflection. In
contrast, Mary never sees herself as a Romantic center: "I did not make
myself the heroine of my tales," she writes in her introduction to *Frankenstein*. "Life appeared to me too commonplace an affair as regarded myself. I could not figure to myself that romantic woes or wonderful events
would ever be my lot".[14] "Unlike her husband," Johnson writes in her
book's opening, "Mary Shelley did not always like to surround herself
with admirers or imitators, but desired rather to be part of *a narrative
group*." To be part of a "narrative group" is not to be its center, but to
be its member, to participate in a collaborative, collective literary conversation whose open-ended, as yet unmastered and unknown creative
implications keep unfolding. For Mary, this participation is first of all
the opportunity to listen: to *listen in the margin* to the polyphony, to the
plurality of voices of the circle. "Many and long," writes Mary in recalling the formation of the narrative group that gave birth to *Frankenstein*,
"were the conversations between Lord Byron and Shelley, to which I was
a devout but nearly silent listener" (p. 168). To listen is to get precisely *out*

of one's own self, to break outside of one's self-centeredness, to pay attention to the other, to put the other at the center. Johnson in turn listens in the margin—to Mary's act of listening, and to her silence.

Listening is a way to forget oneself in others' stories. "The more self-forgetful the listener is," Walter Benjamin wrote, "the more deeply is what he listens to impressed upon his memory . . . [H]e listens to the tales in such a way that the gift of retelling them comes to him all by itself."[15] Such is Mary's gift. Such is—on a different level—Johnson's gift. "For storytelling"—Benjamin says—"is always the art of repeating stories" (*Illuminations*, p. 91).

The "narrative group" in which Mary desires to participate is therefore, first of all, a community of listening: a community of listeners that (upon Byron's challenge: "we will each write a ghost story") undertakes to become a community of storytellers. In his 1817 preface to *Frankenstein*, Shelley narrates how this narrative group came into being.

"The season was cold and rainy," Shelley writes, "and in the evenings we crowded around a blazing wood fire and occasionally amused ourselves with some German stories of ghosts which happened to fall into our hands" (p. 6).

Citing Shelley's preface, Johnson completes her point about listening, and concludes at once her definition of her circle, and her Copernican decentering of the Romantic sky from Shelley's stellar narcissism and from his Romantically poetic, male self-centeredness: "*Mary Shelley's circle*," Johnson declares, "*is the one listening to ghost stories around the fire.*" This statement is deceptively simple: it contains in fact a revolutionary, visionary redefinition of Romanticism and of the Romantic circle. The defining image of Johnson's analysis is at once concrete (having a literal, tangible physical reality) and highly figurative (pregnant with symbolic meaning, toward which its literality is but a sign): "Mary Shelley's circle is the one listening to ghost stories around the fire." At the material center of this generative scene of listening and of storytelling which, in giving birth to Mary's writing, becomes imaginatively the metaphorical and allegorical, visionary frame of Johnson's book, the centerpiece—the very center of "Mary Shelley and Her Circle"—turns out to be neither male nor female, neither wife nor husband, but the incandescence of the blazing fire.

What can be, in Johnson's vision, the meaning of the fire at the center of *Mary Shelley and Her Circle*?

Fire

On the most obvious plane, the fire in the middle of the scene of listening that gives birth to Mary's writing (and to Johnson's book) can be understood as a material presence, a fragment of the corporeal world, that could incorporate as well the radiant force of magnetism that attracts the members of the circle to each other, and that could therefore symbolize in turn, both the fire of desire that sets ablaze Mary and Percy's love affair, and the fire of creation, the spark or "the sudden flash of inspiration,"[16] by which Frankenstein—like the Romantic writers—is (in Johnson's words) "fired with the longing to penetrate the secrets of life and death." [17]

Both Percy's and Mary's works refer to the myth of Prometheus, who steals the fire for the benefit of mankind (Percy in *Prometheus Unbound*, Mary in *Frankenstein, or the Modern Prometheus*). "Prometheus," notes Johnson, "the fire bringer, the giver of both creation and destruction, is also said by some accounts to be the father of the human race."[18]

When Mary and Percy wrote about Prometheus, neither one of them expected that the fire would acquire a concrete reality in their own lives, beyond the mythical and the metaphorical. But it did: the fire trespassed literary bounds when, a few years later, in an unanticipated way, Shelley died by drowning near the coast of Lerici (Italy) and his body, once it washed up on the shore, was burned in a funeral pyre that lasted several hours.[19]

All that remained of Shelley, after his body was reduced to ashes, was his poetry, his writing, including an unfinished poem—*The Triumph of Life*—on which he was working when he went to sea, a poem that his death leaves broken off in midsentence, on a question that gains all the more significance from the event which interrupts it: "'Then, what is life?'—I cried—" writes Shelley. Rising out of the poet's accidental death, in ironic contiguity to Shelley's burned body, this poem and its question—this last line and last residue of Shelley's life—are doomed to remain unanswered, yet the resonance and poignancy of its interrogation continue to reverberate interminably: "'Then, what is life?'—I cried." This unanswered question has survived, along with Shelley's poetry.

～

Speaking of the mystery of the survival of literary works, despite and beyond their authors' deaths, Walter Benjamin compares their fate in history and their endurance, the growing power of their literary "afterlife," to metaphors of fire, ashes, and funeral pyres. Johnson invited us to listen to this Benjaminian passage, since she had cited and highlighted it in her preceding book *The Feminist Difference*.[20] It is my own suggestion to bring back this quotation previously highlighted by her (in an altogether different context) here, because it is still relevant, and could illuminate quite strikingly the reading she accomplishes in her last book. "If," writes Benjamin (and Johnson cites), "to use a simile, one views the growing work [of art] as a funeral pyre, its commentator . . . is left with wood and ashes . . . [while its critic] is concerned only with the enigma of the flame itself: the enigma of being alive. Thus the critic inquires about the truth whose living flame goes on burning over the heavy logs of the past, and the light ashes of life gone by."[21] Johnson underscores what she paraphrases as "this curious conjunction of an image of death (a funeral pyre) with the concept of life (the enigma of being a alive)," and tells us to expect that the surprising paradox of this conjunction will "return in an unexpected way" in her own writing.[22]

Benjamin's comparison of the "growing power" of the surviving literary work to the growing flame of a funeral pyre is reminiscent, in its imagistic metaphorical and philosophical conceptuality, of Shelley's literal cremation and of the actual protracted incandescence of his concrete funeral pyre on the shore of the Italian beach in whose proximity he drowned. Byron, who attended this fiery memorial, described it to a friend: "You can have no idea what an extraordinary effect such a funeral pyre has, on a desolate shore, with mountains in the background and the sea before, and the singular appearance the salt and frankincense gave to the flame. All of Shelley was consumed, except his *heart*, which would not take the flame, and is now preserved in spirits of wine."[23]

Thus, the fire at the center of the circle of listening could refer not just to Byron's fireplace (around which the ghost stories are first heard), or to the fire of desire and creation which consumed the Romantic writers, but also to the funeral pyre of Shelley's burnt body and to his own (preserved) charred heart, a burnt heart which figures at the literal center of the book, at the conclusion of the Shelley chapter. Johnson's style in this last paragraph—as always in this book—is elliptically condensed and understated, swift and minimalist:

> Percy's dead body was supposed to be completely burned on the beach where he washed up, but the heart remained unburned and was given to Mary. She

spent the remainder of her life with it, living with and defending the rights of Percy Florence, her dead husband's only surviving child. When Mary died in 1851, the heart was buried with her.

Romanticism is presumed to be the language of the heart.[24] Yet in *Mary Shelley and Her Circle*, Romanticism rewrites itself as the language—the enigma—of the charred heart.

2. The Affirmation of the Minor

Mary, Johnson writes, "was the only contestant to take the ghost-story contest seriously: Byron and Shelley preferred to work in more respectable genres, and Polidori's imagination took him too far. Mary Shelley thus defined her place in literature in a minor genre (the gothic or sensational novel)."

Johnson's affirmation that it is Mary's choice to *"define her place in literature* in a minor genre"—to *define herself* as positively and affirmatively "minor"—stands in opposition to two symmetrically opposed critical traditions: on the one hand, Johnson challenges and contradicts the canonical, male-centered critical perception of Romanticism, a tradition that discounts Mary through the claim that "true" Romantic writers—those who count—have to be by definition to be "major," while "majority" is naturally perceived as male and described as male appropriation ("My concern," Harold Bloom explains, "is only with *strong* poets, *major figures*, with the persistence to wrestle with their strong precursors, even to the death" [25]). On the other hand, Johnson's emphasis on Mary's (deliberate) minority must also be distinguished from the feminist position of scholars of Romanticism who, in contrast, claim for Mary a centrality, which means for them "majority" as "non-minority": "There seems to be a new, unmistakable and cross-national consensus that Mary Shelley is very far indeed from the passive receptor, the minor figure overshadowed by the major Romantic," write (among many others) the editors of a collective volume on Mary Shelley's writings, entitled *Iconoclastic Departures: Mary Shelley after Frankenstein*.[26]

Among these two extremes (Mary excluded as a "minor," Mary included as a "major"), Johnson's sympathy is rather with the latter view. But her philosophical point is different: "If I put the accent in this way on her marginality, it's not in order to discover for her a new centrality, but in order to analyze the new manner in which the question of marginality is inscribed in and agitates her work."[27] For Johnson, "minority" is not a question of evaluation, but a factual designation of one's location in the world. Johnson is interested in how Mary precisely turns her minoritarian stance into a literary resource, how she makes of her peripheral position an enabling vantage point, which makes it possible for her to see and to disclose aspects of the world that from the center would have remained unseen, invisible. As a woman writer facing a male circle, Mary, Johnson claims, is the unspoken bearer of an affirmation: *assuming* rather than denying her minority (her marginality of gender and of genre), Mary transforms this minority (this negativity) into a powerful new literary vision.

Johnson's concept of "the minor"—used somewhat defiantly (against the grain)—rejoins the innovative vision of the French thinkers Gilles Deleuze and Félix Guattari in their collaborative book *Kafka: Toward a Minor Literature*.[28] This philosophical book defines the (subversive) positivity of "the minor" and of (the re-created concept of) "minor literature," by demonstrating its unique sophistication and its incomparable conceptual importance, which major literature cannot replace and for which it cannot be nor become a substitute. Kafka is their prime example, in his marginal geographical position with respect to German culture, and in his seditious, "minor use" of the "major language"—German—in which he writes and which he radically "deterritorializes." Every minor literature implies a similar (insider's) deterritorialization of the hegemonic (major) language in which the minor writer writes. In Johnson's reading, Mary equally practices "a minor use" of the hegemonic codes of the Romantic circle. *Frankenstein*'s disguised critique of Percy Shelley is one example of such a perniciously seditious twisting or "minorization," "deterritorialization," of the territory of the major. Every minor literature is therefore by its very minor nature inherently political, whether it intends to be or not. Most importantly, a minor (literary) use of language always encroaches on a minority's collective interests, however missing, incoherent, inadvertently expressed, obscure, or utopian those collective interests might be. Therefore, the minor writer—however inarticulate or skeptical—produces "active solidarity." In its very singularity and in its most subjective individual concern, minor literature always implies the value and the function of a *collective utterance*. "[I]f the writer is in the margins or completely outside his or her fragile community," the authors write, "this situation allows the writer all the more the possibility to express another possible community and to forge another consciousness and another sensibility."[29] In Mary Shelley's case (in Johnson's circle), the collective value of the minor utterance, and the "active solidarity" it produces, might point in Johnson's understanding toward the narrative formation of an imagined community of women writers.[30] Johnson agrees, thus, with the basic theoretical insight of Deleuze and Guattari: "That is the glory of this sort of minor literature—to be the revolutionary force for all literature."[31] In the end, minority and literarity are somehow linked, in the sense that literature always proceeds from the language of an otherness, seeking to be recognized and to be liberated. Johnson concretizes, deepens and extends this insight. That is why she holds on to the minority of Mary Shelley.

Through Mary Shelley, Johnson listens to the circle like a musical performer, and replays Romanticism in a minor key.

3. The Autobiographical Writing Competition: The Ghost-Story Contest

The originality of Johnson's book, and the gist of her visionary view of the originality (the distinctiveness) of "Mary 's Circle," hinges on the deepened allegorical significance Johnson lends to the concrete historical event of the writing competition (1816) that gives birth to Mary's writing, as Mary retrospectively narrates in the added (1831) Introduction to the third edition of *Frankenstein*. Johnson cites Mary's account of the origin of her first novel:

> "We will each write a ghost story," said Lord Byron; and his proposition was acceded to. There were four of us. The noble author began a tale, a fragment of which he printed at the end of his poem of Mazeppa. Shelley, more apt to embody ideas and sentiments in the radiance of brilliant imagery, and in the music of the most melodious verse that adorns our language, than to invent the machinery of a story, commenced one founded on the experiences of his early life. Poor Polidori had some terrible idea about a skull-headed lady, who was so punished for peeping through a key-hole . . . The illustrious poets also, annoyed by the platitude of prose, speedily relinquished their uncongenial task.
>
> I busied myself *to think of a story—a story to rival those which had excited us to this task.* ("Introduction to *Frankenstein*, Third Edition, 1831," p. 167; emphasis mine)

Johnson's book articulates the global drama of this linguistic, human, literary, textual, and intertextual competition, in interpreting the competition in its largest human sense yet through the closest textual and intertextual readings, and in narrating simultaneously the story of the rivalry and that of the excitement among these mutually inspiring and mutually competing writers and their "rival stories." "I propose," Johnson explains, "to study both the people and the texts that Mary tried to take in and to measure up to, in entering into the ghost-story writing-contest. Mary engages in this competition with both her writing and her life. Her passion and her art alike proceed from these generative moments of connection and of difference, of *rival stories* inscribed within a circle of entangled lives and of entangled texts." "In this study," Johnson emphasizes at the end of her Introduction, "I want to look at what Mary was competing with."

For Byron, the idea of the ghost-story contest is essentially a game, a bid for supremacy. Shelley, on his side, is caught up in a male struggle against Byron, who is (implicitly) the only real rival that he recognizes, and the only one he wants to beat. Later in life, Shelley writes to Mary: "I despair of rivalling Lord Byron, and there is no other with whom it is worth contending."[32]

Unlike the men, Mary does not compete for supremacy, but for equality. She does not seek to overpower men, but rather to gain power (semantic authority) over herself. As a woman competitor, she claims the right to be, like men, a *subject of desire*, and not merely an object of desire. She claims an equal partnership in the competitive creativity of the narrative group. But Mary, Johnson says, is "the only contestant to take the ghost story contest seriously." "Byron and Shelley," Johnson writes, "preferred to work in more respectable genres, and Polidori's imagination took him too far. Mary thus defined her place in literature in a minor genre (the gothic or sensational novel) . . . Having surrendered the prestigious poetic genres to Byron and Shelley, she chose to compete with other authors for the most vulgar genres of prose."

For Johnson, the writing competition is thus all at once a contest between genders (male and female), a contest between genres (poetry and prose, verse and narrative), and a contest between social classes (the aristocratic origin of Shelley and of Byron and the artistic aristocracy of their poetic practice, versus Mary's lower end, middle-class origin, the non-elitist, wider popular appeal of her chosen genre [the gothic novel], and her basic democratic storyteller's wish, to reach the people and to touch the people).

PART TWO

V

Writing in the Face of Death

Reading this last manuscript that Barbara Johnson wrote against all odds, despite disease, in the last year of her life, and managed to complete a few weeks before her death, I think how fitting it is that she addresses us in this last work not as a theorist, but as a storyteller.

❧

The most famous writer—and the most profound storyteller—who similarly wrote in wrestling with his own disease, who equally completed his literary work just before his death, and who, moreover, made of the confrontation with his own impending death the very center of his novel, is Marcel Proust.

Proust was one of Johnson's most admired and beloved writers, since her youth. As it happens, in the last year of her life, Johnson was rereading Proust, and was inspired by his model to write her own autobiography. This autobiographic writing, which she entitled "Sentimental Education," and which she started—in parallel to the last phases of *Mary Shelley and Her Circle*—was, however, interrupted—after only a few opening pages—by her death.

Proust's influence is present, I submit, in Johnson's last completed work. I thus propose to read *Mary Shelley and Her Circle* in the light of Proust's unique writing endeavor, by making more explicit the Proustian model and the Proustian inspiration in the background of the text.

❧

No one expressed better than Proust what it means to write when one is sick, and what it means to face—precisely through the writing—one's own impending death. No one expressed better than Proust what it means to circle back in time, to reach back to the depths of an unconscious memory, so as to repossess the meaning of one's past, and to recover, rediscover, the significance of the creative origin of one's own being.

I believe that Johnson strives to attain to all these joined meanings, in writing *Mary Shelley and Her Circle*.

> The idea of death [Proust writes] took up permanent residence within me in the way that love sometimes does. Not that I loved death, I abhorred it. But . . . its image adhered now to the most profound layer of my mind, so completely that I could not give my attention to anything without that thing first traversing the idea of death.[33]

It is thus not surprising that, facing her own death, Johnson turns to Proust as an inspiring spiritual support. Proust managed to endure his illness by putting it in the service of his art, and Johnson in some ways tries to do the same, to make her writing transform and reshape her suffering and to give it a new meaning.

Not only has Proust (as a writer) stunningly won his battle with his own disease, through the creation of an autobiographical literary masterpiece accomplished and completed at the very mortal climax of his life. He was also an exquisite reader, and has left his mark as one of the sharpest, most acute and most insightfully original literary critics. As a critic, Proust believed—and put forward the proposition—that artists who are battling with disease are endowed with special powers, and have the ability to reach depths and to access insights that are simply out of reach for writers in good health. Comparing Baudelaire (whom he admires) to Victor Hugo, Proust writes:

> Next to a volume like *Les Fleurs du mal*, Hugo's immense work appears vague, soft, devoid of accent. Hugo never ceased talking about death, but with the detachment of a *bon vivant* and of a man who passionately enjoys life. It may be, alas, that only he who contains approaching death in him, who like Baudelaire is threatened with aphasia, can reach the lucidity in true suffering . . . A Baudelaire, better still a Dostoevsky, in thirty years . . . create something of which not a single paragraph could have been accomplished by a whole line of a thousand artists in fine health.[34]

In the light of Proust's insight, I will suggest that, although Johnson as a critic has always written about death, it is a viscerally, vitally different Barbara Johnson, one who—in Proust's words—has "endured the mortal exhaustions that precede death,"[35] who is now circling back to Mary Shelley and her Circle. A Barbara Johnson who herself is now inhabited by a strong autobiographical impulse (who reads Mary Shelley with her own life), and who, like Proust, is seeking to complete her work before her death, in the acute awareness that she is running out of time.

Recapturing Time, or "Reading Backwards"

As Proust demonstrates, time can be "recaptured," the past can be relived, and can be illuminated, repossessed, and life can be reborn and to some extent "regained" in a literary work which resurrects its drive, its impetus, and which translates both its desires and its disappointments into images of understanding. "Real life," writes Proust, "life at last laid bare and il-luminated—the only life in consequence that can be said to be really lived—is literature" (*TR*, p. 253).[36]

For Johnson as for Proust, the reading of a life (one's own or other lives) entails a necessary deconstruction of the characters'—and of one's own—illusions. Life (in Proust's case, in Johnson's case, and in Mary Shelley's case) is a dramatization of what Lacan would call "the subversion of the subject" by her own desire. The narrative performs an ironic demystifica-tion of life's naïve hopes and of its emotional distortions and self-misper-ceptions. Autobiography and biography alike imply a constant process of correction of what Proust calls "this perpetual error that is, precisely, 'life'."[37] Like Proust, Johnson knows that "that life of ours, . . . which cannot effectually observe itself . . . need[s] to be translated, and often, to be read backwards and laboriously deciphered" (*TR*, pp. 254–255). For Johnson as for Proust, and indeed for Mary Shelley as a storyteller, "The work of art was the sole means of rediscovering Lost Time" (*TR*, p. 258).

Thus, Johnson in her turn is an architect of memory who constructs, in *Mary Shelley and Her Circle*, a highly complex intertextual architecture of narrative threads: "[L]ife is perpetually weaving fresh threads which link one individual and one event to another . . . these threads are crossed and recrossed, doubled and redoubled to thicken the web," forming "a rich network of memories" that creates, in her book as well, "an almost infinite variety of communicating paths to choose from" (*TR*, p. 428).

Impossible Autobiography

Mary Shelley, Johnson says, could not write the story of her own life ex-cept through its repression: she could not write her own autobiography, except through fiction, as a storyteller.[38] I will suggest that in her last book, Johnson writes for Mary her impossible autobiography, through her own semi-autobiographical reading of Mary's life, and her analysis of

Mary's fictional articulation of this life through her displaced activity (her indirect autobiography) as storyteller. I have suggested that Johnson is partaking (autobiographically) of the writing competition (the performative dynamics of the ghost-story contest) which she sets up as a central (visionary) metaphor for Mary's whole life, and which she in turn (in my reading) reenacts. But the writing contest also lives through "time," and ends up in its turn undergoing change and transformation. The struggle for existence as a writer (as a woman writer), the existential writing competition in which Barbara Johnson, like Mary Shelley, is autobiographically engaged, finally translates itself into a poignant competition between life and death. Ultimately, what both women writers, at the limit, are competing with, each in her way, is death.

Mary meets death even while she is born, through the loss of her own mother, who dies in giving birth to her, and whom she consequently will never know except as a living and dead ghost, in the actual ghost story of her life. She then lives through the unexpected death in infancy of three of the four children she has borne, of whom only one survives into maturity. At the age of twenty-four, Mary then lives through the unexpected, horrifying, and disfiguring death of her own husband through an accidental drowning, followed by the burning of his corpse—the extinction through cremation of the poet's body when he has barely reached thirty years of age. Johnson in her turn meets death early on, first through the loss of a beloved pianist (the husband of her piano teacher) who dies young from a car accident, and later through the loss of Paul de Man, her mentor, who dies from a terminal disease. Then, still young and in the very prime of life, she herself is hit with an unexpected diagnosis (and prognosis) of a rare neurological, degenerative—and ultimately terminal—disease.

"Reading is a form of friendship," Proust has written. "And the fact that it is directed at someone who is dead, who is not there, lends something disinterested, almost moving, to it."[39] Through the bond of reading she creates with Mary Shelley so as to articulate for her sister-writer Mary's own impossible autobiography, Johnson understands that the writing competition which starts as a shared bid for female authorship and for feminine equality, ultimately turns into a much more primordial, existential struggle between life and death.

But each one of the women writers thus knotted in this bond of reading lives her fate—confronts death—in a different way. Mary in the end creates a totally idealized romantic myth of an angelic Percy Shelley, in which the reality of life (their mutual life) is lost. Johnson's narrative does not idealize, but on the contrary writes life (the tangled lives of the Romantic circle) as a Proustian de-mythification—a "reading backwards" or a deconstruction—of this idealized romantic myth. "True mourning," as de Man writes (and as Proust and Johnson know) "is less deluded."[40]

VI

Writing's Struggle with the Body

In the end, the storyteller's mourning, and her (allegorical) writing competition, is transformed into Writing's competition with the Body. "It is in moments of illness," Proust writes, "that we are compelled to recognize that we live not alone but chained to a creature of a different kingdom, who has no knowledge of us and by whom it is impossible to make ourselves understood: our body."[41]

> For the fundamental fact was that I had a body, and this means that I was perpetually threatened. . . . Indeed, it is the possession of a body, that is the great danger . . . to our human and thinking life . . . The body immures the mind within a fortress; presently on all sides the fortress is besieged and in the end, inevitably, the mind has to surrender. (*TR*, p. 435)

In her last months, while writing *Mary Shelley and Her Circle*, Johnson in her turn feels "besieged" by an estranged and endangered body, "by whom it is impossible to make ourselves understood." She writes her last book in a competition with her own disease, through a harrowing, heroic contest with her own declining body (yet another autobiographical ghost story, with whose terror she was wrestling for nine years). But Johnson is determined to defy and to transgress the restrictive limits of her failing health, and invents means to outsmart those limits. "I wished to live deliberately," she would later assert in borrowing Thoreau's words. "I did not wish to live what was not life, living is so dear; nor did I wish to practice resignation, unless it was quite necessary." She wants (as Thoreau puts it)—and will in fact try by all means—"to drive life to a corner."[42]

Having suffered from progressive loss of coordination, using keyboards—typing—had become toward the end almost an impossible activity, a skill that demanded all her courage, all her resourcefulness, all her time and all her strength. She sacrificed her e-mail communication even with her closest correspondents (her most intimate and dearest friends)—in order to be able to pursue her writing and to finish this book only weeks before her death, through sheer willpower, in a spirited defiance of her failing strength.

Similarly, Proust describes how the dying storyteller, in "perpetually regrouping his forces," would have "to endure the book like a form of fatigue, to accept it like a discipline, . . . follow it like a medical regime, vanquish it like an obstacle, win it like a friendship——" (*TR*, p. 431).

Disfiguration

Johnson was always interested—quite enigmatically—in figures of (allegorical) disfigurement. Her first book (written when she was radiant with youthful health and beauty), was called (in French), *Défigurations du langage poétique (Disfigurations—Of Poetic Language).*[43] Her early concern with disfigurement applied at first only to rhetoric (to the poetic language of Baudelaire and Mallarmé), but then, with the discovery of Mary Shelley's *Frankenstein*, it was extended to the physicality of life itself, when Johnson's 1980 innovative reading[44] correlates the monster's body with Mary's own disfigured life, first through her unwanted pregnancy (from Percy Shelley, who was still married to another woman), then through her child's death, and later through Shelley's death by drowning and consequent disfiguration and burning of his corpse. Now, twenty years after this early insight, facing the disfiguration of her own life by the illness, Johnson bonds again with Mary's autobiographical writing of her "monstrous" losses, losses grieved and rendered meaningful through Mary's literary triumph in the ghost-story writing competition, which gives birth to *Frankenstein* as (in Johnson's reading) a generalizable allegory of the disfigured, speechless, and repressed autobiography of the female writer. Johnson had always deeply, existentially empathized with the creature's plight. In her stellar youthful essay, she clairvoyantly (to everyone's surprise) insisted: "The reader of *Frankenstein*, too, would be well advised to look beyond the monster's physical deformity, both for his fearsome power and for his hidden beauty."[45] Now that the monster—which she always saw as embedded in the self's autobiography—can be metaphorically likened to her own disease, now that the creature's isolation, his loneliness, and his "defacement," have symbolically become closer to her own, she will inadvertently, astonishingly demonstrate how she can—in actuality—live up to what she described precisely as his hidden beauty.

The Body in the Margin of the Text

Johnson therefore is (unwittingly) "inscribing her own body in the margin of her manuscript," in much the same way Paul de Man had analyzed the death and the disfigurement of Shelley's body as *contained within the text* of his unfinished poem, *The Triumph of Life*. The poem, says de Man, is an unfinished fragment, whose poetry is violently cut off by the poet's death. The poem's meaning, its intelligibility, is thus forever undercut, as though wounded, fractured, by the event of the physical disfigurement of Shelley's body. The poem necessarily encompasses this corporeal wound, includes this silent, inarticulate event—which interrupts it by a sudden allegorical disfiguration. In de Man's analysis, whose lucidity and grief Johnson clearly shares, the limits seem to be undone between the body and the writing. It is as though Shelley's final poem writes its own disfiguration, not by intention but by fate.

". . . Shelley's body," de Man writes, "burnt after his boat capsized and he drowned off the coast of Lerici . . . is present in the margin of the last manuscript page and has become an inseparable part of the poem . . . It may seem a freak of chance to have a text thus molded by an actual occurrence, yet the reading of *The Triumph of Life* establishes that this mutilated textual model exposes the wound of a fracture that lies hidden in all texts."[46]

Similarly, Johnson's body seems to be inscribed in the margin of her final manuscript, particularly in the abbreviated, gasping, racing, almost breathless textuality of her final pages. It is as though Johnson had written the ungraspable physical event of the imminent interruption of her life and writing into her last manuscript.

VII

Writing the End

As a young theorist (who most probably was not yet thinking of her own mortality), in a conference titled "*Les fins de l'homme*"—"The Ends of Man"—in Cerisy, in France, in 1980, Johnson for the first time picks up Mary Shelley (*The Last Man*) as the topic of her lecture, and thereby undertakes to meditate on the significance of death (in Mary Shelley's fiction) through a correlation she brings into focus, between the termination of a book and termination of a human life:

"To write the end," Johnson says in Cerisy in 1980, in the (French) discussion following her Mary Shelley lecture, "To write the end (the end of the book, or the human's end) is manifestly an impossible task. The end cannot (and cannot but) be written" "*La fin ne peut (que) s'écrire.*"[47]

In retrospect, this brilliantly spontaneous statement was prophetically descriptive of her own predicament in writing her last book. In *Mary Shelley and Her Circle*, the termination of the book precisely coincides with the termination of a life (her own), and both terminations—both endings—are experienced as equally impossible, and desperately struggle and "compete" with one another. "In this study, I want to show what Mary was competing with," Johnson had written (in the last words of her introduction). In turn, I propose to show what Johnson is competing with in writing this last book.

Like Proust, in her last months, Johnson competes with time. The end of life endangers and calls into question the termination of the book. To recapitulate her own words, "the end cannot and *cannot but* be written," because fate knocks already on the door: the author's death—inscribed already in the margin of the manuscript—is imminent, and will unavoidably impose an ending to the book in ending life. But simultaneously, "the end *cannot* be written," because, when the end arrives, it is no longer possible to write it: there is no force left in the weakened body, no final breath with which to write the book's end. And thus, it is perhaps symbolic that the last book has no real ending, that there is no closure, no conclusion, no possible totalization (of life, and) of the book's spiral plurality of stories.

The Circular Structure of the Book

However, I would argue that the meaning of the book resides, precisely, in its meaning's *circulation*. "The end of the book"—Johnson's last chapter, on Polidori—does not really conclude the book (does not present a final mastery, a final unifying meaning), but circles back to the beginning, to Johnson's introduction about Mary Shelley. Mary Shelley is now viewed—on both sides of the fracture of her husband's death—as the creator both of *Frankenstein* (disfiguration) and of the Shelley myth (erasure of disfiguration). "Each individual therefore,"—Proust has written—"and

I was myself one of these individuals—was a measure of duration for me, in virtue of the revolutions that like some heavenly body he had accomplished not only on his own axis but around other bodies" (*TR*, p. 429). Likewise, each one of Johnson's portraits (chapters) circulates among and around the others. Johnson's circle keeps revolving, in the perpetual movement of its revolutions.

The end of the book goes back to the beginning, moreover, in returning to the generative drama of the writing competition (the circle of competitors around the fire, the circular frame of the book), now viewed with added elements, from an enlarged circular perspective: exhibiting the fracture at the heart of the Romantic circle, and reinscribing—without words—the literal and allegorical disfiguration which Mary's myth of Shelley (and of the Romantic poet as Creator) has erased.

The end returns also to the introduction's inextricable tangle of death and birth. "The natural supernaturalism of life was at the two ends of it—birth and death," writes Johnson in her final chapter: "Ghost stories covered the uncanniness of death, but Mary Shelley's *Frankenstein* and Polidori's *Vampyre* were about what gave life."

Johnson's book begins and ends with the two winners of the ghost-story writing competition: Mary and Polidori. Indeed, the unforeseen success and popularity of the two works that have come out of the ghost-story contest—Polidori's *The Vampyre* and Mary Shelley's *Frankenstein*—have both exceeded expectations. Johnson notes, however, how Polidori (in this "writing competition") is frustrated and neglected in his love for Byron, just as Mary is frustrated and neglected in her love for Shelley. Despite their winning, neither one of them can claim centrality in their lovers' hearts. In a book that reflects on marginality, it is ironically noteworthy that the two winners remain marginal, outsiders to the glamour and the glory of the circle. Nor can the two winners fully claim the credit of their signatures. Both Mary and Polidori publish their works at first anonymously, and both of them are similarly dispossessed from their proper names, when Polidori's *Vampyre*, inadvertently first published under Byron's name, continues to be publicly attributed to Byron (by Goethe, for example), just as Mary Shelley's novel (in the year of its first publication, and by certain critics, up until today) is attributed to Percy Shelley. The two winners of the writing competition—inadvertent shapers of new literary genres and of unpredictable and unpredictably influential literary and artistic legacies—have therefore in themselves remained to some extent ghost writers.

~

What Does It Mean to Be a Storyteller?

Facing the inexorable end, Johnson, like Proust, writes the epic of the writer (in Johnson's and in Mary's case, the epic of the female writer) who is "searching for lost time" (searching for time as loss, and for the time of loss) in the present moment of the writing.

In her essay *The Last Man*, Johnson talked about "a certain relation to language which ends as at once affirming and denying the end, solitude, the possibility of speaking."[48] In her last book, through her own weaving of the chain of her linked stories, Johnson in her turn lives precisely this relation she described, of simultaneously "affirming and denying the end, solitude, the possibility of speaking." In so doing, she also duplicates and mirrors Mary Shelley's affirmation and denial of the end, through her own career as storyteller.

Johnson in her turn becomes a storyteller. Situated on the threshold between life and death, on the border between two temporal impossibilities, the past and the future, she, like Scheherazade, tells stories so as to remain alive, writing so as not to die, but to begin again (and to begin again) the present moment, in tying one story to the next, one chapter to the next, in such a way as to forestall the fatal end.

"Memory," writes Benjamin, "passes a happening on from generation to generation. It starts the web which all stories together form in the end. One ties on to the next, as the great storytellers have always known. In each of them there is a Scheherazade who thinks of a fresh story whenever the tale comes to a stop."[49]

No wonder, then, that Johnson, who lived as a theorist, dies as a storyteller. The story is a sufferance, an endurance. It is not just narrated: it endures and is endured. "What I have endured," writes Mary Shelley (in the letter following her husband's death), "is not to be alleviated by time."[50] In *Mary Shelley and Her Circle*, Johnson questions the endured and the unendurable—"the wound of a fracture that lies hidden in all texts"[51]— with an embodied patience, an attunement, a resilience, a duration, a stubborn durability. All sorrows can be borne if they are borne witness to. As a storyteller facing her own death and poised against it, Johnson bears witness to *endurance*—in all the senses of the word. She precisely shares with Mary Shelley the remarkable capacity to bear and to survive.

"Survival," Audre Lorde says, "is not an academic skill. It is learning how to stand alone, and how to make common cause with others."[52] In the excruciating circumstances of her last year, when she herself can no longer give lectures and can hardly speak, Johnson survives, communicates, and bears witness to survival—Mary Shelley's and her own—through her amazing gift for listening and for storytelling. Her book becomes her final tool for learning (and for demonstrating) how, against excruciating odds, to find the strength to stand alone and yet, in writing, how to continue to communicate and to make common cause with others.

This book should thus be read as what it is: not just a work of literary criticism (that itself reads like a novel), but a life act and a life event in its own right; an ultimate life tool, that perhaps can also stand as emblem for the embodied life act and for the specimen life struggle of the woman writer and the woman reader (and beyond them, of the writer and the reader), wherever they might be.

∾

"When we have arrived at reality," writes Proust, "we must . . . express it and preserve it" (*TR*, p. 256). "And when we seek to extract from our grief the generality that lies within it, we are to some extent consoled"(*TR*, p. 261). Literature enables to makes peace with death: "Let us accept," says Proust, "the physical injury which is done to us for the sake of the spiritual knowledge which grief brings; let us submit to the disintegration of our body . . . Ideas come to us as substitutes for griefs, and griefs, at the moment when they change into ideas, lose some part of their power to injure . . . ; the transformation itself releases suddenly a little joy" (*TR*, pp. 267–268). "If we succeed at least in explaining it, is not even our infirmity transformed into strength of a new kind?" (*TR*, p. 264).

VIII

Mortality: "The Privilege of Humans"

Johnson starts the writing competition with her medical diagnosis by producing, one after the other, several extraordinary books, of which the first two (*Mother Tongues*, Mallarmé's *Divagations*) devote themselves to poetry and its translation (studying poetic language, the relations between poetry and life, and the meaning of poetic destinies). Her third book (during illness), *Persons and Things*, devotes itself to a rethinking of what constitutes the human.

Johnson's trajectory of loss and of increasing deprivation becomes, thus, a trajectory of intensified linguistic, philosophical, poetic, and critical creation. Work and life interpret one another, but the work, rather than passively and helplessly reflecting life, has the function of actively transfiguring it, reshaping it, and humanizing it.

Persons and Things is the first book that Johnson wrote when speaking in public became physically impossible and she was forced to take her retirement from Harvard (from the teaching that she loved, from the community she serviced and which gave her a strong sense of belonging: a loss of community that, incidentally, recalls Mary Shelley's loss of her Romantic circle, rendered as the plague in *The Last Man*).

In *Persons and Things*, Johnson goes beyond the mere fact of confronting death and writing in the face of death: she philosophically defines humanity as an insight into what it means to be a mortal. Humanity, in Johnson's definition, is the capacity to be addressed, concerned, by the idea of mortality. She goes as far as to describe, call, and define mortality as "the privilege of humans."[53] She situates in this "capacity for being mortal" the human capacity par excellence. I call it a "capacity" (it is not her term: it is my name for what I understand she is describing) because, in *Persons and Things*, as in her own life, Johnson transforms this awareness of mortality (awareness also of her own mortality)—into an enabling insight, a capacity for owning one's own transience, a paradoxically enriching capability. It is precisely this concern with mortality that, in her conception, differentiates a person from a thing: it is what makes both men and women human, what endows them with inalienable humanity and personhood. But personhood, in Johnson's understanding, is contingent on its own vulnerability, fragility, mortality. Personhood—like life—is what precisely can be lost; it is that of which a person can quite easily be stripped.

When the disease becomes the monster in her own "ghost story," Johnson struggles, pointedly, not to let her illness *deface her personhood*: she would not let this disintegration of her reality undercut her courage, compromise her stubborn self-reliance, her fierce independence even in conditions of physical dependence. She adopts an absolute stand toward her fate. In embodying precisely the humanity, the (inadvertent) magnanimity of "the capacity for being mortal," and in making of her own personal mortality an exemplary impersonal, philosophical symbol of the "privilege of humans," she succeeds in preserving her humanity intact despite the disfiguring disease, and thus becomes, herself, a symbol of how utmost human grandeur can be lived, experienced and expressed—through utmost human destitution.

Indeed, in its epigraph (about beauty and disfiguration) and in two of its reflective chapters on what gives life ("Animation," "Artificial Life"), *Persons and Things* returns to Mary Shelley's *Frankenstein* (Johnson's youthful "aha" moment, and one of her favorite parables or pedagogical tales), which here becomes one of the key philosophical references of the book. In passing, Johnson recapitulates Percy Shelley's last unfinished question in "The Triumph of Life": "'What is life?' I asked,"—writes Shelley in his (interrupted) last words. "What is life?," she writes. "There are many who attempt to answer [that] . . . question, . . . but very few focus on mortality" (*PT*, p. 156).

Shelley's question was surrounded by his silence. Johnson hears the silence. It is out of silence that *Persons and Things* precisely speaks, in the shadow of the threat of the eventual loss of the possibility of speaking (what she herself in her own youth spoke of as "the end, solitude, the possibility of speaking").[54]

Yet, for Johnson, at that stage, silence interacts with speech as mortality interacts with life. Like a caesura that—by interrupting verse—enhances its poetic quality and its poetic resonance, mortality, which interrupts and limits life, intensifies its paradoxical vitality, enhances its potential poetry.

As can be attested in the pages of this book, when life becomes equal to mortality, mortality returns as increased appetite for life, and can be transformed into an enhanced life. Indeed, in *Persons and Things*, even in the face of death, even in the failure of articulated speech, life is vibration, resonance, expression, shortage, shortage of time: "anxiety": "excitement." "What are the origins and aims of this book? It is not organized chronologically, although it may well be about the anxiety and excitement of being historical" (*PT*, p. 3).

In the face of our historic finitude, only literature can perhaps give our story an infinitude. Thus, at last—again—Mary Shelley, and her Circle. Beyond the polarity of gender, it is the Romantic writers' shared concern with mortality ("the privilege of humans") that now appears to Johnson to be the defining feature of their (our) humanity and personhood. Johnson shares with them the "capacity for being mortal": the common denominator of men and women alike, and specifically the great earthly rallying point of the men and women of *Mary Shelley and Her Circle*.

Daringly imaginative, like the bold romantic heroes in the story that she tells, Johnson, like them, will die young, before her time. "Death," says Walter Benjamin in his famous essay "The Storyteller," "Death is the sanction of everything the storyteller has to tell. He has borrowed his authority from death."[55]

"The prospect of death," Johnson has written in *Persons and Things*, "may be what human beings have in common . . . Mortality may infuse all human speaking with a kind of pathos that something that can neither live nor die cannot have. So that if a person 'has something to say,' it is first and foremost 'I am alive,' but in the face of death" (*PT*, p. 155).

～

IX

The Flame

The first book Johnson wrote during her illness, *Mother Tongues*,[56] ends with a citation from Benjamin's essay on the Storyteller. Since this relatively long quotation figures on the last page of the book, as part of its conclusive paragraph, Johnson must have found it particularly meaningful, something important she wanted to express.

"Seen in this way," Benjamin writes (and Johnson quotes), "the storyteller joins the ranks of the teachers and sages. For it is granted to him to reach back to a whole lifetime (a life, incidentally, that comprises not only his own experience but no little of the experiences of others . . .). His gift is the ability to relate his life; his distinction, to be able to relate his entire life. The storyteller: he is the man who could let the wick of his life be completely consumed by the gentle flame of his story."[57]

The way the storyteller is depicted as a writer touched by fire, whose life and body are literally consumed by, and as though burning through, the flame of his (her) story, carries us back to the fire at the center of *Mary Shelley and Her Circle*: it evokes the central points of incandescence in the text—the image of the burning corpse of Shelley, together with the Benjaminian visual image of the afterlife of literary works as funeral pyres which continue to burn, to grow, and to intensify their power and their flame, beyond their author's death. Beyond the ashes of the writer and of the writer's life, there remains within the writing an indestructible inscription, a living embodiment of "the enigma of the flame itself: the enigma of being alive."[58]

Through the fire that permeates her writing and burns in her work, Johnson as a dying storyteller reaches back to a whole lifetime: going over a whole life of thinking, feeling, reading, writing, living, suffering, teaching. In this, she "joins the ranks of the teachers and sages." "Her gift is the ability to relate her life; her distinction, to be to able to tell her entire life." As a storyteller in *Mary Shelly and Her Circle*, Johnson tries to signify precisely life in its entirety. Yet, to signify life in its entirety is to let life be consumed by its own fire. Thus, in writing her last book, Johnson quite precisely, literally "lets the wick of her life be completely consumed by the gentle flame of her story."

～

X

"It's in the Writing that there is Something Obscure"

It was a mystery how Johnson (who was no longer writing to any one of us, because she could not type), nonetheless typed this last text. Only one person—a very close friend—dared to ask. This friend, Barbara Rietveld, shared with me the following astonishing description. I cite her e-mail word by word.[59]

> On one visit to her, [Rietveld narrated,] I asked her to describe to me *how* she typed—which was with one finger. Why? I asked. Is it because you cannot maneuver all 10 fingers, or because it takes too much energy?
>
> Her answer was nothing that I had imagined. She needed one hand to hold on to the table because she no longer had any sense of balance. If she did not hold on to "right" herself, the room started to spin, she lost her sense of what was up and what was down [on the screen], and she couldn't focus on finding the letter on the keyboard.

～

This fire of the will that melts the body's weakness; this final image of the writer at the limit of the possible and the impossible, writing from beyond the possible, converting disability into ability and finitude into infinitude by means of language, turning fate into expression, and turning its own absolute stand toward its fate into infinite resourcefulness—this final image of the writer, in the absoluteness of her affirmation, holds for me a power and a mystery that cannot be forgotten, and whose enigma— whose opaque illumination—cannot be reduced to simple intelligibility.

"There must be something occult deep inside everyone," Stéphane Mallarmé—Johnson's most beloved poet—wrote in the volume of poetic prose that Johnson lovingly translated in her final years: "decidedly I believe in something opaque, a signification sealed and hidden, that inhabits common man . . . , it's in the writing—not in oneself—that there is something obscure."[60]

Proust—Johnson's other love—in turn knows that a book's "depth" can be measured only by "the shadow which we have had to traverse": "Real books," Proust says, "should be the offspring not of daylight . . . but of darkness and silence" (*TR*, p. 257).

～

Triumph of Life

As a teacher who became a storyteller, and as a storyteller who—in *Mary Shelley and Her Circle*—"has joined the ranks of the teachers and the sages," Johnson keeps imparting her own courage, her own gathered knowledge, and "above all, her real life."

"It is characteristic," Benjamin writes, "that not only a [wo]man's knowledge and wisdom, but above all [her] real life—and this is the stuff that stories are made of—first assumes transmissible form at the moment of [her] death."[61]

Transmissible is here the key word. The unexpected revelation that profound storytellers open up is that of a miraculous *transmissibility of life through death*, a transmission suddenly made possible and meaningful, communicable, even in its unfathomability.

Thus it is that at the moment of her death, Johnson accomplishes a *triumph of transmission*—of communication—not merely of her Mary Shelley story, but of the dignified meaning of her own life; a triumph that transmits the fire at the center of the circle of her writing and her life, that passes on the flame of life, and that, at the very heart of the impossible, continues to dispense its wisdom and its courage, to share its humanity (its fragility and strength), and to yield—through the articulation of its bond of reading—a surprisingly redemptive literary warmth, "the warmth which we never draw from our own fate."[62]

> With this comes to light the innermost basis for the "narrator's stance." For it is [s]he alone who, in the feeling of hope, can fulfill the meaning of the event . . . Thus, hope finally wrests itself from it . . . like a trembling question . . . This hope is the sole justification for the faith in immortality, which must never be kindled from one's own existence.[63]

In narrating the impossible autobiography of Mary Shelley through her reading's autobiographical participation in, and enactment of, the ghost-story competition and the writing contest between life and death, Johnson triumphs over the restrictive circumstances of her malady and of her destiny, and wins her own race against time, in managing against all odds to finish her last book, and to bring thus to completion the circle of her writing: a circle that preserves at once the indestructibility of the charred heart, and the creative spark, the inextinguishable literary fire at its center.

This last manuscript embodies therefore Johnson's ultimate, unique *triumph of life*. It is the luminosity and the opaqueness of this triumph which is at the source of her story, and which endows her writings with their aura, and with their living and enduring textual authority.

Notes

Part One: Early Essays

Foreword

1. This phrase is used in Felman's Afterword to Part Two of this book.

2. Barbara Johnson, "Gender Theory and the Yale School," in Barbara Johnson, *A World of Difference* (Baltimore: Johns Hopkins University Press, 1987), p. 33. Reproduced in Part One of this book.

3. Ibid.

4. The allusion, here, is to James Whale's film *The Bride of Frankenstein* (1935), a sequel to his critically acclaimed first film, *Frankenstein* (1931), which was adapted from Mary Shelley's novel. In the novel, as the reader will remember, the scientist-creator Victor Frankenstein begins to construct—then destroys—the female monster, the "Bride" that the monster desires but that is dismantled and obliterated almost as soon as she is created.

Introduction

1. Originally published as "Le dernier homme," in *Les fins de l'homme. A partir du travail de Jacques Derrida. 23 juillet–2 août 1980*, ed. Philippe Lacoue-Labarthe and Jean-Luc Nancy (Paris: Editions Galilée, 1980). Johnson's essay was later translated by Bruce Robbins, and published in its English version as Barbara Johnson, "The Last Man," in *The Other Mary Shelley: Beyond Franken-stein*, ed. Audrey A. Fisch, Anne K. Mellor, and Esther H. Schor (New York: Oxford University Press, 1993). Derrida's essay "Les fins de l'homme" was later translated by Alan Bass as "The Ends of Man," in *Margins of Philosophy* (Chicago: University of Chicago Press, 1982).

2. *The Other Mary Shelley*, p. 262.

3. Mary Shelley, *The Last Man*, ed. Hugh J. Luke, Jr.; introduction to the

Bison Book Edition by Anne K. Mellor (Lincoln: University of Nebraska Press, 1995), p. vii.

4. Esther Schor, ed., *The Cambridge Companion to Mary Shelley* (Cambridge: Cambridge University Press), p. 2.

5. (New York: Routledge, 1988), p. 39.

6. (New York: Oxford University Press), p. 99; *Studies in Romanticism* 15, no. 2 (Spring 1976): pp. 165–195.

7. (New Haven, Conn.: Yale University Press), p. 237.

8. (Berkeley: University of California Press), pp. 88–119.

9. *PMLA* 95 (May 1980): pp. 332–347.

10. *The Last Man* is not actually Mary Shelley's last novel, but her third.

11. "Women's, Gender, and Sexuality Studies at Yale: Reflections, Celebrations, and Visions," http://wgss.yale.edu/womens-gender-and-sexuality-studies-yale-reflections-celebrations-and-visions, January 28, 2012.

12. *Feminist Literary History* (New York: Routledge, 1988), p. 3. At the time of the publication of *Feminist Literary History*, Johnson was no longer at Yale, having moved to Harvard in 1983.

13. *diacritics* 5, no. 4 (Winter 1975): pp. 2–10.

14. (Princeton, N.J.: Princeton University Press).

15. *diacritics* 12, no. 2 (Summer 1982): pp. 2–10.

16. Elizabeth Abel, "Editor's Introduction," *Critical Inquiry* 8, no. 2 (Winter 1981): 173. Abel later collected articles from this and other issues of *Critical Inquiry* as *Writing and Sexual Difference* (Chicago: University of Chicago Press, 1982), where the quotation from Johnson appears on p. 1.

17. "*Frankenstein*, Feminism, and Literary Theory," in *The Cambridge Companion to Mary Shelley*, p. 49.

18. "Committee on Degrees in Studies of Women, Gender, and Sexuality: History," http://wgs.fas.harvard.edu/icb/icb.do?keyword=k53419&tabgroupid=icb.tabgroup86304 , January 28, 2013.

19. "Celebrating 20 Years of Women's Studies at MIT," http://web.mit.edu/wgs/about/history.html, January 28, 2013 .

20. (New York: Methuen), pp. 205–219; *Critical Inquiry* 12, no. 1, pp. 278–289, reprinted in *Race, Writing, and Difference* (Chicago: University of Chicago Press, 1986), pp. 317–328. "Metaphor, Metonymy, and Voice" was also reprinted in *Textual Analysis: Some Readers Reading*, ed. Mary Ann Caws (New York: Modern Language Association of America, 1986), pp. 232–244. Both essays are also reprinted in *A World of Difference*.

21. Schor, "Introduction," *The Cambridge Companion to Mary Shelley*, p. 1.

22. Ed. Stephen C. Behrendt.

23. *Modern Critical Interpretations* (New York: Chelsea House Publishers, 1987).

24. Ed. J. Paul Hunter (New York: W. W. Norton, 1996), pp. 241–251.

The Last Man

1. Originally published as "Le dernier homme," in *Les fins de l'homme. A partir du travail de Jacques Derrida. 23 juillet–2 août 1980*, ed. Philippe Lacoue-Labarthe and Jean-Luc Nancy (Paris: Editions Galilée, 1980).

2. Friedrich Nietzsche, *Human, All-Too-Human: A Book for Free Spirits,* Part I, trans. Helen Zimmern (New York: Russell and Russell, 1964), p. 20.

3. Jean-Jacques Rousseau, *The First and Second Discourses,* trans. Roger D. and Judith R. Masters (New York: St. Martin's Press, 1964), p. 91.

4. Jacques Derrida, "The Ends of Man," in *Margins of Philosophy,* trans. Alan Bass (Chicago: University of Chicago Press, 1982), p. 115.

5. *Time,* June 30, 1980, p. 52.

6. Albert Camus, *The Plague,* trans. Stuart Gilbert (New York: Knopf, 1977), p. 35.

7. Percy Bysshe Shelley, Preface, "The Revolt of Islam," *Poetical Works* (London: Oxford University Press, 1970), p. 33.

8. Mary Shelley, *The Last Man,* ed. Hugh J. Luke (Lincoln: University of Nebraska Press, 1965), p. 5.

9. Maurice Blanchot, *The Last Man,* trans. Lydia Davis (New York: Columbia University Press, 1987), p. 89.

My Monster/My Self

1. Nancy Friday, *My Mother/My Self* (New York: Dell, 1977); Dorothy Dinnerstein, *The Mermaid and the Minotaur* (New York: Harper Colophon, 1976); Mary Shelley, *Frankenstein; or, The Modern Prometheus* (New York: Signet, 1965). Ed.—As is narrated both in the general Introduction to this volume and in Felman's Afterword (to Part Two), Johnson's initial teaching and lecturing on Mary Shelley's *Frankenstein* (a teaching which will soon give birth to the splendid "My Monster/My Self") takes place in a Yale course on narrative (1980), in which the assigned classroom text of *Frankenstein* (determined in advance by the course's team of teachers) is the 1965 Signet edition, from which Johnson will cite Frankenstein in this and other essays. Johnson remains attached to this first object of her teaching— and all her subsequent citations of *Frankenstein*, both in her early essays (in Part One) and in her last book, *Mary Shelley and Her Circle* (in Part Two)— are to this Signet Classics 1965 edition, which reproduces *Frankenstein* in its third (1831) historical edition.

Shelley was seventeen when she completed her writing of the novel in May 1817, and *Frankenstein* was first published in January 1818 by a small London publishing house. This original edition was issued anonymously, with a preface written for Mary by Percy Bysshe Shelley (but without signature), and with a dedication to philosopher William Godwin—her father. The second edition of Frankenstein was published in two volumes in France in 1823, and credited Mary Shelley as the author. In October 1831, the first "popular" edition in one volume appeared. This edition was heavily revised by Mary Shelley, partially because of pressure to make the story more conservative. It importantly included a second, longer preface, an author's introduction, in which Mary for the first time claims authorship in her distinct (and distinctly public) voice. In contradistinction to the edition used by Johnson, the editors elected to cite the original 1818 edition in their Afterwords, using for this purpose the Norton Critical Edition, Second Edition (2012). As mentioned above, there are differences between the text of the original edition of *Frankenstein*, and the text of the third edition, but these differences are not relevant to Johnson's arguments and insights, with the exception of the third edition's duplication of the Prefaces, which Johnson analyzes, an analysis which grounds her pathbreaking, innovative points here.

2. See Ellen Moers, "Female Gothic," and U. C. Knoepflmacher, "Thoughts on the Aggression of Daughters," in *The Endurance of Frankenstein*, ed. George Levine and U. C. Knoepflmacher (Berkeley: University of California Press, 1979), and Mary Poovey, "My Hideous Progeny: Mary Shelley and the Feminization of Romanticism," *PMLA* 95 (May 1980): pp. 332–347.

Gender Theory and the Yale School

1. This chapter, as the text makes clear, is very much a cry of its occasion: a conference entitled "Genre Theory and the Yale School" held May 31–June 1, 1984, at the University of Oklahoma at Norman.

2. Jonathan Culler, *On Deconstruction* (Ithaca, N.Y.: Cornell University Press, 1982), p. 289.

3. Jacques Derrida, "The Law of Genre," in *Glyph 7: Johns Hopkins Textual Studies* (Baltimore: Johns Hopkins University Press, 1980), pp. 203–204.

4. Geoffrey Hartman, *The Fate of Reading* (Chicago: University of Chicago Press, 1975), p. 248, and *Beyond Formalism* (New Haven, Conn.: Yale University Press, 1970), p. 351.

5. Hartman, "Words, Wish, Worth: Wordsworth," in *Deconstruction and Criticism*, ed. Harold Bloom (New York: Continuum, 1979), p. 215. Hereafter cited as *DC* followed by a page number.

6. Harold Bloom, *A Map of Misreading* (New York: Oxford University Press, 1975), p. 33. I would like to thank Susan Suleiman for calling this quotation to my attention.

7. The story of Jael is found in *Judges* 4. Jael invites Sisera, the commander of the Canaanite army, into her tent, gives him a drink of milk, and then, when he has fallen asleep, drives a tent peg through his head and kills him. Sima Godfrey suggested this pun.

8. Paul de Man, "The Epistemology of Metaphor," *Critical Inquiry* 5 (1978): pp. 13–28.

9. Barbara Johnson, *The Critical Difference* (Baltimore: Johns Hopkins University Press, 1980).

Afterword. Animating Autobiography:
Barbara Johnson and Mary Shelley's Monster

1. Barbara Johnson, *A World of Difference* (Baltimore: Johns Hopkins University Press, 1987).

2. Mary Shelley, *Frankenstein*, ed. J. Paul Hunter, a Norton Critical edition, 2nd ed. (New York: W. W. Norton, 2012).

3. For a further consideration of the various meanings of "correspondence" in Barbara Johnson's work, see *Mother Tongues: Sexuality, Trials, Motherhood, Translation* (Cambridge, Mass.: Harvard University Press, 2003), 94–140.

4. Victor Frankenstein relays that when he kissed Elizabeth, his love, she turned suddenly into a deathly thing, and he felt himself to be holding the corpse of his dead mother (p.51). Such transformations may well be read as an effort to deprive Elizabeth of her life through the kiss and to mourn the mother's death on the occasion of a sexual encounter. The dead mother thus already exercises a power of transformation to turn the living into the dead. Thus, the turning of inanimate matter into life seems to be in the service of compensating for a loss. It seems to be significant as well how often the monster is referred to as a "mummy."

5. For a position that resonates with Barbara Johnson's views on the invariable recurrence of aggression within social forms, see Lee Edelman, *No Future: Queer Theory and the Death Drive* (Durham, N.C.: Duke University Press, 2004).

Part Two: Writing in the Face of Death

Mary Shelley and Her Circle, Introduction

1. Ed.—The collection was the creation of the financier Carl H. Pforzheimer, Sr. (1879–1957), who took special interest in the lives and works of the poet Percy Shelley and his contemporaries. The manuscripts of the collection, today archived in the New York Public Library, are published in *Carl H. Pforzheimer Collection of Shelley and His Circle, 1773–1822*, ed. Kenneth Neill Cameron and Donald H. Reiman, 10 vols. (Cambridge, Mass.: Harvard University Press, 1961–2002).

Endnote references are Johnson's, except where noted. Endnotes added by the editors are always prefaced by the abbreviation "Ed.—"

2. Mary Shelley, *Frankenstein* (New York: Signet, 1965). Parenthetical page numbers in Johnson's citations of *Frankenstein* refer to this edition.

3. Ed.—"Standard British Novels," also called "Bentley's Standard Novels," refers to a series of inexpensive reprints of classic novels, published between 1831 and 1862 by Henry Colburn and Richard Bentley.

4. Ed.—Compare the way in which Johnson explores the question of genre in relation to gender (and monstrosity), in her essay "Gender Theory and the Yale School" (reprinted in Part One of this book): "After all, Aristotle, the founder of the law of gender as well as of the law of genre, considered the female the first distortion of the genus 'man' en route to becoming a monster" (p. 33). Barbara Johnson, *A World of Difference* (Baltimore: Johns Hopkins University Press, 1987), 32–41. Hereafter cited in text and notes as *WD*.

5. *The Complete Works of Percy Bysshe Shelley*, ed. Roger Ingpen and Walter E. Peck, vol. 8 (New York: Gordian Press, 1965), pp. 232–233.

Chapter One: William Godwin

1. See Mary Poovey, *The Proper Lady and the Woman Writer: Ideology as Style in the Works of Mary Wollstonecraft, Mary Shelley, and Jane Austen* (Chicago: University of Chicago Press, 1984).

2. Ed.—In Mary Shelley's novel, the monster kills Victor Frankenstein's young brother, William, but Justine (a servant woman) is unjustly accused and executed for the crime.

3. Mary Shelley, *The Last Man*, vol. 4 of *The Novels and Selected Works of Mary Shelley*, ed. Nora Crook with Pamela Clemit (London: William Pickering, 1996). Parenthetical page numbers in *Mary Shelley and Her Circle* refer to this edition.

4. William Godwin, *Caleb Williams*, ed. Maurice Hindle (New York: Penguin Classics, 2005). Parenthetical page numbers refer to this edition.

5. William Godwin, *Enquiry Concerning Political Justice* (New York: Penguin, 1985). Parenthetical page numbers refer to this edition.

6. Ed.—See Michel Foucault, *Discipline and Punish: The Birth of the Prison* (New York: Vintage, 1995), originally published as *Surveiller et punir: naissance de la prison* (Paris: Gallimard, 1975).

7. See John Bender, *Imagining the Penitentiary: Fiction and the Architecture of Mind in Eighteenth-Century England* (Chicago: University of Chicago Press, 1987).

8. Harriet Jacobs [Linda Brent, pseud.], "Incidents in the Life of a Slave Girl," in *The Classic Slave Narratives*, ed. Henry Louis Gates, Jr. (New York: Mentor, 1987). Parenthetical page numbers refer to this edition.

9. Janet Todd, introduction to *Mary* and *Maria*, by Mary Wollstonecraft, and *Matilda*, by Mary Shelley, ed. Janet Todd (New York: Penguin, 1991). Parenthetical page numbers refer to this edition.

10. Percy Bysshe Shelley, *Poetical Works*, ed. Thomas Hutchinson, notes by

Mary Shelley (1905; reprint, with corrections by G. M. Matthews, Oxford: Oxford University Press, 1970), pp. 336–337.

11. Ed.—See Phyllis Chesler, *Women and Madness* (New York: Doubleday, 1972).

12. William Godwin, *Memoirs of the Author of A Vindication of the Rights of Woman* (Oxford: Woodstock Books, 1990), p. 112.

Chapter Two: Mary Wollstonecraft

1. Susan Gubar, "Feminist Misogyny: Mary Wollstonecraft and the Paradox of 'It Takes One to Know One,'" in Gubar, *Critical Condition: Feminism at the Turn of the Century* (New York: Columbia University Press, 2000), pp. 135–142.

2. Mary Wollstonecraft, *The Vindications*, ed. D. L. Macdonald and Kathleen Scherf (Ontario: Broadview Press, 1997). Parenthetical page numbers refer to this edition.

3. Ed.—The two last quotations are chapter titles, announcing the agenda of Wollstonecraft's insistent argument (Chapters 7 and 8, respectively, of the second *Vindication.*)

4. Ed.—Walpole's much-quoted comment first appeared in a letter to Hannah More, dated January 24, 1795. *The Yale Edition of Horace Walpole's Correspondence*, ed. W. S. Lewis (New Haven, Conn.: Yale University Press, 1961), vol. 31, p. 397.

5. William Wordsworth, *Poetical Works [of] Wordsworth*, ed. Thomas Hutchinson and Ernest de Selincourt (Oxford: Oxford University Press, 1969), p. 570.

6. Wollstonecraft, "Advertisement" to *Mary*, in *Mary* and *Matilda*, p. 3.

7. Wollstonecraft, *Mary* and *Maria.*

8. Cited by Poovey, p. 118.

9. Ed.—For an in-depth discussion of the lingering legacy of animistic beliefs, see Barbara Johnson's "Surmounted Beliefs," in *Persons and Things* (Cambridge, Mass.: Harvard University Press, 2008), pp. 131–152.

10. Edmund Burke, *Reflections on the Revolution in France*, ed. Conor Cruise O'Brien (New York: Penguin, 1969). Parenthetical page numbers refer to this edition.

11. Claudia Johnson, *Equivocal Beings: Politics, Gender and Sentimentality in the 1790s. Wollstonecraft, Radcliffe, Burney, Austen* (Chicago: University of Chicago Press, 1995), pp. 4–5.

12. Introduction by Walter Scott to Horace Walpole, *The Castle of Otranto* (New York: Macmillan, 1963), p. 115.

13. William Godwin, *Godwin on Wollstonecraft: Memoirs of the Author of* The Rights of Woman, ed. Richard Holmes (1898; London: Harper Perennial, 2005), pp. 60–61.

14. Mary Wollstonecraft, *Letters Written During a Short Residence in Sweden, Norway, and Denmark*, ed. Carol H. Poston (Lincoln: University of Nebraska Press, 1976), p. 5.

15. William Shakespeare, *The Winter's Tale*, ed. Barbara A. Mowat and Paul Werstine (1998; New York: Simon and Schuster, 2005).

Chapter Three: Percy Bysshe Shelley

1. Godwin, *Political Justice*.

2. "Notes on *Queen Mab*," in Mary Shelley, P. B. Shelley: *Poetical Works, Notes by Mary Shelley*.

3. Percy Bysshe Shelley, *Zastrozzi and St. Irvyne,* ed. Steven C. Behrendt (Oxford: Oxford University Press, 1986), p. 88.

4. William Wordsworth, first preface to the *Lyrical Ballads*, in *Poetical Works*, p. 735.

5. Ed. "To Harriet," in *Poetical Works*, p. 522.

6. Ed.—"To Mary Wollstonecraft Godwin," in *Poetical Works*, p. 522.

7. Ed.—("Yet look on me"), in *Poetical Works*, p. 523.

8. Ed.—Johnson elaborates on this point in her essay "Apostrophe, Animation, and Abortion," in *WD*, pp. 184–199.

9. Ian Gilmour, *The Making of the Poets: Byron and Shelley in Their Time* (London: Chatto & Windus, 2002), pp. 290–291.

10. Ann Wroe, *Being Shelley: The Poet's Search for Himself* (London: Jonathan Cape, 1997), pp. 139–140. Poems excerpted from *The Revolt of Islam*, Canto IV, ll. 1666–71 (in *Poetical Works*, p. 78) and *Alastor*, l. 466 (in ibid., p. 25).

11. See Wroe, *Being Shelley*, pp. 81–104.

12. Percy Bysshe Shelley, *Shelley's Prose; or, The Trumpet of a Prophecy*, ed. David Lee Clark (Albuquerque: University of New Mexico Press, 1954). Hereafter abbreviated *Shelley's Prose*. Parenthetical page numbers will refer to this edition.

13. Mary Shelley, *The Last Man*.

14. Ann Radcliffe, *The Mysteries of Udolpho*, ed. Jacqueline Howard (New York: Penguin, 2001). Parenthetical page numbers refer to this edition.

15. Lynn Hunt, *Inventing Human Rights: A History* (New York: Norton, 2007), p. 136.

16. Ed.— *"Le sujet supposé savoir"*—"the subject presumed to know"—is a Lacanian concept, describing the role assigned to Authority in any situation of psychoanalytic "transference" (i.e., love is a projection of knowledge on a subject presumed to know, irrespective of the subject's real knowledge). See Jacques Lacan, *Seminar XI: The Four Fundamental Concepts of Psychoanalysis*, ed. Jacques-Alain Miller, trans. Alan Sheridan (London: The Hogarth Press and the Institute of Psycho-Analysis, 1977).

17. Mary Shelley, *Mary Shelley's Journal*, ed. Frederick L. Jones (Norman: University of Oklahoma Press, 1947), pp. 104–105. Quoted in Poovey, *Proper Lady*, p. 114.

18. *Lodore*, ed. Fiona Stafford, vol. 6 of *The Novels and Selected Works of Mary Shelley*. Parenthetical page numbers refer to this edition.

19. J. C. L. de Sismondi, *A History of the Italian Republics* (London: J. M. Dent, 1907), p. 122.

20. Machiavelli, "The Life of Castruccio Castracani of Lucca," in *The History of Florence and Other Selections*, ed. Myron Gilmore (New York: Twayne Publishers, 1970), p. 49.

21. Mary Shelley, *Valperga*, ed. Nora Crook, vol. 3 of *The Novels and Selected Works of Mary Shelley*.

22. Doucet Devin Fischer, "Introductory Note" to Mary Shelley, *The Fortunes of Perkin Warbeck*, ed. Fischer, vol. 5 of *The Novels and Selected Works of Mary Shelley*, p. xiii . Hereafter cited as *Perkin Warbeck*. Parenthetical page numbers refer to this edition.

23. Ed.—There are various accounts about how the heart came to be buried with Mary. According to one of these accounts, narrated by the family, some time after Mary Shelley's death, her son Percy Florence Shelley and his wife, Jane, opened her box-desk. Inside they found the journal Mary had kept with Shelley in their 1814 elopement year. With it was a folded copy of one of Shelley's last poems, *Adonaïs*, mourning Keats's premature death. Unwrapping the paper, they found that it contained the charred remains of Shelley's heart, which Mary had kept with her all those years. The heart was buried with the son, Sir Percy Florence, at his request, in the family vault where his mother's body was also entombed. All accounts agree that the remains now lie in the family sepulcher in the churchyard of St. Peter's Church, near their home on the property purchased by Mary in Boscombe, Bournemouth, England.

Chapter Four: Lord Byron

1. *Benét's Reader's Encyclopedia*, ed. Katherine Baker Siepmann (New York: HarperCollins, 1987), p. 145.

2. Lord George Gordon Byron, *Poetical Works*, ed. Frederick Page, 1904, revised by John Jump (New York: Oxford University Press, 1970), p. 209.

3. The expression is from Jerome Christensen, *Lord Byron's Strength: Romantic Writing and Commercial Society* (Baltimore: Johns Hopkins University Press, 1993).

4. *Lord Byron: Selected Letters and Journals*, ed. Leslie Marchand (Cambridge, Mass.: Belknap Press, 1982). Quotations from this work refer to this edition.

5. Mary Shelley, *The Last Man*, vol. 4 of *The Novels and Selected Works of Mary Shelley*, ed. Nora Crook with Pamela Clemit (London: William Pickering, 1996).

6. Homer, *The Odyssey*, trans. Robert Fitzgerald (New York: Farrar, Straus, and Giroux, 1998).

7. Byron, *Letters and Journals*, p. 95.

8. Byron, *Poetical Works*, p.192.

9. Ibid., p. 212.

10. Byron, *Letters and Journals*, pp. 149–150.

11. Debate on the "Frame-Work Bill," in the House of Lords, 27 February 1812, quoted in Gilmour, *The Making of the Poets*, p. 325.

12. Wordsworth, *Poetical Works*, p. 148.

13. William Veeder, *Mary Shelley & Frankenstein: The Fate of Androgyny* (Chicago: University of Chicago Press, 1986), p. 119.

14. "The 'Uncanny,'" in *The Standard Edition of the Complete Psychological Works of Sigmund Freud*, ed. and trans. James Strachey, vol. 17 (London: Hogarth Press, 1955), pp. 219–256.

15. Byron, *Poetical Works*, pp. 635, 638, 639.

16. Byron, *Letters and Journals*, p. 45.

Chapter Five: John Polidori

1. David L. Macdonald, *Poor Polidori: A Critical Biography of the Author of The Vampyre* (Toronto: University of Toronto Press, 1991). The biographical facts about Polidori are often taken from this volume, to date (as far as I know) the only biography in existence of Polidori.

2. Ed.—This line, from the diary of Polidori, is from a page that later got torn away; the line is reconstructed from Rossetti's memory, who attested he (Rossetti) had read it in Polidori's diary before the page was torn.

3. Ed.—Frances Polidori married Gabriele Rossetti and became the mother of Maria, Dante Gabriel, William, and Christina Rossetti. All of the children had literary gifts, but Dante Gabriel and Christina became particularly famous as poets.

Afterword: Barbara Johnson's Last Book

1. *diacritics*, Summer 1982. Reprinted in *A World of Difference*, pp. 144–154. Hereafter abbreviated *WD*.

2. Barbara Johnson, "Le dernier homme," in *Les fins de l'homme: à partir du travail de Jacques Derrida, colloque de Cerisy*, 23 juillet–2 août 1980 (Paris: Galilée,1980), p. 87. Later translated into English by Bruce Robbins, and published as Barbara Johnson, "The Last Man," in *The Other Mary Shelley*, pp. 258–266. Reproduced in this volume as Chapter 1, Part One.

3. Barbara Johnson, *Persons and Things* (Cambridge, Mass.: Harvard University Press, 2008), pp. 1–2, 153–167, 168–175.

4. Barbara Johnson, "Gender Theory and the Yale School," originally published in *Genre*, Summer 1984; reprinted in *WD*, pp. 32–41, and reproduced here in Part One.

5. Hegel, *The Phenomenology of Spirit*, trans. A. V. Miller (Oxford: Oxford University Press, 1977), # 475, p. 288.

6. Freud, *The Interpretation of Dreams*: "What is clearly the essence of the dream-thoughts need not be represented in the dream at all. The dream is, as it were, *differently centered* from the dream thoughts—its content has different elements as its central point" (translated by James Strachey; London: Penguin Books, The Pelican Freud Library, vol. 4, ch. 6, p. 414; Freud's italics).

7. "The Last Man," in *The Other Mary Shelley*, pp. 258–259 (italics mine).

8. In her lapidary conceptual condensations, Johnson sums up those divisions as "the difference-versus-equality debates, the essentialism-versus-postmodernism debates, the black-feminist critiques of white feminism, the lesbian critiques of normative heterosexuality within feminism, the international feminist critiques of first-world-feminism," etc. Barbara Johnson, *The Feminist Difference: Literature, Psychoanalysis, Race, and Gender* (Cambridge, Mass.: Harvard University Press, 1998), p. 2.

9. See Barbara Johnson, *WD*, p. 15: "Therefore, the one imperative a reading must obey, is that it follow, with rigor, what puts in question the kind of reading it thought it was going to be. A reading is strong, I would therefore submit, to the extent that it encounters and propagates the surprise of otherness. The impossible but necessary task of the reader is to set herself up to be surprised."

10. Cited by Mario Vargas Llosa, in *The Perpetual Orgy: Flaubert and Madame Bovary* (English translation from the Spanish by Helen Lane; New York: Farrar, Straus, and Giroux, 1975, 2011), p. 61.

11. Mary functions in all chapters as a sort of leitmotiv that disappears and reappears sporadically and unpredictably within each chapter, but whose thematic and acoustic burden persistently recurs from one chapter to another, returns to resume its intermittent, under-current, contrapuntal doubling story. Johnson's counter-narrative evolves—discreetly, understatedly—through intermittent subterranean repetitions of the burden, which keep moving the story forward, through its changing variations and its circular, melodious, yet disruptive and subversive, contrapuntal recapitulations.

12. Johnson, "The Last Man," in *The Other Mary Shelley*, p. 259.

13. At various stages of her life, Mary is disowned from the name Shelley, remaining as nameless as her monster: first, in her capacity as the eloped sexual companion of a poet and a lover married to another; later, after Shelley's death, as the disputed holder of the aristocracy and the inheritance of Shelley's father's name, which she desires only so as to transfer its privileges to her late husband's sole surviving son, Percy Florence (Shelley).

14. Mary Shelley, "Introduction to *Frankenstein*, Third Edition (1831)," in Mary Shelley, *Frankenstein*, ed. J. Paul Hunter, Norton Critical Edition, 2nd ed. (New York: W.W. Norton, 2012), p. 166. Hereafter, citations from *Frankenstein* (followed by page numbers) refer to this edition.

15. Walter Benjamin, "The Storyteller," in Walter Benjamin, *Illuminations:*

Essays and Reflections, ed. and with an introduction by Hannah Arendt (New York: Schocken Books, 1968), p. 91. Benjamin's collection will be cited as *Illuminations*.

16. Barbara Johnson, "My Monster/ My Self," in *WD*, p. 151.

17. Ibid., p. 150.

18. Ibid., p. 149.

19. Mary did not have the heart to watch the burning of her husband's corpse, so Shelley's friend Trelawny took care of it and physically assisted in it. Byron, who attended the incineration of the disfigured body, could not bear it and went swimming in the sea. In a letter to her friend Maria Gisborne, Mary narrates the burning impact of this pyre she could not bring herself to witness, but experienced physically, belatedly, in later holding Trelawny's burned hands. "What I have endured," Mary tells Maria Gisborne, "is not to be alleviated by time . . . . Trelawny . . . supported us in our miseries . . . —& when I shake his hand I feel to the depth of my soul that those hands collected those ashes—yes—for I saw them burned & scorched from the office—no fatigue—no sun—or nervous horrors deterred him, as one or the other of these causes deterred all others—he stood on the burning sand for many hours beside the pyre—if he had been permitted by the soldiers he would have placed him there in his arms—I never, never can forget this." (Mary Shelley, Letter to Maria Gisborne, November 22, 1822, in *The Letters of Mary Wollstonecraft Shelley*, ed. Betty T. Bennett, 3 vols. (Baltimore: Johns Hopkins University Press, 1980), vol. 1, pp. 290–291.

If he could, says Mary, Trelawny would have held the burning Shelley in his arms, with the fire at the center of the circle. The catching fire has a communicative function: it materially communicates itself from hand to hand within (the broken chain of) the Romantic circle, from the burning hand of the dead to the scorched hand of the living (Trelawny) and from there to Mary's hand: unable to face the fire, Mary witnesses the funereal pyre through her sense of touch.

20. *The Feminist Difference*, pp. 165–166.

21. Ibid. Johnson refers to Arendt, citing from Benjamin's essay "On Goethe's Electives Affinities" in her introduction to Benjamin's *Illuminations*, p. 5.

22. *The Feminist Difference*, p. 166. Johnson is reviewing the flamboyant (fiery critical legal) style of another woman writer, Patricia Williams ("The Alchemy of Style and Law," on Williams's book, *The Alchemy of Race and Rights: Diary of a Law Professor*).

23. Cited in Dorothy and Thomas Hoobler, *The Monsters* (New York: Little, Brown, 2006), p. 271.

24. "I was overcome by my own heart alone," says Rousseau as Shelley's double, in *The Triumph of Life. The Selected Poetry and Prose of Shelley*, ed. Bruce Woodcock (London: Wordsworth Poetry Library, 1998), p. 546, ll. 240–41. The poetic figure of Rousseau stands both for Shelley's literary guide and for his political and

philosophical (revolutionary) mentor. Rousseau, like Shelley, is not overcome by life, but "by his heart alone." The language of the heart is equally referred to by the young Tennyson, who writes after the death of Byron: "Such writers as Byron and Shelley, however wrong they may be, did yet give the world another heart" (cited in Hoobler and Hoobler, *The Monsters*, p. 270).

25. Harold Bloom, *The Anxiety of Influence: A Theory of Poetry* (New York: Oxford University Press, 1997), p. 5. In line with this "masculine" conception, Bloom's anthology—*Romanticism*—includes no women.

26. Introduction to *Iconoclastic Departures: Mary Shelley after* Frankenstein, ed. Sindy Conger, Frederick Frank, and Gregory O'Dea (London: Associated University Presses, 1997), p. 12.

27. *The Other Mary Shelley*, pp. 258–259.

28. Gilles Deleuze and Félix Guattari, *Kafka: Toward A Minor Literature*, trans. Dana Polan (Minneapolis: University of Minnesota Press, 1986; French original ed. 1975). I'm not sure whether Johnson actually read Deleuze and Guattari, but her philosophical conception of the "minor" is aligned with theirs.

29. Deleuze and Guattari, *Kafka*, p. 17.

30. On this point, and on Johnson's own elaborated emphasis on the political implications and the collective value of the figure (and the minor utterance) of Mary Shelley, see especially Johnson's essays "Gender Theory and the Yale School" and "My Monster / My Self," reprinted at the beginning of this volume.

31. Deleuze and Guattari, *Kafka*, p. 19.

32. Cited in Dorothy and Thomas Hoobler, *The Monsters*, p. 141.

33. Marcel Proust, *In Search of Lost Time*, vol. 6, *Time Regained*, trans. Andreas Mayor and Terence Kilmartin, rev. D. J. Enright (London: Vintage Books, 2000), p. 444. Citations from this work will henceforth be marked by the abbreviation *TR*, followed by page number.

34. Marcel Proust, *Sur Baudelaire, Flaubert et Morand* , ed. Antoine Compagnon (Paris: Editions Complexe, "Le regard littéraire," 1987), pp. 118–119; English translation, "Apropos de Baudelaire," in *Twentieth Century Views: Baudelaire*, ed. Henri Peyre (Englewood Cliffs, N.J.: Prentice-Hall, 1962), pp. 113–114.

35. Ibid. (French ed.), p. 118, my translation.

36. "But art," continues Proust, "if it means awareness of our own life, means also awareness of the lives of other people . . . Through art alone are we able to emerge from ourselves, to know what another person sees of a universe, which is not the same as our own . . . Thanks to art, instead of seeing one world only, our own, we see that world multiply itself." (*TR*, pp. 253–254).

37. "*Cette perpetuelle erreur, qui est, precisément, la 'vie.'*" (*Albertine Disparue: The Fugitive*). Proust, *In Search of Lost Time*, vol. 5, *The Captive* and *The Fugitive*, trans. Terence Kilmartin and C. K. Scott Moncrieff, rev. D. J. Enright (London: Vintage Press, 1996), p. 656.

38. See "My Monster/My Self."

39. Proust, in *Days of Reading*, trans. John Sturrock (New York and London: Penguin, 1988, 2008); "On Ruskin," p. 81.

40. Paul de Man, "Anthropomorphism and Trope in the Lyric," in *The Rhetoric of Romanticism* (New York: Columbia University Press, 1984), p. 262.

41. Proust, *Remembrance of Things Past*, vol. 3, *The Guermantes Way*, trans. C. K. Scott Moncrieff (New York: Modern Library, 1933). (Modified translation) *In Search of Lost Time*, vol. 3, *The Guermantes Way*, trans. Terence Kilmartin and C. K. Scott Montcrieff, rev. D. J. Enright (London: Vintage Press, 1996), p. 341.

42. Citation from the epitaphic speech Johnson prepared in advance for her memorial. Cited from Thoreau, *Walden, or Life in the Woods*, Chapter 2, in Thoreau, *Walden, Civil Disobedience and Other Writings*, 3rd ed., ed. William Rossi (New York: Norton, 2008), p. 219. See Shoshana Felman, "Barbara's Signature," in *The Barbara Johnson Reader* (Durham, N.C.: Duke University Prress, 2014).

43. Barbara Johnson, *Défigurations du language poétique: La seconde révolution baudelairenne* (Paris: Flammarion, 1979).

44. First in the class on *Frankenstein*, and later in "My Monster/My Self" (*diacritics*,1982), and in the later version of this essay in *WD* (1987), reproduced here in Part One.

45. "My Monster /My Self," in *WD*, p. 149.

46. Paul de Man, "Shelley Disfigured," in *The Rhetoric of Romanticism* (New York: Columbia University Press, 1984), pp. 120-121.

47. Johnson, "Le dernier homme," p. 87 (discussion: my translation from the French).

48. Johnson, "The Last Man," in *The Other Mary Shelley*, p. 265.

49. Benjamin, "The Storyteller," in *Illuminations,* p. 98.

50. Letter to Maria Gisborne, November 21, 1822, in *The Letters of Mary Wollstonecraft Shelley*, ed. Betty T. Bennett (Baltimore: Johns Hopkins University Press, 1980), vol. 1, p. 290.

51. Paul de Man, "Shelley Disfigured," in *The Rhetoric of Romanticism*, p. 120.

52. Audre Lorde, *Sister Outsider*, cited by Barbara Johnson as an epigraph to *A World of Difference*, pp. 1–2.

53. Barbara Johnson, *Persons and Things*, p. 156. Hereafter abbreviated as *PT* (followed by page number).

54. Johnson, "The Last Man," in *The Other Mary Shelley*, p. 265.

55. Walter Benjamin, "The Storyteller," in *Illuminations*, p. 94.

56. Barbara Johnson, *Mother Tongues: Sexuality, Trials, Motherhood, Translation* (Cambridge, Mass.: Harvard University Press, 2003).

57. Benjamin, "The Storyteller," in *Illuminations*, pp. 108–109; excerpt quoted by Johnson at the conclusion (on the last page) of *Mother Tongues*, p. 187.

58. Johnson, citing Walter Benjamin, in *The Feminist Difference*, p. 166; John-

son borrows the quotation (in Benjamin's essay "Goethe's *Elective Affinities*") from Hannah Arendt's Introduction to Walter Benjamin, *Illuminations* , p. 5.

59. Barbara Rietveld was of Johnson's age; they studied together at Yale University, and were of the same generation of graduate students in French. In their student days at Yale, they became best friends. Graduating, they lost touch with each other, and reconnected after twenty-five years of separation, when Rietveld heard about Johnson's illness. They became very close again, and maintained their friendship through a regular e-mail correspondence, since they did not live in the same city. When Johnson withdrew from writing e-mails, they talked on the phone and Rietveld visited Johnson occasionally. Rietveld was initially supposed to be one of the editors of the present volume, as she was a vital part of Johnson's small circle of involved friends during the last phases of her illness. But several months after Johnson's death, Rietveld herself unexpectedly also passed away from an aggressive terminal disease that took her life in February 2010. In her last months, Rietveld took care of editing one of Johnson's final manuscripts, *Moses and Multiculturalism*, which could thus posthumously see the light (out of the University of California Press in 2010) thanks to her devoted care, when Johnson had become too weak to do it. The e-mail from Rietveld that I am citing here was written and sent to me on October 15, 2009, four weeks after Johnson's death, and four months before Rietveld's own unexpected death. It should also stand as testimony and memorial for their unique, humanly exceptional friendship.

60. Stéphane Mallarmé, "The Mystery in Letters," in *Divagations*, trans. Barbara Johnson (Cambridge, Mass.: Harvard University Press, 2007), p. 231.

61. Walter Benjamin, "The Storyteller," in *Illuminations*, p. 94.

62. Ibid., p. 101.

63. Walter Benjamin, "Goethe's *Elective Affinities*," trans. Corngold, in Walter Benjamin, *Selected Writings*, vol. 1, *1913–1936*, ed. Marcus Bullock and Michael W. Jennings (Cambridge, Mass.: Harvard University Press, 1996), p. 355.

Index

Abel, Elizabeth (*Writing and Sexual Difference*), xix

action: Lord Byron as man of, 107; Mary Shelley on lack of relation between knowledge and, 11

"An Address to the Irish People" (P. Shelley), 85

"An Address to the People on the Death of the Princess Charlotte" (P. Shelley), 85

Aeschylus (*Prometheus*), 92–93

"African American Women Writers" course (Harvard University), xxii

"Afterword, Animating Autobiography: Barbara Johnson and Mary Shell's Monster" (Butler), 37–50

"Afterword: Barbara Johnson's Last Book" (Felman): on bringing Mary Shelley forth as a shadow story of Romanticism, 125; on "circling back" to beginning of Johnson's work on Shelley, xii–xiii, 124, 128–29; on circular structure of *Mary Shelley and Her Circle,* 149–50; comparing "Shelley and His Circle" and "Mary Shelley and Her Circle," 131, 133, 134–35; exploring the revolutionary implications of the, 127; on fire as the symbol of Mary's circle

engagement in listening, 135–36; on *Frankenstein's* disfiguration theme, 147–48, 149; on fresh vision of Romanticism through marginality of Mary Shelley, xviii, 15, 126, 127, 132; on the ghost-story writing competition being an autobiographical competition, 133, 140–41; on Johnson' art of juxtaposition and multilayered textual architecture, 130, 144; on Johnson inscribing her own body into the margin of the manuscript, 148; on Johnson's affirmation of Mary as "minor" author in, 138–40; on Johnson's affirmation of right to ambivalence in struggle for freedom, 128–29; on Johnson's Introduction explaining her project, 132–33; on Johnson's lasting literary and theoretical influence, 123–24; on Johnson's *naming* of Mary Shelley, 131, 132; on Johnson's re-definition of Romanticism, 133–40; on Johnson's "to write the end" spontaneous statement, 149; on Johnson's triumph of transmission, 157–58; on Johnson's work as collective biography of circle of Romantic writers, 129; on Johnson's writing while facing

M E R I D I A N

Crossing Aesthetics

Deborah Esch, *In the Event: Reading Journalism, Reading Theory*

Winfried Menninghaus, *In Praise of Nonsense: Kant and Bluebeard*

Giorgio Agamben, *The Man Without Content*

Giorgio Agamben, *The End of the Poem: Studies in Poetics*

Theodor W. Adorno, *Sound Figures*

Louis Marin, *Sublime Poussin*

Philippe Lacoue-Labarthe, *Poetry as Experience*

Ernst Bloch, *Literary Essays*

Jacques Derrida, *Resistances of Psychoanalysis*

Marc Froment-Meurice, *That Is to Say: Heidegger's Poetics*

Francis Ponge, *Soap*

Philippe Lacoue-Labarthe, *Typography: Mimesis, Philosophy, Politics*

Giorgio Agamben, *Homo Sacer: Sovereign Power and Bare Life*

Emmanuel Levinas, *Of God Who Comes To Mind*

Bernard Stiegler, *Technics and Time, 1: The Fault of Epimetheus*

Werner Hamacher, *pleroma--Reading in Hegel*

Serge Leclaire, *Psychoanalyzing: On the Order of the Unconscious and the Practice of the Letter*

Serge Leclaire, *A Child Is Being Killed: On Primary Narcissism and the Death Drive*

Sigmund Freud, *Writings on Art and Literature*

Cornelius Castoriadis, *World in Fragments: Writings on Politics, Society, Psychoanalysis, and the Imagination*

Thomas Keenan, *Fables of Responsibility: Aberrations and Predicaments in Ethics and Politics*

Emmanuel Levinas, *Proper Names*

Alexander García Düttmann, *At Odds with AIDS: Thinking and Talking About a Virus*

Maurice Blanchot, *Friendship*

Jean-Luc Nancy, *The Muses*